1230 9100 224 312 8

327.4105 Smi
Vietnam and the unravelling of
empire : General Gracey in Asia,
1942-1951
Smith, T. O.

WITHDRAWN

Vietnam and the Unravelling of Empire

Also by T.O. Smith

BRITAIN AND THE ORIGINS OF THE VIETNAM WAR: UK Policy in Indo-China 1943–50

CHURCHILL, AMERICA AND VIETNAM, 1941–45

Vietnam and the Unravelling of Empire
General Gracey in Asia 1942–1951

T.O. Smith
Associate Professor of History, Huntington University, USA

© T.O. Smith 2014

All rights reserved. No reproduction, copy or transmission of this publication may be made without written permission.

No portion of this publication may be reproduced, copied or transmitted save with written permission or in accordance with the provisions of the Copyright, Designs and Patents Act 1988, or under the terms of any licence permitting limited copying issued by the Copyright Licensing Agency, Saffron House, 6–10 Kirby Street, London EC1N 8TS.

Any person who does any unauthorized act in relation to this publication may be liable to criminal prosecution and civil claims for damages.

The author has asserted his right to be identified as the author of this work in accordance with the Copyright, Designs and Patents Act 1988.

First published 2014 by
PALGRAVE MACMILLAN

Palgrave Macmillan in the UK is an imprint of Macmillan Publishers Limited, registered in England, company number 785998, of Houndmills, Basingstoke, Hampshire RG21 6XS.

Palgrave Macmillan in the US is a division of St Martin's Press LLC, 175 Fifth Avenue, New York, NY 10010.

Palgrave Macmillan is the global academic imprint of the above companies and has companies and representatives throughout the world.

Palgrave® and Macmillan® are registered trademarks in the United States, the United Kingdom, Europe and other countries.

ISBN 978–1–137–44869–9

This book is printed on paper suitable for recycling and made from fully managed and sustained forest sources. Logging, pulping and manufacturing processes are expected to conform to the environmental regulations of the country of origin.

A catalogue record for this book is available from the British Library.

A catalog record for this book is available from the Library of Congress.

For Tom, Helen, Ellie and my students

Blessed are those who find wisdom, those who gain understanding, for she is more profitable than silver and yields better returns than gold. She is more precious than rubies; nothing you desire can compare with her. Long life is in her right hand; in her left hand are riches and honour. Her ways are pleasant ways, and all her paths are peace.

Proverbs 3: 13–17

Contents

List of Tables	viii
Acknowledgements	ix
List of Abbreviations	xii
Introduction	**1**
1 The Prelude: Burma 1942–1945	**10**
The war in the Far East	11
The triumph of Gracey's 20th Indian Division	12
2 The Power Vacuum: Vietnam 1945	**32**
Vietnam during the Second World War	34
Gracey's intervention in Vietnam	42
3 The Sideshow: Cambodia 1945	**57**
Cambodia during the Second World War	58
Gracey's intervention in Cambodia	62
4 The Enforcement: Indo-China 1945–1946	**78**
Protecting the peace: Military aid	79
Protecting the peace: Humanitarian aid	93
5 The Aftermath: Bengal and Kashmir 1946–1951	**103**
Gracey and the crises in Bengal and Kashmir	107
Conclusion	**131**
Select Chronology	138
Select Personalia	141
Notes	146
Bibliography	169
Index	181

Tables

4.1 British minimum French Indo-China programme
    September 1945   95

Acknowledgements

As with my previous books, I have incurred a number of debts, which is a pleasure to acknowledge and credit. Although, once again, it should be noted that the usual disclaimer applies that none of the following bear any responsibility for this book's shortcomings or conclusions.

My principal debt of gratitude is to Professor Martin Thomas (Chair of Colonial History at the University of Exeter). It was Martin who, in his role as external examiner for my PhD thesis, first discussed and then later encouraged that a book project considering General Sir Douglas Gracey and peace enforcement was missing from the decolonisation historiography. Unfortunately, two other books and numerous articles took precedence over a 'Gracey' project. Therefore, it has taken me more than a decade to return to this subject and to develop my initial nebulous ideas into a more workable tome. In the meantime, articles about peacekeeping and rice production have hopefully reassured Martin that I had not forgotten about the several future publication projects that were discussed during the *viva voce*.

Similarly, I am greatly indebted to my dear friend Dr Larry Butler (Reader in Imperial History at the University of East Anglia). As always, Larry has been most generous with his time, offered much needed encouragement and painstakingly read and commented upon large portions of the draft typescript. If all historians replicated such patience and kindness then the profession would be a far better one.

I owe a note of thanks to previous scholars in the fields of imperial and diplomatic history for their research into South and Southeast Asian decolonisation. Indeed, the size of the bibliography testifies to the rich vein of academia that I have had the privilege to build upon. I am particularly grateful to Professor John Charmley (University of East Anglia), Professor Benedict Kiernan (Yale University), Professor Thomas Otte (University of East Anglia), Dr David Roberts (Loughborough University), Ms Jennifer Reeves (University of East Anglia) and Mr Chris Sutton (Lingnan University), who have all taken a personal interest in my work. They have frequently offered much needed encouragement, helpful observations and sage advice during the long evolution of this book.

Likewise, a special note of thanks is also due to my colleagues in the History Department at Huntington University – Professor Dwight Brautigam, Professor Paul Michelson and Professor Jeffrey Webb. Despite the philistine climate, which currently prevails in Anglo-American higher education, the Huntington University History Department has continued to provide the intellectual conditions in which serious historical research can thrive and for which I am deeply thankful. I am also grateful to the Faculty Appointments and Tenure Committee at Huntington University, which sanctioned sabbatical leave to work on the manuscript.

I am indebted to the staff, trustees and individual copyright holders of the following libraries and archives: the British Library, London; the Cadbury Research Library, University of Birmingham; the Centre for the Archives of France Overseas, Aix en Provence; Huntington University Library; the Liddell Hart Centre for Military Archives, King's College, University of London; the Mountbatten Archive, University of Southampton Library; the Middle East Centre Archive, University of Oxford; the National Archives, Public Record Office, London. Portions of this book were road tested in much different and earlier forms as: 'Britain and Cambodia, September 1945–November 1946: A Reappraisal', *Diplomacy and Statecraft*, vol. 17, no. 1, 2006, pp. 73–91 and 'Major-General Sir Douglas Gracey: Peacekeeper or Peace-Enforcer?' *Diplomacy and Statecraft*, vol. 21, no. 2, 2010, pp. 226–39. They are reproduced here by kind permission of Taylor and Francis Group. A version of the introduction was published as 'Britain in Vietnam: A Myth Re-examined', *Historical Yearbook*, the Nicolae Iorga History Institute of the Romanian Academy, vol. 10, 2013, pp. 68–76. It is gratefully reproduced here with permission. The epigraph quotation is taken from the Holy Bible, New International Version. Copyright 1973, 1978, 1984 by International Bible Society. Used by permission of Hodder & Stoughton Ltd. All rights reserved.

I am very grateful for the assistance of my publishers Jenny McCall, Clare Mence, Angharad Bishop and Emily Russell at Palgrave Macmillan, who have once again demonstrated enormous patience, understanding and support beyond the call of normal duty.

Finally, I owe an immense debt of gratitude to my family. The love, encouragement and support of my parents, Victor and Joan Smith, have been invaluable. My wife Elizabeth, who has lived with this project from the beginning, clearly deserves a medal. But I also owe much to my brother and his wife, Thomas and Helen Lyman Smith, along with their daughter Eleanor, and also the students whom Elizabeth and

I have adopted over the years and who have become an integral part of our family: Katie Fager, Kris Burgess, Paul Hageman, Steve and Ashlee Edinger and many others. The joy of these relationships means that it is only fitting that this book should be dedicated to them.

Abbreviations

CCS	Combined Chiefs of Staff
COS	Chiefs of Staff (British)
JIC	Joint Intelligence Committee
JSM	Joint Service Mission (Washington)
PM	Prime Minister
SEAC	Southeast Asia Command
SOE	Special Operations Executive
UN	United Nations

Introduction

> Gracey, after brilliantly commanding his division, carried out in an outstanding manner a most difficult military-political task in Indo-China.[1]
>
> Field Marshal Viscount Slim

Hitherto there have been a number of excellent studies concerning Britain's brief but controversial involvement in the origins of the Vietnam War. Yet despite the quantity of sophisticated Anglo-centric accounts with reference to Britain's involvement in Vietnam in 1945, mainstream historians have been too content to follow like sheep the doyens of the past. The result has been to either prosecute or defend the actions of the British commanding officer in Saigon – Major-General Sir Douglas David Gracey. But in doing so, little attention has been given to either the context of Gracey's Indo-Chinese deployment (the Burma Campaign 1942–1945) or the consequence (the First Kashmir War 1947–1948) of these first British brushes with post-war Asian nationalism. The present volume therefore argues for a reappraisal of Gracey's French Indo-China deployment outside of the narrow confines of the Vietnam War (to include Burma, Cambodia and Kashmir within the Gracey narrative) in order to understand more broadly British foreign policy and the decline of the British Empire.

At the time of his death in 1964, General Sir Douglas David Gracey had enjoyed 13 years of a modest and tranquil retirement from military life. During this period, he lived in the affluent British county of Surrey

---

An earlier edition of this introduction was published as T.O. Smith, 'Britain in Vietnam: A Myth Re-examined', *Historical Yearbook*, the Nicolae Iorga History Institute of the Romanian Academy, vol. 10, 2013, pp. 68–76.

and indulged in his passion for the gentleman's game of cricket with membership of the Marylebone Cricket Club – otherwise known as the MCC or Lord's. Even in this idyllic environment, Gracey displayed a deep-seated paternalistic concern for the common soldiery – an intense duty of care that had been exhibited throughout his military career. Therefore, it was only natural in retirement that he should serve as the chairman of the Royal Hospital for the Incurables in Putney.[2] He also indulged in his affection for his 'boys' with an immensely glowing foreword to the privately published diaries of Major Anthony Bickersteth who, during the Burma Campaign 1942–1945, had commanded Princess Mary's 4/10th Gurkha Rifles in Gracey's 20th Indian Division.[3]

The affectionate, proud and yet unassuming closeness to his officers and men was not surprising. These were the veterans of the long forgotten 14th Army – led by Slim. They had desperately fought one of the most brutal British campaigns of the Second World War along the Burma front and then, following the Japanese surrender in 1945, dutifully stepped in to police the power vacuum in Southeast Asia on behalf of the newly established United Nations Organisation. In comparison to the bravado of the fighting 8th Army and the familiar household name of Field Marshal Montgomery, or even the Whitehall chiefs such as Field Marshal Alanbrooke, Air Chief Marshal Portal and others, it was unsurprising that the dynamic and inspirational men (Slim and his divisional commanders: Major-General Harold Briggs, Gracey and Major-General Frank Messrvy) who had led British, Indian and Gurkha troops through some of the world's toughest jungle terrains – while others clamoured for glory and honour closer to home – stood silent guard over their comrades while nursing the wounds of the past.

It could have remained thus, with Gracey being remembered with modest praise by Slim for his diligent command of the 20th Indian Division both in wartime and retirement. But Slim considered Gracey worthy of greater commendation. In Gracey, Slim found a dynamic divisional commander who was 'full of energy and ideas'. Furthermore, Slim observed during the Burma Campaign that with the forces under Gracey he 'had never seen troops who carried their tails more vertically'.[4] Despite the obvious risk of encountering the Japanese, Gracey's troops also had to contend with malaria, the harsh jungle foliage, insects, leeches, snakes, leopards, tigers, elephants and saltwater crocodiles.[5] In these hazardous circumstances, Gracey developed a happy, tight-knit and confident division that – due to the unusual length of his tenure – was justly proud of its commanding officer.[6]

Nevertheless after Gracey's retirement, with the advent of the Cold War, a number of Anglo-American writers sought to reassess Gracey's legacy. The Burma Campaign did not attract their attention but rather Gracey's management of the power vacuum in southern Vietnam in 1945. In doing so, it became overly fashionable to attack Gracey's command in Saigon in order to blame Britain – and specifically Gracey – for the American entanglement in what would later become known as the Vietnam War.[7] In such circumstances, an outstanding military reputation built during the Burma campaign became first of all soiled, then damaged and finally destroyed, by the complexity of Allied liberation duties. In addition, and perhaps more unfairly, all of the evils of empire – to a greater or a lesser degree – were bestowed upon Gracey. He embodied the servitude of the past. At the same time, the indigenous Vietnamese became the victims of the future.

As early as 1955, nine years before Gracey's death, the American author Ellen Hammer set out in her book, *The Struggle for Indochina 1940–55* (1955), the hypothesis that Gracey, a rabid imperialist, had actively sought to ensure a French return to Vietnam vis-à-vis the birth of an independent indigenous Vietnam.

> Gracey took it upon himself to restore Indo-China south of the sixteenth parallel to the French and thereby engaged the British Government in a responsibility for the war which followed.[8]

This was followed by a slew of works: *Vietnam: A Dragon Embattled*, Volume 1 (1966) by Joseph Buttinger; *Abuse of Power* (1967) by Theodore Draper; *The United States and Vietnam* (1967) by George Kahin and John Lewis; *The British in Vietnam* (1970) by George Rosie; *Why Vietnam?* (1980) by Archimedes Patti – a former Office of Strategic Services officer and commander of the first Office of Strategic Services team in Hanoi in 1945; *The March of Folly: From Troy to Vietnam* (1984) by Barbara Tuchmann; and *The Politics of Continuity: British Foreign Policy and the Labour Government 1945–1946* (1993) by John Saville. All of these books highlighted Gracey's pro-imperialist management of southern Vietnam in 1945.[9]

Patti, in particular, regarded Britain's actions as directly contributing to the outbreak of the First Vietnam War (1946–1954).[10] According to Patti, Gracey's liberation actions were 'ill-considered', 'highly questionable' and 'highhanded'. In a devastating assessment of Gracey's command, Patti concluded that Gracey was 'a man without a plan. He merely reacted to events as they occurred, neither anticipating them nor appreciating their impact after the fact'. Ho Chi Minh, the Vietnamese communist leader of the nationalist Vietminh coalition, naturally shared Patti's poor evaluation of Gracey. Patti recorded that

'Gracey was an inveterate colonial official dedicated to the perpetuation of the old order'.[11]

Likewise the British journalist, Rosie, was exceptionally damning in his criticism of events in southern Vietnam. The 20th Indian Division had been 'implicitly ruthless' in their actions. This had immediately resulted in 'alarming directness' by the British, which had 'cost the lives of thousands of Vietnamese'. In his analysis, Rosie argued that Gracey was naturally 'highly suspicious of the Vietminh' and displayed 'evidence of strong pro-French feelings'. Rosie concluded that in taking such brutal measures the forces at Gracey's disposal had become 'overtly political'. Therefore, instead of overseeing United Nations post-surrender duties 'the general [Gracey] took sides' and prevented a more consultative and conciliatory homecoming for French imperialism.[12]

More recently, Mark Lawrence's book, *Assuming the Burden: Europe and the American Commitment to War in Vietnam* (2005), argued that Gracey had acted 'boldly' with a 'naked policy of suppression' towards the Vietnamese. In doing so, Gracey had pursued a 'brazenly pro-French policy', which had resulted in Allied liberation forces 'burning down houses' and carrying out other such insalubrious tasks. French colonial rule had in this grubby manner been 'returned behind a temporary shield provided by Britain'.[13]

As a result, these authors have made certain that Gracey has been vilified by an inundation of criticism. This has created the myth that, had it not been for the on-the-ground actions of the Allied liberation commander in Saigon (Gracey) in 1945, Vietnamese nationalism would have flourished, and thereby Gracey could have prevented a further 30 years of needless bloodshed.

In this regard, Gracey certainly did not help his own reputation. He greatly assisted his detractors by allowing them to condemn him with his own words. At a meeting of the Royal Central Asian Society in 1953, Gracey stated that in Saigon:

> I was welcomed on arrival by the Vietminh who said 'Welcome' and all that sort of thing. It was a very unpleasant situation, and I promptly kicked them out.

Dennis Duncanson later argued that the comment was 'spontaneous and unconsidered'.[14] But the damage was done. The protagonist had readily supplied proof that, at heart, he was an uncompromising imperialist, an old style colonialist and a racist who belonged to the forgotten age of the mid-Victorian Empire.

Yet if the case for Gracey's prosecution has been well supported, so too have been the grounds for his defence. F.S.V. Donnison's book, *British Military Administration in the Far East 1943–1946* (1956), skilfully emphasised the complex issues surrounding inadequate British troop numbers being deployed to police an intricate power vacuum in Southeast Asia in 1945. In southern Vietnam, the Vietminh had 'no authority and there was not effective administration, and no maintenance of order whatsoever'. Gracey therefore had to act in order to ensure the well-being of the civilian population and also of his own forces. In doing so, this had to be achieved against a number of 'brutal methods adopted by the Vietminh extremists'.[15]

Later Peter Dunn in *The First Vietnam War* (1985) and Dennis Duncanson, in an article for the *Journal of the Royal Central Asian Society* (1968), both offered full-bodied justifications for Gracey's actions vis-à-vis his detractors.[16] Duncanson, in particular, highlighted that despite the unusual modus operandi and the difficult operating conditions in southern Indo-China, Gracey always acted completely within the confines of British military policy, The Hague Convention and international law:

> The authority of the power of the state having passed de facto into the hands of the occupant, the latter shall do all in his power to restore, and to ensure as far as possible, public order and safety, respecting at the same time, unless absolutely prevented, the laws in force in the country.[17]

While at the same time, Dunn was vehemently critical of the Supreme Allied Commander for Southeast Asia, Admiral Lord Louis Mountbatten, for failing to support Gracey with an adequate number of liberation forces. As a result Dunn portrayed Gracey as a proficient soldier betrayed by his superiors and held hostage to fortune.[18]

Peter Dennis' book the *Troubled Days of Peace: Mountbatten and South East Asia Command 1945–46* (1987) offered an important comparative history of the power vacuum in Vietnam and the power vacuum in the Dutch East Indies during the same time period. Although this work was even-handed in its assessment of Gracey, tellingly, Dennis' analysis was far more supportive in its defence of Mountbatten than the commanding officer on-the-ground in Saigon.[19] More recently, John Springhall's spirited defence of Gracey for the *Journal of Contemporary History* (2005) argued that Gracey had unfairly become the general embodiment for the rebirth of French colonialism in Southeast Asia.[20]

Most of these conventional historical works – for either the prosecution or the defence – have focused upon an Anglo-centric approach towards the crucial year of 1945. But in contrast to such studies, Peter Neville's impressive book *Britain in Vietnam: Prelude to Disaster 1945–46* (2008) has sought to defend Gracey's actions by placing British actions within a wider geopolitical context up until the end of 1946. After all 'Gracey was ultimately the servant of British diplomatic and military strategy'. In consequence, Neville has usefully examined a broader chronological and politico-military framework concerning Britain, China, France, the Soviet Union, the United States and a constantly changing plethora of Vietnamese nationalist groupings.[21]

Finally, although historians should avoid writing in the first person, I must acknowledge that this is not my first foray into the Gracey debate. As an academic interested in British decolonisation and international history in Southeast Asia, it has been necessary to pass comment on Gracey's liberation of Vietnam as part of a number of wider studies concerning the dynamics of British foreign policy in the region. Indeed, my article 'Britain and Cambodia, September 1945–November 1946: A Reappraisal' for the journal *Diplomacy and Statecraft* (2006) re-examined British policy towards Cambodia and provided a much needed contrast to British policy towards Vietnam.[22] This was recognised by Neville who highlighted how the article 'usefully discussed' British and French participation in Cambodia.[23] Although the article's remit was far broader in scope than a study of Gracey and British liberation duties in the Cambodian capital Phnom Penh, the article sought to build upon Dennis' earlier comparison of British policy towards Vietnam and the Dutch East Indies and offer a contrast between British approaches within French Indo-China (Cambodia and Vietnam).[24] Similarly my subsequent tome, *Britain and the Origins of the Vietnam War: UK Policy in Indo-China 1943–50* (2007), again examined British liberation duties as part of a wider discussion of British foreign policy towards Vietnam between the Second World War and the Cold War.[25] Later, in an early attempt to develop some of the central themes for this study, I returned to the circumstances surrounding Gracey's role in Saigon and Phnom Penh with an article in 2010 that questioned whether Gracey practised peacekeeping or peace enforcement in the delivery of his Indo-Chinese liberation duties.[26]

Thus amidst the richness of these Anglo-centric studies, the question that needs to be asked is why does British foreign policy – and in particular the actions of Gracey – warrant further examination? The answer is fairly simple. In notable contrast to the studies mentioned above,

Vietnam and the Unravelling of Empire: General Gracey in Asia 1942–1951 expands the debate in four significant ways.

First, to understand Gracey's modus operandi in Vietnam, this study briefly looks at Gracey's role in the Burma Campaign of 1942–1945. Gracey himself wrote an unpublished history of the 20th Indian Division and its operations along the Burma front.[27] It is not the intention of this book to reproduce that account here but rather to re-examine the Burma Campaign in order to understand more fully both the military context of the power vacuum in Asia, the experience of the soldiers that were being expected to police the peace, and the leadership attributes of the central character – Gracey – for what followed in Vietnam, Cambodia and Kashmir.

Second, this study integrates Gracey's operations in Cambodia into the narrative of his operations in Vietnam. This vital French Indo-Chinese comparison sheds a new light on previous claims concerning Gracey's fanatical imperialism and racism. Had Gracey truly been an old school colonial warrior, he would have ruthlessly pursued similar policies in Cambodia and Vietnam in a uniform attempt to restore the French Empire with little care for either the indigenous Cambodian or Vietnamese populations – as his accusers have often argued, based purely upon his actions in Vietnam. For example in Cambodia:

> the Anglo-Indian troops of General Gracey rapidly put an end to the independence proclaimed by Prime Minister Son Ngoc Thanh, opening the country to French troops.[28]

Yet at the same time, Gracey had actually argued for Cambodia that Britain should 'condone the past actions of the P.M. [Son Ngoc Thanh] and to enlist his support; in fact to treat him in the same manner that we had dealt with Aung San in Burma'. In other words, Gracey radically proposed for Britain to work alongside the emergent Cambodian nationalist movement.[29]

Third, this study uniquely examines the aftermath of Gracey's intervention in French Indo-China not by analysing subsequent events in Vietnam but by instead examining Gracey's next crucial command in Asia – Pakistan. The simple fact that Mountbatten personally recommended Gracey to Mohammed Ali Jinnah (the Governor-General of Pakistan) as the temporary Governor of East Bengal highlighted both Gracey's sensitivity and skill in dealing with indigenous nationalist struggles. Indeed, Mountbatten specifically chose Gracey 'in view of his great experience as an administrator in French Indo-China'.[30] This

8 Vietnam and the Unravelling of Empire

revelation directly contradicts much of the negative historiographical analysis concerning Gracey and Vietnam. And it certainly creates a new perspective on the Gracey–Mountbatten relationship.

In regard to Pakistan, it is also imperative to look at Gracey's role in the outbreak of the First Kashmir War – another Asian power vacuum scenario. The East Bengal recommendation and the Kashmir crisis are deeply revealing. Mountbatten's assessment of Gracey's actions in Saigon had only been sent to the British Chiefs of Staff in June 1947. The subsequent pessimistic historical debate surrounding Gracey's command in Vietnam has focused on Mountbatten's appraisal. In the report, Mountbatten had praised Gracey's 'courage and determination in an extremely difficult situation', but Mountbatten had also been critical of Gracey for exceeding his orders. He even bluntly accused Gracey of giving 'permission' for the French coup d'etat. Yet two months after writing this evaluation, Mountbatten was personally recommending Gracey to Jinnah for his crisis management skills.[31]

Fourth, rather than focusing this book on purely British foreign and military policies towards Vietnam or even attempting a service biography of Gracey, this study builds upon previous narratives of British actions towards Cambodia, Vietnam and Kashmir and creates a wider commentary on the dynamics of one of Britain's first contemporary Asian peace enforcement activities (a fusion of British foreign and military policies). The newly born United Nations emerged in a humanitarian maelstrom at the end of the Second World War. Faced with numerous power vacuums, economic dislocation, social displacement and global famine, it did not possess the experience, the expertise or the resources to practise effective peacekeeping. Instead, peace enforcement was the only option available as the old world colonial order began to disintegrate and the new world's clamour for decolonisation gathered pace.

In this context, readers should not therefore view this study as an apology for Gracey. It is also not a detailed military history of events on the ground in Vietnam, Cambodia and Kashmir. But rather this book is a re-examination of the early practice of peace enforcement – particularly high-policy decisions concerning military and humanitarian aid. In addition, it is a defence of the fog of war thesis, both in the power vacuum in French Indo-China at the end of the Second World War and also in the first Kashmir conflict between India and Pakistan in 1947–1948. In doing so, this work is not only concerned with the maintenance of law and order but also with other pertinent issues such as food supply, dockyard provision and essential services. Thus the origins of modern United Nations peacekeeping duties may be found in one of Britain's first crude attempts at peace enforcement (another example being British 1945 liberation duties in the Dutch East Indies). Over time the interface of peace enforcement with what would later be recognised as peacekeeping has been blurred by the nature of geopolitics – for example in Afghanistan and Iraq. But in those early years of the new United Nations order, peace enforcement was the emergent paradigm, and the seemingly more noble concept of neoliberal peacekeeping was as yet undiscovered.[32]

For these four reasons, this book attempts to reappraise three of Britain's most curious episodes of peace enforcement following the Second World War – Vietnam, Cambodia and Kashmir. In doing so, the main focus of the work is not upon Pakistan but rather upon Indo-China. Kashmir is used only to discuss the aftermath of Vietnam. In Indo-China, Gracey did not create the First Vietnam War; the French did, with a little help from the Vietnamese. Nor did Gracey create the First Kashmir War between India and Pakistan; Jinnah, Mountbatten and Jawaharlal Nehru (the Indian Prime Minister) must take most of the responsibility. Yet it has become fashionable – in light of the subsequent American involvement in Vietnam – to seek a non-American military scapegoat for the failings of politicians. Further work is thus needed to see the wood for the trees. This study therefore attempts, in part, to redress this balance.

1
The Prelude: Burma 1942–1945

In many respects, Douglas David Gracey epitomised the high-Victorian ideals of the British Empire. He was born in Gorakhpur in India in 1894. The progeny of a civil servant, Gracey was, as one would have expected, sent to England for his education. First of all he attended Blundell's independent boarding school in Devon. From there Gracey progressed to the Royal Military College at Sandhurst, in Berkshire. Upon graduating from Sandhurst in 1914, he was commissioned to the 1st King George's Own Gurkha Rifles in the Indian Army. It was a natural appointment. Gracey was fluent in the Gorkhali language, and he could therefore easily converse with his Gurkha troops in their native tongue.

During the First World War, Gracey initially fought in France with the Royal Munster Fusiliers. But from 1916 onwards, he saw action in Palestine and Syria with the Gurkha Rifles. Wounded twice, Gracey was awarded the Military Cross for gallantry in 1917, to which was later added a bar. He was also mentioned in dispatches.

After the First World War, Gracey was appointed as an instructor back at his alma mater, the Royal Military College at Sandhurst. However, after two years he was transferred from the college to India. Once in India, Gracey served in a variety of training instructor, staff officer and front-line commands. As a new war in Europe materialised in 1939, Gracey took charge of the 2/3rd Gurkha Rifles on the Northwest Frontier. In 1940, he was appointed as the Assistant Commandant of the Indian Army Staff College in Quetta (modern Pakistan). He married in 1931.

In 1941, Gracey experienced his first action of the Second World War when he led the 17th Infantry Brigade in Iraq and Syria. During this campaign, he was awarded the Order of the British Empire. In the

Middle East, despite acute supply issues, Gracey and the 17th Infantry Brigade successfully secured northeast Syria against Vichy-French forces, including the all-important Mosul to Aleppo railway. It was intended that Gracey's brigade would also assist in the greater defence of the region if the German armies smashed their way through the Caucasus region and threatened British interest in the wider Middle East.[1]

The war in the Far East

In the meantime, the Second World War in South and Southeast Asia had not gone at all well for the western colonial powers. During 1941 and 1942, the Japanese Army forced its way into: French Indo-China; British Hong Kong, Malaya and Singapore; the American-led Philippines; and the Dutch East Indies. Old school western colonialism had been routed by a new, modern and dynamic Asian imperialism. A blend of formal and informal Japanese control emerged from the ashes of western empires to hold sway over Southeast Asia.

The denouement of the British colonial administration and the defence of Singapore were particularly gruesome for Britain. In Singapore, a force of 85,000 British and Commonwealth troops was defeated by 30,000 Japanese.[2] The speed and size of the British capitulation surprised everyone including the Prime Minister, Winston S. Churchill, who was 'stupefied' with the magnitude of the defeat and the nature of the British 'disgrace'. Britain had lost its most prestigious base in the Far East.[3] Furthermore, in order to protect the acquisition of their new assets and to take full advantage of the disintegration of the British Empire in the Far East, the Japanese Army also turned its attention towards other targets. This led to the invasion of Burma and subsequently India.

During the invasion of Burma, the Japanese Army replayed the similar devastating success of the campaign against British forces in Malaya. British rule was rapidly swept aside in an Asian *Blitzkrieg*, and Japanese imperial control was established in Burma in its stead. Nonetheless, with the commencement of the Burmese monsoon season, the Japanese advance eventually came to a standstill in May 1942. This enabled the Japanese Army to consolidate its hold upon Burma even further, but it also permitted the British Empire a respite to organise its colonial resources for the defence of India.[4] Thus, it was against this worsening geopolitical background to the war in the Far East that Gracey was recalled from Syria to assist in the vital defence of the most important component of the British Empire, India.

The triumph of Gracey's 20th Indian Division

On 1 April 1942, Gracey took command of the newly established 20th Indian Division.[5] Gracey believed passionately that his new division should receive thorough preparation and training for undertaking arduous jungle operations. He therefore set about creating a specialist educational programme for the instruction of the 20th Indian Division in jungle warfare. Gracey took a special interest in the development of the teaching course. This reflected his own deep-seated desire to educate his troops to the best of his ability in order that they performed at their optimal levels upon the battlefield. It also indicated an inner passion to oversee and improve the well-being of his men in the field. Thus, on 13 April, Gracey personally began to draw up a comprehensive training manual for the 20th Indian Division in jungle battle-craft.[6] In doing so Gracey, surprisingly, created the only division in Slim's 14th Army that had been specifically trained for warfare in Burma.[7] It was a far-sighted decision that later reaped huge dividends for both Gracey and Slim.

It was remarkable that up until this point in the Second World War the British Army in India had developed so few specialist units for undertaking jungle operations. The leadership of the British Army in India was not ignorant of the terrain in which it expected its units to operate. Indeed, the repeated failure of the British to stem the Japanese advance into South and Southeast Asia revealed the necessity of developing new jungle tactics to halt the seemingly relentless march of the Japanese Army towards India.

The British Army in India had decided that there were three degrees of jungle density, which British forces would face in the field. These received the uninspiring names of – dense, thick and thin.

> Dense: so thick that a man on foot could not get through without cutting his way.
>
> Thick: in which a man could force his way through with the aid of a stick but without having to cut.
>
> Thin: in which a man could move at a fair pace, without cutting or damaging his clothes, picking his way.

The types of foliage within such jungle densities could be most varied. For example, they might include 'bamboo, tree, palm, forest and scrub-mangrove swamp'.[8]

In contrast to a widely held belief within the British Army in India, Gracey advocated that jungle terrain and foliage were both in actual fact the soldiers' friend. It was his deeply held conviction that units under his command could be highly mobile even in the densest of jungle foliage, and that they should certainly not under any circumstances become merely 'lorry bound'.[9] Gracey appreciated the need for both speed and surprise. With limited logistical infrastructure in jungle warfare, road based units would quickly become highly predictable in their movements and thus be a relatively straightforward enemy target. Similarly, during a major Japanese offensive, it was also possible for a non-road based foe to easily circumnavigate its lorry bound opponent, thus rendering motorised units operationally impotent. Furthermore, motorised units on unpaved jungle roads were frequently at the mercy of the weather. Torrential rain often made motorised transport slow and slippery. Moreover, the weather sometimes made it impossible for motorised transport to move forward at all. This was certainly the case if, for example, a sudden storm had either produced a large rockslide or simply turned an innocuous road into a fast flowing stream.

Gracey therefore developed transportation for the 20th Indian Division using both animal and motorised sources. This meant that the division was no longer solely reliant upon road transportation. This benefited the British defence of India in two ways. First, it enabled Gracey to move his units with intense speed and surprise across difficult terrain. Second, it freed up a large number of vehicles that could be transferred to other divisions within the British Army in India. This made it possible for a number of under-resourced units to become highly mobile.[10] It was an intuitive decision that greatly impacted the operational capabilities on a wider scale than just his division. Brigadier E.C.J. Woodford, who commanded the 32nd Indian Infantry Brigade within the 20th Division during the Burma Campaign, later noted that two of Gracey's greatest leadership strengths were his ability to undertake 'clear thinking' and his aptitude for making 'decisive' management decisions.[11]

The training manual that Gracey drew up naturally bore the imprint of its author. It was full of 'practical common sense'. Indeed, it eventually proved to be so comprehensive and successful that it did not require any updating as the Burma Campaign progressed. Gracey's vision for jungle warfare reflected his style of leadership. He was not a great orator but he was a 'highly capable and respected' leader in the field. Yet his leadership skills went far deeper than merely a new and specialist approach to jungle training. Gracey was not just interested in the educational endeavours of his troops or the strategic machinations involved in the specialist study of jungle warfare. He also took a deep and personal interest in the general welfare of his troops.[12] Major Malins, who served under Gracey in Burma, noted that his commanding officer at all times regarded his men as 'though he was personally responsible for the lives of every single man under his command'. As was clearly evident to Malins, Gracey had never forgotten the needless human slaughter and suffering he had witnessed during the Battle of the Somme in the First World War. Indeed, Gracey readily informed Malins and the other officers within his division that 'men are the most important and precious thing we've got'. He therefore instructed his officers always to use their men 'with the greatest care'.[13]

In mentoring his officers and training them to highly appreciate their men, Gracey introduced what he later modestly called a strong 'team spirit' into the 20th Indian Division.[14] Gracey's self-effacing admission camouflaged a zealous concern and a passionate regard for the wellbeing of his troops. It was worth the investment: Brigadier Woodford noted that 'his [Gracey's] constant concern for his men and their trust in him were responsible for the exceptional standard of discipline and efficiency it [the 20th Indian Division] always maintained'.[15] This was certainly aided by the strong interpersonal bond and deepseated self-worth that Gracey shared with his officers. Major Bickersteth, for example, was convinced that deep down at heart his commanding officer remained, like him, a company commander. Thus, Gracey's lectures to his officers did not consist of dull military theory or dry academic rhetoric. But rather, Gracey's briefings were always full of what Bickersteth called 'immense practical value'. In return, Gracey's officers greatly valued their divisional commander due to his experience of, and his intense empathy with, the characteristics of their roles.[16] In doing so, Gracey aimed to create a large interconnected family within the 20th Indian Division. Just as Gracey appreciated his company and platoon commanders, they in turn were expected to be familiar with their men, and their families, and indeed their problems. The 20th Indian Division thus became a very personal division 'instilled with Gracey's own spirit'.

In addition to Gracey's concern for the well-being of the troops under his command, he was also worried about the treatment of any civilians upon the battlefield. He particularly despised the Japanese Army for its maltreatment of civilians during the Burma Campaign.[17] Nevertheless, Gracey did not let this hatred, concerning Japanese humanitarian atrocities, cloud his operational judgement. He had a healthy respect for his Japanese foe. Gracey regarded the Japanese Army as a formidable enemy whose military achievements one could not fail to acknowledge.[18] Again, reflecting his deep-seated commitment to education, Gracey exhorted his officers to study and apprise themselves of Japanese Army tactics.[19] In doing so, Gracey certainly demonstrated due respect for the Japanese Army, but he always maintained a profound self-assurance in the justice of an ultimate British victory.[20] This without doubt rubbed off on his officers and men. Indeed, Slim later noted how 'confident' the 20th Indian Division had become under Gracey's leadership.[21] Slim's unswerving trust in Gracey's leadership abilities was not without just cause. Gracey had taken time to develop a highly mobile and well-trained division, who had eagerly become specialists in Southeast Asian warfare. To illustrate this point, at the end of 1942, the 20th Indian Division took part in an intra-division jungle warfare exercise on the island of Ceylon; following the successful completion of the war games Gracey's division was deemed ready for deployment to the war in the Far East.[22]

Hence the 20th Indian Division was moved from the tranquillity of Ceylon to Ranchi in eastern India. Once located at Ranchi, Gracey's division was rapidly absorbed into the hustle and bustle of Slim's XV Corps. Slim previously knew Gracey from the Syria Command of 1941, and Slim already held Gracey in high regard as being 'full of energy and ideas'.[23] Gracey now quickly became part of Slim's inner circle.[24] Gracey's motivational and man-management skills within the 20th Indian Division were evident for all to see. Slim openly commented that Gracey possessed a 'great hold' over his men. In addition, he regarded Gracey's leadership of the 20th Indian Division as an exemplary tour de force.[25] While based at Ranchi, Gracey continued to train and educate the 20th Indian Division in jungle warfare techniques. Extensive patrols were sent out. Forward positions were established and then dismantled. Live firing practice and firing discipline became critical training exercises. Above all, the division was repeatedly drilled in the necessity of producing proper and accurate reports that could be rapidly dispatched to Gracey's tactical headquarters from any sector his troops patrolled or occupied.[26] Discipline, mobility, speed, education and information had become the hallmarks of Gracey's command and his division readily bore their impression.

During October 1943, the 20th Indian Division was moved into its pre-allocated position for the defence of the Indian–Burmese frontier close to the city of Imphal.[27] In doing so, the 20th Indian Division was transferred from XV Corps over to IV Corps. Gracey thus became part of Lt.-General Geoffrey Scoones' command. At the same time Slim, his former commander, was promoted to lead the 14th Army. This comprised of the IV, XV and XXXIII Corps. Lt.-General Philip Christison replaced Slim at XV Corps. Once the 20th Indian Division was established in its new location, Gracey quickly dispatched extensive patrols to all sectors within his purview. Detailed reports soon began arriving at 20th Indian Division headquarters. The strong learning culture that Gracey had developed during training was now put into practice. Extensive and rapid patrolling enabled the 20th Indian Division to acquire an immense amount of information that could be used to their advantage.

Gracey initially had neither the knowledge nor the understanding of either the terrain or enemy movements on the other side of the frontier. But after an intense period of information gathering, in late 1943 and early 1994, he began to move the 20th Indian Division forward from Imphal and into Burma.[28] In November, the 20th Indian Division occupied and fortified the village of Tamu. This was positioned just the other side of the Indian–Burmese frontier. The occupation of Tamu enabled Gracey to secure one of the main routes from Imphal into Burma. It also gave him the ability to protect the access road from Imphal to the crucial British airfield and supply base located at Palel. This was located just inside the Indian frontier.[29] As the 20th Indian Division moved forward, mules transported food and other supplies including luxuries such as alcohol for the officers.[30]

By February 1944, Gracey had succeeded in advancing his units much further forward into Japanese controlled Burma. The 20th Indian Division had successfully moved ahead from the village of Tamu, and it had occupied the Kabaw Valley in the Burmese highlands. In addition, the division was now actively sending out patrols even further afield: across the Chindwin River and deep into central Burma.[31] During this offensive, Gracey had discovered that it was not just the Japanese Army the 20th Indian Division had to be wary of. The Kabaw Valley was proven to be a notorious malarial death trap. But despite such risks, the move forward into Burma appeared to have been a great jungle warfare accomplishment for the previously untried and untested 20th Indian Division. Gracey successfully used air power to assist with clearing the Japanese forces, and he experienced an early triumph when units of his division effectively captured the village of Kyaukchaw.

At all times during the advance, Gracey continued to send out multiple units probing forward. Extensive patrols were dispatched to reconnoitre the terrain ahead, monitor the movements of the Japanese Army and keep Gracey's headquarters alive with information. It was through these patrols that Gracey first discovered the Japanese Army moving in large numbers up the Chindwin River towards Imphal. This represented the start of a major Japanese offensive against the British defence of India.[32] Intensive and continuous patrols had been the key to Gracey's early success with the 20th Indian Division, and he was now greatly aggrieved at having to fall back in the face of a new and formidable Japanese attack.[33]

In the Burmese jungle, there was no conventional front line. Gracey had been pushing the 20th Indian Division forward with aggressive and intensive patrolling. This provided him with detailed knowledge as to the Japanese Army's whereabouts and a more general idea as to his enemy's intended movements.[34] But the sheer size and scale of the Japanese advance now threatened to overwhelm both Gracey's ability to patrol forward and his intelligence gathering operations. The Japanese forces that Gracey faced were trying to capture the airfield and supply base at Palel. It was vital for Japan to secure Palel not only for the advance upon Imphal but also for any sustained Japanese offensive into India. Thus, unbeknown to Gracey, the 20th Indian Division now faced the best troops and the heaviest firepower in the Japanese Army. As the Japanese Army built up its forces for the offensive upon Palel, Gracey was met with stubborn and sustained Japanese attacks in the Kabaw valley. This posed Gracey with numerous difficulties in pulling his units back from the Valley, where they were by now heavily outnumbered and outgunned by the Japanese Army.[35]

Slim, however, did not want the 20th Indian Division to be extracted from Burma too prematurely. It was therefore decided by his command that the 20th Indian Division would first of all withdraw from the Kabaw Valley and then be concentrated at the town of Moreh, which was located just inside the Burmese frontier. If Moreh could not be held against the Japanese offensive then the division would be withdrawn further still across the Indian frontier towards the city of Imphal. In these circumstances, the division would be expected to hastily regroup and take up a defensive position in the hills surrounding the Shenam Saddle. Slim believed that Shenam was crucial to the defence of Imphal, and he therefore ordered Gracey to hold the Shenam Saddle at 'all costs'.[36] The hilltop positions that the 20th Indian Division eventually established on the Shenam Saddle thus became crucial to the defence of Imphal and British India.

In the meantime, the town of Moreh had become a large British base and supply centre for the 20th Indian Division. By February 1944, Gracey had amassed at Moreh 2,400 tons of ammunition and other military supplies, as well as 64,000 gallons of fuel. This was a highly unusual divisional treasure trove. It equated to nearly 15 days of supplies for the 20th Indian Division compared to the normal allocation of only six days. In addition to the large amount of supplies assembled at Moreh, the town had also become the home for Gracey's tactical headquarters and the divisional engineering centre.[37] Thus, due to the considerable value of material located at Moreh, Gracey ordered that the 20th Indian Division would only withdraw from the town upon his personal orders. In the meantime, Scoones instructed Gracey to speed up the evacuation of all civilian labour from Moreh. At the same time, the 20th Indian Division ceaselessly continued its patrols to monitor the Japanese advance.

Night patrols by the 20th Indian Division soon discovered that large numbers of Japanese military units were continuing to pour cross the Chindwin River.[38] The division's situation at Moreh appeared to be just as exposed and vulnerable to being overwhelmed by the Japanese Army advance as its previous positions in the Kabaw Valley. In consequence, on 20 March Gracey was ordered to withdraw from the town. Gracey set up a series of defensive boxes to provide cover for the retreat. In addition, 221 Group of the Royal Air Force supported the extraction with aerial cover. Despite the intensity of the Japanese offensive, in the end the 20th Indian Division somehow managed to produce a fairly orderly withdrawal.[39] Nonetheless, Gracey was not at all best pleased with either Scoones' order to retreat or at having to destroy all of his 'excessive' stores to prevent them falling into Japanese hands.[40] But in the broader scheme of the 14th Army, the professional nature of Gracey's retreat did at least preserve fundamental lines of communication and assist in protecting the city of Imphal.

In addition, as Slim readily noted, Gracey's 20th Indian Division certainly experienced a great deal of 'excitement' during the actual extraction. In order to purchase as much time as possible to orchestrate the retreat from the town of Moreh, it had been necessary for Gracey to deploy a number of units in an active campaign of offensive–defensive manoeuvres. This was to keep the Japanese advance under constant pressure, confuse the enemy as much as possible and prevent the Japanese offensive from simply overrunning Moreh before Gracey had effectively departed.[41] Throughout the retreat from Kabaw, Tamu and Moreh, Gracey maintained full confidence in his patrols and his troops. However, it was not all plain sailing for the 20th Indian Division. One of Gracey's units, the 4/3rd Gurkha Rifles, proved themselves to be a most incapable and defensive-minded battalion during the extraction from Moreh. This battalion subsequently had to be intensively re-educated in order that it could learn from its mistakes and become much more capable and aggressively minded during future patrolling duties.

The 20th Indian Division was therefore ordered by Scoones to take up its new location on the Shenam Saddle on 25 March. The speed and the sheer size of the Japanese advance made it imperative for Gracey to achieve this as soon as possible. The position at Shenam was not just strategically important for the defence of the city of Imphal. It also overlooked the road to the airfield and supply base at Palel. Heavy fighting now accompanied Gracey and the 20th Indian Division as they established their defences at Shenam.[42] In addition, Gracey's sector was not the only area under attack. Brigadier Geoffrey Evans to the north desperately pleaded for Gracey to lend him a brigade from the 20th Indian Division in order to reinforce the northern sector against the Japanese offensive. Gracey was neither happy with the nature of the appeal nor the apparent poor planning of his contemporary. Nonetheless Gracey, as a team player, was compelled to oblige Evans' request.

Gracey also found time during the initial deployment at Shenam to complain bitterly to Scoones at having to abandon the town of Moreh. He was greatly aggrieved with having lost his well-endowed citadel. Gracey's grievance was no doubt clouded by the loss of his stores. For, as the 20th Indian Division had been faced with an overpowering Japanese advance, there was little that the division could have actually done to protect the town. That said, Gracey certainly suffered at other times, during his sojourn with IV Corps, from Scoones' poor communication skills. All the same, on this occasion, Scoones had been right to fear that Gracey's position at Moreh was simply too exposed to the main Japanese advance upon Imphal. Scoones' rationale, which in the end prevailed, was that if the 20th Indian Division had remained at Moreh then it would have been badly battered by the Japanese offensive. Gracey's complaint was also shown to Slim, who in this instance decided to align himself with Scoones' assessment. Slim therefore firmly agreed with Scoones against Gracey. In this case, it had been strategically important enough to the 14th Army as a whole for the 20th Indian Division to be withdrawn from Moreh.[43]

By April Gracey's troops had successfully dug a series of defensive networks in a desperate attempt to hold on to the territory within the Shenam Saddle. The Shenam defence system was not maintained via a continuous forward line but by the division occupying a string of fortified boxes across a 25-mile-long sector. These boxes were linked together by 'constant and aggressive patrolling' by the 20th Indian Division. For seven weeks, Gracey effectively held on to the hill top positions at Shenam against highly aggressive and repeated Japanese assaults, which included large numbers of infantry, tanks and artillery.[44] The defence was no mean feat. The positions on the Shenam Saddle rapidly became an intense battle for survival, which one historian has aptly called 'the most dreadful [battle] of all'.

On 1 April, the Japanese captured Nippon hill. This was part of the Shenam Saddle defence network. It took Gracey and the 20th Indian Division three brutal weeks to successfully retake the position. In the meantime, on 12 April, the 20th Indian Division temporarily retook Nippon hill only to lose it again to the Japanese on 16 April. During the Japanese assault, the hills within the Shenam sector frequently passed back and forth between British and Japanese control. On 20 and 21 April the Japanese Army successfully overran the British positions at Crete East. Gracey was thereby forced to order that the defensive box at Cyprus also had to be abandoned. However, this eventually proved to be the limit of the Japanese advance at Shenam. The hills at Crete West and Scraggy within the Shenam Saddle system became an impenetrable front line for the next three months. This was certainly aided by the massive aerial support that Gracey received for the defence of his positions. But the 20th Indian Division also withstood assault after assault from the Japanese forces trying to break the Shenam defences. The heaviest casualties naturally occurred during combat for the strategically higher ground. The severity of the fighting within the Shenam Saddle should not be underestimated. Indeed, it has been stated of the battle fought within the 20th Indian Division network that '[t]here can have been few places during the war the possession of which, in proportion to their size, was more costly in human life'.

The Japanese Army had without doubt exerted severe pressure upon the 20th Indian Division at Shenam. After seven weeks of almost continuous fighting, Gracey knew that his men were exhausted. On one occasion, troops of the Indian National Army who had been fighting alongside the Japanese against the British were brutally massacred by Gurkha troops as they surrendered. The Japanese assault had brutalised and dehumanised the British defenders at Shenam. They had experienced wave after wave of Japanese attacks by day and by night. Furthermore, the counterattacks organised by Gracey only brought temporary relief before the Japanese war machine wound itself up to attack the Shenam defences once more.[45]

During the second half of May, the 20th Indian Division was moved northwards to cover Kameng and Nungshigum. The Japanese assault upon Imphal still had to be defeated, but the 20th Indian Division desperately needed to be rested from the relentless assaults at Shenam. The move to Kameng and Nungshigum was therefore intended to act as a mild respite.[46] However because the position at Shenam was so vulnerable, Gracey could only withdraw the 20th Indian Division from the defensive network at Shenam a battalion at a time.[47] The 20th Indian Division's opportunity for relief, however, proved to be short-lived. With the Japanese offensive showing no signs of easing, the 20th Indian Division was transferred to Lt.-General Montagu Stopford's XXXIII Corps in order to attack the Japanese communications centre located at Ukhrul. This would also put pressure upon the Japanese forces along the Kohima–Imphal road.[48]

In appalling conditions, Gracey was ordered to move the 20th Indian Division forward. The division advanced along hill tracks and in torrential rain. It was forced to carry not only its supplies but also its wounded.[49] Eventually, the 20th Indian Division reached its forward positions. From here the 14th Army intended to use the division as 'beaters' to flush out the Japanese who had become lodged at Ukhrul.[50] The 20th Indian Division had good ammunition and armour for the offensive. Nevertheless, the 20th Indian Division experienced heavy fighting at Ukhrul. In addition, the weather made conditions on the battlefront extremely difficult. The poor weather also made both air power and air supply almost impossible. Driving rain turned the battlefield to mud. In these conditions, tracks quickly became too slippery for either the mules or the troops to move along. Gracey's soldiers were soon wet and hungry. Their continuous ascent and descent of hills was physically draining. The 20th Indian Division experienced intense heat in the valleys, and the troops were cold and wet on the mountaintops. Fatigue, 'dysentery, scrub typhus, and skin diseases' quickly set in.[51]

Nonetheless, by 4 July, Japan had been forced by the 14th Army to abandon its Imphal offensive.[52] This ultimately enabled the 20th Indian Division to be rested and re-equipped from the beginning of August.[53] As Gracey pulled his units back from forward areas for retraining, he ordered his officers to begin cataloguing and analysing the experiences of the past few months. Prior to the advance into Burma, the 20th Indian Division had been well trained but untested against the Japanese Army. It was now imperative for combat lessons to be learned and plans developed for the next stage of the Burma Campaign. Therefore, the battalion officers quickly became the educators for their individual units. They were expected to evaluate their previous operational activities and readdress any perceived deficiencies within their commands. In addition, battalion commanders were also required to report all operational insights for Gracey and his staff to analyse at divisional headquarters.[54]

Gracey and the 20th Indian Division represented just one small but vital component in Slim and the 14th Army's defence of Imphal. When the battlefield was finally cleared of the Japanese assault and assessed by the British Army in India, they discovered that there were just fewer than 16,700 British casualties at Imphal whereas the Japanese Army had lost 53,505 troops.[55] Imphal had demonstrated the fortitude of the British 14th Army against the Japanese war machine. This was later proven to have been the turning point for Britain in the war with Japan along the Indian–Burmese frontier. Furthermore, the victory at Imphal also illustrated to Britain the advantage of using air power in supporting jungle warfare operations. This knowledge would be deployed to great effect during the subsequent British counteroffensive into Burma.[56]

Meanwhile, between August and October, the 20th Indian Division was rested, reequipped, resupplied and retrained with Gracey's usual meticulous attention to detail. Thus, in November a rehabilitated and confident 20th Indian Division was moved back towards the front line against the Japanese.[57] On 3 December, the 20th Indian Division spearheaded the British 14th Army assault across the Chindwin River. The main crossing point was situated 30 miles north of the town of Kalewa.[58] By moving forward into Burma under the cover of the rainy season, the 20th Indian Division was more favourably placed to attack the Japanese Army during the forthcoming dry season.[59] The plan was to commence a surprise dry season offensive by rapidly advancing downstream along the Chindwin to its convergence with the Irrawaddy River.[60] This time, Gracey got the better of the Japanese Army. He confused the Japanese defenders along the Chindwin with multiple landings at multiple locations across the river at the same time. Thus, the Japanese forces simply did not know which position contained the main British landing party. As soon as the first units of the 20th Indian Division had successfully crossed the river, Gracey set up roadblocks and ambushes behind the enemy lines to harass the Japanese Army and create further disarray and confusion. As the 20th Indian Division successfully completed the crossing of the Chindwin, Gracey eagerly prepared to move the division further east.[61]

Back on the opposite bank of the Chindwin River, a number of units from the 20th Indian Division now found themselves once again in the Kabaw Valley. The valley had been previously abandoned at the onset of the Japanese offensive upon the city of Imphal. However, this time there would be no retreat from this forward position; the momentum was now with the 20th Indian Division. As the rest of the 20th Indian Division surged forward across the Chindwin, the 4/10th Gurkha Rifles used roadblocks and ambush tactics to dislodge the Japanese troops embedded in the Wainggyo Gorge.[62] Gracey was highly pleased with the battalion's operation within the gorge, and he described the attack itself as 'brilliant'. He had every reason to be pleased with the 4/10th Gurkha Rifles. Their success at Wainggyo demonstrated not only the fortitude of Gracey's jungle training programme but also the complete trust and confidence that he had managed to instil at all levels within his division. Colonel B.R. Mullaly later described the 4/10th Gurkha Rifles' endeavour in the Wainggyo Gorge as 'one of the best independent battalion operations of the Burma Campaign and was a fine example of what resolute troops skilled in patrol work and led by officers of initiative and determination can do'.[63]

As the 14th Army offensive continued, the Japanese forces in Burma now sought to fall back to defend the line of the Irrawaddy River. However, the Japanese command simply did not appreciate the strength, the resolve or the tempo of Gracey's 20th Indian Division.[64] As the 20th Indian Division hurried towards the Irrawaddy, it first of all had to capture the town of Monywa. The subsequent attack upon Monywa was not without its problems. The initial advance had to be delayed for a number of days as Gracey had discovered that the majority of the eastern bank of the Chindwin River was trackless. This meant that the 20th Indian Division's progress along the east bank had become slow and arduous. Therefore, with characteristic clarity of minded, Gracey decided that a number of his units would have to cross the Chindwin and then recross the river further downstream in order to speed up the assault upon Monywa.

As the 20th Indian Division moved towards the town of Monywa, it also faced renewed Japanese resistance from the Japanese airfield located at the village of Budalin. For two days, Gracey attacked the airfield but with little success. The Japanese military hold on either the village or the airfield simply could not be broken. On 6 January 1945, torrential rain prevented another British attack upon Budalin. The weather also prevented urgently needed supplies from reaching the 20th Indian Division. The next day, Gracey was left with no choice but to implement half rations, in order for the division to eke out its already meagre food supplies. It took a further three days for the weather to clear enough for Gracey to capture Budalin and establish British control over the airfield and the village.

The episode at Budalin demonstrated not only how tough the Japanese resistance to the 14th Army offensive had become but also how heavily dependent the 20th Indian Division was upon airdrops for its provisions. Weather was once again a major factor limiting aerial supplies. Another important factor was that Gracey could not advance too quickly, otherwise his units would soon operate outside the range of their air tactical support. This would also deprive Gracey of his fighter-bomber support. Thus, the successful capture of the airfield at Budalin was strategically important to Gracey. It enabled him to maintain both adequate supplies and his aerial defence coverage. Nevertheless, even when the weather permitted aerial supply, the airdrops were not always accurate and the Royal Air Force sometimes dropped the wrong supplies upon the wrong units. Nonetheless, because Gracey's advance followed the course of the Chindwin River, the 20th Indian Division was also able to use water transport to supplement its aerial logistical support.[65]

By mid January, the 20th Indian Division had begun to close in on Monywa. The town was an important prize as it was the largest river port on the Chindwin River before it converged with the Irrawaddy River. From 14 to 16 January, the 20th Indian Division cleared all of the approaches to the town. The battle for Monywa itself began in earnest on 16 January. For the next six days, the 20th Indian Division was engaged in a most intense struggle against the Japanese Army for the control of the town. Gracey was also forced to keep Japanese forces outside of the Monywa sector busy with constant patrols. This was to prevent a relief force from reaching the town and alleviating the 20th Indian Division's siege.

However, the assault upon Monywa was not easy to facilitate. The Japanese Army positions within the town were well constructed and keenly defended. The attack by the 20th Indian Division was significantly slowed down by the strength of the Japanese resistance. Gracey thus had to call in intensive aerial support to dislodge the resolute defenders. For three days, the Royal Air Force pounded Monywa with rocket strikes. Three squadrons of Hurribombers, 12 Mosquitoes, 82 Hurricanes and Thunderbolts flew more than 200 sorties against the Japanese positions during the attack. On the last day of the assault, 100 sorties were flown. The water tower was hit and the Japanese troops, who were totally demoralised by the ferocity of the aerial onslaught, quickly surrendered.[66] A day later, the village of Myinmu, located approximately halfway between Monywa and the city of Mandalay on the north bank on the Irrawaddy River, fell to the 20th Indian Division. At Myinmu, 24 Japanese soldiers walked into the Irrawaddy River to commit suicide rather than be taken prisoner by the British advance.[67] The seizure of Myinmu was strategically important as it enabled Gracey to prepare to cross the Irrawaddy River.[68]

Slim now took the opportunity to visit Gracey's triumphant units. The 20th Indian Division had achieved a most impressive and rapid advance. It clearly deserved a call from the commander in chief of the 14th Army.[69] But despite the visit, this was no time for a respite. The spectacular success of the dry season offensive meant that it was now imperative for the 14th Army to seize control of Rangoon before the monsoon season set in.[70] Although the 14th Army had moved at a great pace, the unconventional nature of the offensive did not assist it with moving any faster. As there was no definitive front line during the Burma advance, every evening many of the British divisions had to establish defensive boxes for the protection of their troops and to receive air supplies. The 20th Indian Division was no exception. This enterprise naturally slowed down the pace of the 14th Army's progress. All of the defensive boxes required intensive mobile patrols to be sent out to identify enemy positions and to maintain communication between the boxes. It was a mammoth daily undertaking. Thus, the defensive box structure proved time and again to be a highly effective method of protecting the divisions as they moved forward, but it was also not without its faults. Nevertheless, the boxes were well guarded, and the individual boxes could in theory indefinitely hold out against a Japanese assault upon their own merits or for as long as they received adequate aerial support.

Hence by the end of January, units from the 20th Indian Division had successfully occupied the village of Myinmu and begun intensively patrolling within the surrounding countryside in order to learn as much as possible about Japanese Army movements.[71] The 20th Indian Division now effectively controlled the northern bank of the Irrawaddy River. Gracey therefore set about searching for suitable places to cross the river and to continue the advance. Patrols were sent across the river to reconnoitre the Japanese military positions on the opposite bank and to survey potential sites for completing the crossing. However, the large girth of the Irrawaddy River meant that a deception plan was also needed to put the Japanese Army in the wrong place. This was required to buy crucial time for the initial crossing teams to establish a successful bridgehead. Counterfeit papers and maps were produced by the 14th Army, which identified a number of phony crossing points. Japanese forces conveniently managed to capture these fictitious documents. At the same time, 50 Royal Air Force Liberator bombers and squadron of Lightning fighter planes attacked Japanese troop positions on the opposite side of the Irrawaddy with flame throwing bombs. As the 20th Indian Division prepared to cross the river, patrols were constantly sent out to monitor the latest Japanese troop movements.[72]

The 20th Indian Division began to cross the Irrawaddy River on the night of the 12 February under heavy Japanese fire.[73] By the next day, the bridgehead was approximately 2,500 yards long by 1,000 yards wide.[74] The deception plan and other British diversionary attacks had worked. The 20th Indian Division had been able to move anti-tank guns, mortars, jeeps and even two bulldozers across the Irrawaddy River.[75] On 15 February, the Japanese Army launched a major counterattack against the bridgehead. The 20th Indian Division now encountered stiff Japanese resistance.[76] At the same time as the Japanese military counterattack, patrols from the 20th Indian Division reported increased Japanese activity within their general sector.[77] The 20th Indian Division's advance was clearly regarded by the Japanese Army as a threat that simply had to be halted. Any Japanese units that were available were urgently being moved towards the bridgehead. Nevertheless, by 27 February, the 20th Indian Division had enlarged its initial bridgehead to an area of approximately eight miles long by two and half miles wide. It was an astonishing feat for the 20th Indian Division to have accomplished and one that Slim duly noted as having been achieved during the 'hardest fighting of the campaign'.[78]

The official history of the Indian armed forces during the Second World War later described the successful institution of the Irrawaddy bridgehead as the 20th Indian Division's 'finest hour'. This was quite an accolade considering the division's previous actions, especially the defence of the Shenam Saddle. But the Japanese Army counteract attack upon the Irrawaddy bridgehead was most severe. It was plainly imperative for the Japanese to hold the line of the Irrawaddy against the British. The effective establishment of the bridgehead now required the Japanese military to throw the 20th Indian Division back across the river. Thus, 'The fighting from the middle of February to the first week of March was marked by bitter attacks by the Japanese, repelled only by the equal ferocity and valour of the Indian troops'.[79]

On 5 March, the 20th Indian Division's artillery crossed over the Irrawaddy River to the bridgehead. At the same time, the 4/10th Gurkha Rifles attacked and took the village of Talington. Gracey was most pleased with the battalion's success: 'my heartiest congratulations and thanks to comdt. and all ranks for most brilliant and successful battle. This is the finest victory and best killing of the campaign so far'. For the next five days, the Japanese Army launched a number of assaults upon the 4/10th Gurkha Rifles in a desperate attempt to retake the village. Gracey later reflected on the 'staunchness in bitter and sustained fighting at Talington... Talington was, I think, their [the 4/10th Gurkha

Rifles] finest hour'.[80] Units from the 20th Indian Division also attacked the village of Myotha in order to disrupt important Japanese lines of communications based there.[81]

Gracey continued to be supported during the advance by 221st Group of the Royal Air Force. Air supplies, fighter cover and aerial bombardment enabled the 20th Indian Division to move forward at a rapid rate.[82] Now that the Irrawaddy had been successfully breached Gracey was ordered to co-ordinate his advance with the 2nd Indian Division. Together the 2nd Indian Division and 20th Indian Division were to clear the area between Mandalay, Maymyo, Wundwin, Mahlaing and Myingyan of enemy forces.[83] It was an audacious and daring endeavour to expel the Japanese Army from the sector. But the plan was also highly susceptible to the weather. Torrential rain could still, at a moment's notice, halt motorised transport and result in half rations being hastily ordered by the divisional commanders.[84] Despite such fears, both divisions now managed to advance much faster than the Japanese expected.[85]

The 20th Indian Division soon began to threaten the city of Mandalay. This was the traditional home of the kings of Burma.[86] A British advance from the south would cut both the city and northern Japanese units off from all road and rail communications to Rangoon.[87] The 20th Indian Division now demonstrated its operational adaptability by successfully combining both jungle and conventional warfare tactics during the advance upon Mandalay. These would again be evident when the 20th Indian Division later pressed southwards down the Irrawaddy River towards Rangoon.[88]

In the meantime on 6 March, the 20th Indian Division relentlessly moved forward towards the village of Kyaukse; Gyo and Dwehla were also soon captured. Slim proudly observed that the 20th Indian Division was swiftly 'clearing village after village' in its path. The speed of the 20th Indian Division's assault certainly caught the Japanese Army by surprise, and the Japanese command was quickly forced to postpone its planned counteroffensive as events on the ground rapidly overtook them.[89] The speed of the advance also did wonders for the confidence of the 20th Indian Division. By 20 March, the 20th Indian Division was swiftly advancing through villages, plantations and groves. Slim recorded that 'the moment had come to strike boldly, and no one was more fitted to do it than Gracey and his men. I have never seen troops who carried their tails more vertically'.[90] The 20th Indian Division was consequently ordered to capture the city of Meiktila. Once again Gracey acted quickly and decisively. To capture Meiktila, it was necessary for the

20th Indian Division to first of all take the town of Wundwin. Gracey formed an impromptu-motorised column of lorries and tanks for the dash of over 70 miles.[91]

At the same time, on 21 March units of the 20th Indian Division were still engaged in the assault upon the fort at Mandalay. This eventually fell to Gracey the next day.[92] Gracey openly recognised that team spirit and speed were the key to his success.[93] Slim acknowledged that the 20th Indian Division's advance was 'a spectacular achievement'. He readily concluded that 'only a magnificent division, magnificently led, could have staged after weeks of the heaviest defensive fighting' such a triumph.[94] But there was still more to come. The 20th Indian Division soon captured the villages of Kume and Wundwin in the race to Meiktila. The speed of the advance once again caught the Japanese Army totally by surprise. In multiple directions, Japanese lines of communication were quickly overrun and Japanese military units were forced to flee into the hills for cover.[95]

Speed obviously remained the key to Gracey's success. On 30 March, the town of Kyaukse fell to the 20th Indian Division as it pressed ahead. Kyaukse was an important road and rail junction.[96] Slim attributed the speed and continuing triumph of Gracey's division to its commanding officer's 'characteristic energy'.[97] But the rapid advance was not without its failings. There remained constant food shortages and many British units were often placed on half rations. British supply lines within Burma were by now stretched to the very limit. The push towards Rangoon was rapidly becoming a crucial race for the 14th Army to seize the port area and secure adequate supply lines for the British forces situated further upcountry.[98]

By driving the Japanese forces into the hills, the 20th Indian Division could afford the luxury of a few days rest. After this, Gracey was ordered to cut the Japanese Army's communication and supply routes by seizing the city of Magwe. On 10 April, the 20th Indian Division therefore resumed its offensive.[99] The rapid nature and sheer intensity of the advance meant that during the move forward Burmese logistical infrastructure was often destroyed. Bridges, administrative buildings, sea harbours, river ports, railway stations, boats and railway carriages were all heavily damaged by both the British and the Japanese; often beyond repair. The 14th Army soon discovered, in particular, that rice and oil were in very short supply. In such circumstances, the Burmese population suffered with food shortages and disease increased. Civilian tempers were frayed and riots sometimes broke out.[100] The speed of the liberation had not helped the 14th Army in this respect. As Slim took hold of Burma, he needed to set up military administrations in the cities and towns that he captured. But the pace of liberation and the speed of the Japanese military capitulation had caught the British totally unawares. The 14th Army was particularly slow in establishing its administrative control over liberated territory despite being keen to do otherwise. Nevertheless, the civilian population generally gave the 14th Army a warm welcome despite the inherent food shortages and occasional riots.[101]

Gracey now added two further motorised brigades to his division in order to aid his mobility in what had become a conventional as well as a jungle warfare setting. This enabled him to move at even greater speed to what he had achieved thus far. On 11 April, there were no British troops within a 60 miles radius of the town of Taungdwingyi. By 14 April, Gracey had seized the town.[102] This was a significant British victory. The 20th Indian Division had severed the Japanese eastern and western fronts in Burma.[103] The town of Taungdwingyi served as a vital communication point for all rail and road transportation at the highly crucial and strategic intersection of the Irrawaddy and Sittang Valleys. On 19 April, Gracey surprised the Japanese Army once again. This time units of the 20th Indian Division arrived at the outskirts of Magwe. By nightfall all roads leading into the city had been blocked by Gracey's troops. A day later Magwe itself was cleared of its Japanese occupiers.[104]

The speed and the force of 20th Indian Division time and again surprised the Japanese Army. On 28 April, after stubborn resistance by the Japanese military, Gracey captured the city of Allanmyo.[105] By mid April, the pace of Gracey's advance was certainly aided by the revolt of the Karen people against the Japanese occupation. This also gave Gracey an insightful experience of working alongside a Southeast Asian militia movement. The Karen eventually killed over 5,000 Japanese soldiers making them a significant British ally. At approximately the same time, the Burmese nationalist leader Aung San similarly switched sides and transferred his support from the Japanese Army into the arms of the advancing British forces. This likewise aided the 14th Army offensive. Slim believed that Aung San was a true nationalist and thus Slim was extremely anxious to secure his full support against the Japanese forces. During Aung San's subsequent revolt against Japanese rule in Burma, his Burmese National Army claimed to have killed 20,000 Japanese troops. The Burmese National Army certainly caused the Japanese Army a great deal of significant trouble, nevertheless the claim to have killed 20,000 Japanese troops appeared to have been a sanguine over-exaggeration. A more pragmatic estimation of the Burmese National Army's contribution to the British cause would have been more likely to be closer to 8,826 Japanese casualties.[106]

30   *Vietnam and the Unravelling of Empire*

A British conference was quickly convened at the city of Allanmyo to assess the British advance to date and to plan for the final drive towards the Burmese capital, Rangoon. Stopford conferred with Gracey, Evans and Brigadier G.M. Dyer, the commanding officer of 268th Indian Infantry Brigade, to speed up the advance towards the capital. On 1 May, Gracey gave orders for the 20th Indian Division to advance towards the city of Prome. Two days later, Gracey occupied the city. The Japanese military defences in Burma were now in total disarray and British Army units easily overran their positions.[107] Gracey later noted that the 'great speed between each action and in action confounded the Japanese time and again'.[108]

With the city of Prome firmly under his control, Gracey was now instructed to clear the road from Prome to Rangoon. At this moment, the Japanese Army launched a major counterattack at the village of Shwedaung against the 20th Indian Division. But the 4/10th Gurkha Rifles and a number of other units from the 20th Indian Division readily defeated the embittered Japanese military assault. As the 20th Indian Division proceeded to secure the main strategic positions upon the Prome-Rangoon axis, Gracey also ordered the division to begin intensive patrolling of the Pegu Yomas mountain range in order to seek out the remaining Japanese Army units within his sector of operations. In the Pegu Yomas, Gracey hunted down numerous Japanese units who had fled from the previous British advances. The Japanese military responded by engaging the 20th Indian Division with counterinsurgency warfare tactics, and the 20th Indian Division was repeatedly forced to dispatch patrols into the mountain range to mop up the pariah Japanese units.[109]

At the same time, Gracey's advance from Prome to the town of Tharrawaddy met with very little resistance. The 20th Indian Division now effectively controlled the Prome to Rangoon Road.[110] With the ever-improving military situation, the supply lines for the 20th Indian Division also embarked upon the road to recovery. Major Bickersteth was grateful for resumption of normal rations and even the odd luxury. Although, this did not prevent Bickersteth from the odd waspish quip when he was subsequently offered a subpar fix during one particularly rowdy session in the officers' mess: 'I stuck to whisky – it is some pretty vile American type, not Scotch unfortunately'.[111]

In June, Gracey's troops liberated the townships of Paungde and Hmawbi. For the next two months, most of the 20th Indian Division operated along the Prome to Rangoon axis. There they remained until the Japanese surrender in early August. Their lives were frequently interrupted by sporadic clashes with local Japanese forces.[112] But as the Japanese military threat in Burma diminished, Gracey and the 20th Indian Division began to prepare for the British invasion of Malaya.[113] Thus, on 10 August units from the division were sent to Rangoon to assemble for Operation Zipper.[114] However, events further afield now significantly altered the destination of Gracey and the 20th Indian Division. The Allied decision to drop two atomic bombs upon Japan dramatically cut short the war in the Far East. Gracey and his troops were now required to participate in the liberation of Japanese controlled Southeast Asia rather than its conquest.[115]

As the British military planners scrambled to draw up new liberation directives, Gracey, the 4/10th Gurkha Rifles and a number of other units from the 20th Indian Division prepared to be deployed to southern French Indo-China.[116] Gracey had no idea as to how his liberation forces would be received by the Japanese Army or by the Cambodian, Vietnamese and French populations. But what he could be assured of was that he was taking into Vietnam and Cambodia troops that readily bore his trademarks of mobility, pace, self-control, education and information. Furthermore, during the Burma Campaign these troops had excelled themselves in pragmatically organising roadblocks and ambushes in jungle and conventional warfare settings. They had also demonstrated their adaptability in the Pegu Yomas mountain range by effectively engaging Japanese forces in a counterinsurgency conflict. In addition, they had successfully worked alongside indigenous Southeast Asian forces such as the Burmese National Army and the Karen militias. The war in the Far East was over and confidence was high.

2
The Power Vacuum: Vietnam 1945

The Second World War in Europe ended in May 1945, but the war in the Far East awaited resolution. The victorious Allied leaders met at the town of Potsdam, just outside of Berlin, in July 1945 to formulate an adequate punishment for Germany and the shape of the post-war world order. Detailed Allied negotiations at the Potsdam Conference, concerning the ongoing war in the Far East, resulted in southern Indo-China being positioned within the range of Southeast Asia Command (SEAC) operational activities. By this stage in the Second World War, the French administration in Indo-China had been overthrown by the Japanese military. The Japanese established in Vietnam, Laos and Cambodia independent national regimes. These were little more than puppet administrations. In reality, French Indo-China was a Japanese occupied territory similar to British Malaya, British Singapore and the Dutch East Indies. In the corridors of power, in London and Washington, Anglo-American war planners naturally expected the war in the Far East to continue well into 1946.

With this in mind, the Combined Chiefs of Staff attached two French divisions to SEAC. This appeared logical. French Indo-China was under hostile occupation and plans were already well underway to ensure the liberation of Southeast Asia from Japanese imperial control. Admiral Lord Louis Mountbatten, the Supreme Allied Commander for Southeast Asia, who was present at Potsdam, welcomed the addition of French troops into his operational purview. These would be the ideal forces to assist in the liberation of French Indo-China. As Mountbatten concluded, he would be willing to be relieved of the 'problem' (the restoration of French colonialism), which could only be realistically accomplished by France.[1]

Very few of the delegates who attended Potsdam foresaw that the war in the Far East would end so abruptly. The dropping of the two atomic bombs upon Japan, in early August 1945, dramatically cut short the war in the Far East. In doing so, the sudden cessation of hostilities caught Anglo-American military planning staff completely off guard. They were simply unprepared to begin the task of administering a Japanese surrender across the whole of Southeast Asia. They lacked any detailed knowledge as to the local circumstances on the ground in French Indo-China or elsewhere.[2] The British Foreign Office welcomed the change in priorities from Europe and America to the Far East.[3] But even the Foreign Office staff were just as ill prepared as their War Office counterparts to deal with the realities of the Japanese capitulation and the outbreak of political violence in Indo-China. The Second World War had induced the violent birth of Vietnamese nationalism and unleashed what eventually proved to be a fatal blow to French colonialism in Indo-China.

For the moment, however, London remained blissfully unaware of the daunting complexities that awaited the arrival of British–Indian forces on the ground in Indo-China. The Potsdam Conference had symbolically bisected French Indo-China at the 16 parallel. This wartime compromise had been made in order to resolve a high-policy political dispute between SEAC and China Theatre concerning which Allied theatre held operational jurisdiction over Indo-China.[4] What had appeared a logical resolution at Potsdam in July now compromised Allied duties in Southeast Asia during August and September. In northern French Indo-China, the Chinese nationalists would be responsible for administering the Japanese surrender. In southern French Indo-China, SEAC would be in charge. Laos was mostly located in the Chinese nationalist sphere. Cambodia was positioned under British control. Vietnam was roughly divided into two equal halves. Allied planners simply drew a line on a map to make this division, and it cut across kinship ties and local relationships. The division naturally complicated political, economic and social stability on the ground during Allied liberation duties. At the same time, throughout July and August, Vietnam felt the initial tremors of an indigenous nationalist revolution. Thus commenced the political evolution of a divided peninsula, with Ho Chi Minh eventually dominating northern Vietnam.

Britain and the United States fully supported a French return to Indo-China. But because of the Potsdam Conference the successful manifestation of any French colonial regime would now depend upon how well France could work with its American, British and Chinese Allies.[5]

In southern Indo-China, SEAC planned for French military units to be attached to Gracey's liberation forces.[6] In the south, despite the machinations of the Vietnamese, some sort of rudimentary French return appeared certain. In the north, the Chinese showed a certain degree of favouritism towards emergent Vietnamese nationalism. The stage was therefore set for future misunderstandings, argument and confrontation.

Vietnam during the Second World War

The situation in Vietnam during the Second World War was complex. France had initially become interested in Vietnam during the reign of Louis XIV (1643–1715). Catholic missionaries led much of the early French activity in Vietnam. The French state later became increasingly drawn into Indo-Chinese affairs in order to protect the Catholic Church, which had invariably aggravated and then threatened various local indigenous rulers. In a series of stages, from 1858 onwards, France gradually assumed the control of what is today known as Vietnam, Laos and Cambodia.[7] When metropolitan France fell to the German invasion of 1940, the French Government in Vietnam, as in the rest of Indo-China, sided with the newly created administration of Vichy France. The Vichy Government was established by Nazi Germany as part of the armistice terms that it imposed upon France. Unoccupied France and its colonies (named as Vichy France after the town of Vichy, which became the bureaucratic centre for the new government) under the leadership of Field Marshal Henri Petain dissolved the French Third Republic and commenced a notoriously abusive relationship with Nazi Germany.

In the Far East, in the autumn of 1940, Japanese troops entered French Indo-China unopposed by the officials of Vichy France. The Japanese armed forces easily took over French airfields and naval bases. In doing so, the Japanese secured vital logistical supplies for their imperial expansion into the rest of Southeast Asia, China and India.[8] Vichy France's Indo-Chinese officials were content to coexist with their new Japanese overlord. A similar degree of comfort existed in the relationship between metropolitan France and Nazi Germany. The Axis powers, Germany in the west and Japan in the east, had grotesquely proved how impotent France had become. The myth of French imperial strength had been cruelly exposed. In 1940, France simply ceased to exist as an independent great power.

In reality, although Vichy France was still the colonial power responsible for the administration of Indo-China, the Japanese military was pleased to act as the colonial overlord. Japanese imperialism needed to take full advantage of the current French frailties. Japan wanted to use the Vichy regime with its local knowledge and history, to make Vietnam into a highly productive outfitter for the Japanese war effort. In this context, the Japanese saw it as prodigious for white colonialism to continue its exploitation of Asiatic peoples. The French possessed the necessary technical expertise to best develop Indo-China for the Japanese. In addition, any subsequent economic adversity or social unrest could be conveniently attributed to harsh French management rather than poor Japanese oversight. It was a highly profitable venture for the Japanese to pursue. If the French complained about the unjust state of affairs, the Japanese would merely remove them from power thereby depriving the local French population of their wealth and status vis-à-vis the indigenous Indo-Chinese. This strategy of divide and rule suited the Japanese well. However, the French had a lot to lose.

In the short term, therefore, the Japanese military was content to coexist alongside the French administration in Vietnam. As the Japanese Empire expanded in the east, the relationship with Vichy France worked to their advantage. Yet by 1945, the Japanese Empire in the Far East had begun to retract following a series of sustained Allied attacks. In such circumstances, Japan needed to strengthen its hand in French Indo-China in order to reinvigorate its war effort. This could be achieved by Japan removing the Vichy France administration and imposing its own imperial control on Indo-China behind a new façade of indigenous Vietnamese, Cambodian and Laotian Governments.

As a result, a fatal blow to French colonial control was struck. On 9 March, 1945, the Japanese launched a coup d'état against the Vichy France authorities in Indo-China. The relationship of convenience was over. French assistance in Indo-China was no longer regarded as a benefit to the Japanese war effort. Following the Allied liberation of France in 1944, Indo-China was the sole Vichy France regime loyally collaborating with the Axis powers. The presence of large numbers of Japanese troops in Indo-China ensured that this was the case. An earlier separation would not have produced an amiable divorce. But now with the turning of the tide in the war in the Far East, Japan desperately needed to secure French Indo-China and prevent Vichy France from suddenly switching sides. With British victories in Burma, a potential French rebellion in Indo-China would drain vital military resources from the front line and unnecessarily tie down troops needed for the defence of Greater Asia. Hence the ambiguity, concerning the existence of a Vichy administration when mainland France was now an Allied power, could not be permitted to continue any longer.

In the meantime, in Vietnam, Bao Dai, the Vietnamese Emperor, was permitted by the Japanese to declare Vietnamese independence from France. He naturally established Vietnamese self-government within the sphere of Japanese controlled Greater Asia. Bao Dai appointed the patriotic academic Professor Tran Trong Kim as his Prime Minister. But true power inevitably rested with the Japanese. Bao Dai was an indigenous figurehead. For the Vietnamese people, little changed. Japan had merely replaced France as the colonial power. Vietnamese sovereignty was purely symbolic. By using Bao Dai as its vassal and a willing conduit, Japan had been both pragmatic and magnanimous. After all, it could afford to be. It required Vietnamese support against a possible Allied invasion. It also needed to replace the Vichy France administration within the diminishing Japanese imperial sphere. Vietnamese self-determination similarly required the French colonial government to be overthrown and, with a large resident French population in Indo-China, it needed a powerful ally to protect it from any later French return.

In the end, the Vichy regime posed little threat to imperial Japan. The Japanese coup d'état proved both ruthless and effective. The Vichy France administration rapidly fell apart when faced by the superior number of Japanese forces and equipment. A limited number of French troops under the command of General Marcel Alessandri did attempt to stand firm against the Japanese action. But for the most part the resistance was futile. Under such circumstances, Alessandri was forced to lead a retreat from Hanoi towards the Vietnamese border with China. The long march north became a symbolic attempt to reinvigorate French pride in the region. Hopelessly outnumbered and outgunned by the Japanese, French troops fought an intense rearguard action as they stumbled towards Allied lines.

Alessandri initially led his troops towards the town of Son La in Tonkin. This was approximately halfway between Hanoi and the Chinese border. In Son La, Alessandri hoped to be able to establish an emergency headquarters. This would enable him to regroup and revitalise his brutally decimated forces. For the moment, an independent French spirit survived, hastily making for Son La. But in the rest of Indo-China, the chains of French colonialism had been broken. Japanese imperialism had prevailed.[9]

Nevertheless, Alessandri continued to resist the Japanese and refused to surrender. A remnant of the French Empire in the east was at least prepared to fight for its pride. French forces were now in combat against the Japanese deep behind enemy lines in Greater Asia. London and Washington therefore scrambled to get to grips with the new situation. Winston Churchill, the British Prime Minister, asked for an urgent briefing to be prepared. He had been caught out by the developments in Indo-China. As a result, the Prime Minister's preliminary response to the crisis was both vague and hesitant. French Indo-China had been a backwater to other affairs of state in the Far East. As French troops fought against the Japanese in Indo-China, Churchill was forced to admit that he had no idea if there were actually any French troops still based there.[10] The Prime Minister conceded: 'I have not followed the affairs in the country for some time'.[11]

While the Allied high-policy vacuum continued, and the bureaucratic wheels of state caught up with the actual circumstances on the ground, American Major-General Robert McClure stepped into the breach and ensured that American military aid was sent without delay to Alessandri. For a week, McClure's American Army Air Force units assisted Alessandri's forces by flying 28 relief sorties. Force 136 of the British Special Operations Executive also helped Alessandri against the Japanese.[12] The race was on to save the remaining French troops trapped behind enemy lines. In Washington, French General de Saint Didier directly approached the Joint Service Mission for formal British aid.[13] At the same time, Rene Massigli (the French Ambassador in London) approached Anthony Eden (the British Foreign Secretary) with another formal request for immediate British assistance. Massigli specifically asked the Foreign Secretary if Britain could urgently expedite the French military unit, the *Corps Leger*, to the Far East.[14]

Eight days after the start of the Japanese coup in Indo-China, and with French troops still insufficiently equipped and greatly outnumbered by the Japanese military forces pursuing them, Churchill stirred into action. The Prime Minister personally approached the American President, Franklin D. Roosevelt, to request a solution to the intra-Allied logistical dispute between SEAC and China Theatre.[15] Nothing had as yet been resolved regarding French forces fighting the Japanese, but Indo-China had been raised to the summit of Anglo-American diplomacy. Churchill's special relationship with Roosevelt was being used to iron out a logistical dispute concerning who was permitted to conduct Allied operations in French Indo-China.[16]

The British War Cabinet Joint Intelligence Committee Sub-Committee was asked to consider in what circumstances it would be reasonable for British–Indian forces to assist the French forces in Indo-China. The committee recommended that SEAC urgently send provisions to the beleaguered Alessandri.[17] But the Japanese military controlled all of the Indo-Chinese airfields. The only way for SEAC to deliver supplies to the French forces was to prepare a series of parachute drops of arms and ammunition.[18] On 19 March, Churchill gravely informed General George Marshall, the Head of the American armed forces, that:

> The Prime Minister feels that it would look very bad in history if we were to let the French force in Indo-China be cut to pieces by the Japanese through shortage of ammunition, if there is anything we can do to save them them. He hopes therefore that we shall be agreed in not standing on punctilio in this emergency.[19]

Delay was no longer possible. Churchill followed up on his warning to Marshall with an instruction to the British–Indian armed forces to intervene vigorously and aid the retreating French units. SEAC had thereby been ordered by the Prime Minister to take direct action in Vietnam.[20]

Meanwhile Alessandri, with limited supplies and facing a far superior opponent, continued to resist the Japanese. Elsewhere in French Indo-China small pockets of resistance to Japanese control persisted, but for the most part the rest of Indo-China simply accepted the accession of their new colonial master.[21] On 22 March, Alessandri reached the town of Son La. The town was located in the mountains between Hanoi and the Chinese border. Here French forces resisting the Japanese coup converged and regrouped. Alessandri was able to use the town as a rallying point for forces fleeing to China. Yet his time was running out. Alessandri believed that he could only hold the town for another couple of days.[22] But with the arrival of significant numbers of troops, over the next few days, Son La still remained in French hands on 27 March. Alessandri eventually managed to rally 4,500 troops to Son La and a further 2,000 to Luang Prabang in Laos.

With sustained resistance by the French in Son La, and additional numbers of troops finding their way to the rallying points, Alessandri was compelled to request further provisions from the Allies.[23] Britain readily assisted with financial aid and medical supplies.[24] But in reality, it was impossible for SEAC to sustain a French force of 6,500 men in two different locations deep behind Japanese lines and under constant Japanese attack. With all of the airfields held by the Japanese, SEAC airdrops just could not provide the quantities of supplies needed. SEAC planes were attacked and parachuted supplies often went astray. Alessandri was left with little choice but to commence the long march from Son La to China. By early May, most of his forces had reached the Indo-Chinese frontier and had crossed over into Chinese nationalist territory.[25]

In the meantime, Bao Dai sought to establish a Vietnamese regime under his tutelage. This government was, in many respects, merely a puppet of imperial Japan. True independence had not been achieved. But the removal of the French colonial administration did allow for more radical groups to flourish in Vietnam. One of these groups was the Vietminh. The Vietminh was not a single, unified, political party. It was, in fact, a general umbrella organisation that brought together a disparate and wide-ranging coalition of Vietnamese nationalist political entities. The Indo-Chinese Communist Party was therefore just one of a number of parties within the Vietminh movement. With the fall of French colonialism to the Japanese, and the institution of a weak puppet administration under Bao Dai, a power vacuum began to develop in which the Vietminh hoped to be able to take full advantage. At this crucial juncture, the American Office of Strategic Services decided to aid the Vietminh. The Office of Strategic Services was the forerunner of the Central Intelligence Agency. From 16 July onwards, an American intelligence team worked alongside the Vietminh movement in northern Vietnam.[26]

As Japanese power in Indo-China waned, so did the power of the Bao Dai administration.[27] The Vietminh decided that now was the time to strike. On 6 August, the Vietminh publically announced its intention to disarm the Japanese military and welcome Allied liberation forces into Indo-China. It was an audacious and timely ploy to establish the Vietminh as the only legitimate political entity in Vietnam.[28] Four days later, Japan indicated its desire to surrender to the Allies. As the Japanese situation in the Far East fell apart, the Indo-Chinese Communist Party met to consider and co-ordinate a more direct response. The Central Committee of the Vietminh subsequently issued a cry for a wave of political violence to engulf Vietnam. This reflected the growing strength of the Indo-Chinese Communist Party within the Vietminh movement. The insurrection was focused upon seizing control of Hanoi.[29]

Events now unfolded rapidly. The Vietminh was ideally placed to take advantage of the power vacuum. On 17 August, the Vietminh symbolically demonstrated the size of their popularity. A mass rally of Vietminh supporters took place in Hanoi. The next day, the Vietminh broke into the city armoury and seized weapons and ammunition. The Japanese military merely turned a blind eye. On 19 August, Ho Chi Minh, the leader of the Vietminh and also the Indo-Chinese Communist Party, arrived in Hanoi to establish a new Vietnamese administration. Ho immediately needed to consolidate his regime in the north. Therefore, the Vietminh quickly sent out nationalist emissaries into the rest of Tonkin. Bao Dai abdicated as the Vietnamese Emperor.[30]

While the Vietminh took full advantage of the power vacuum and seized control of northern Indo-China, General Douglas MacArthur, the American Supreme Allied Commander in the Pacific, dithered. MacArthur crucially held back Gracey's forces from landing in southern Vietnam until MacArthur had received the formal Japanese surrender. This elongated the power vacuum. The Japanese military had unofficially stood down. But Allied liberation forces had not yet arrived. MacArthur's motives appeared reasonable. He feared that any Allied troops sent in to administer Japanese disarmament duties, before the formal surrender had been undertaken, would face staunch Japanese resistance from a proud foe that had not as yet experienced defeat in Indo-China.[31]

The French were naturally eager to resume control of Indo-China as quickly as possible. Large numbers of French citizens lived in the south, and Indo-China was regarded as the most valuable part of the French Empire. France therefore pushed for a swift Allied deployment.[32] Time was of the essence. The Chief of Staff to Force 136 (the British Special Operations Executive in the Far East) ominously forewarned that in Malaya Britain needed to issue clear instructions to the indigenous resistance groups that had been fighting the Japanese during the Second World War lest they be tempted to seize power.[33] The same could be said for French Indo-China. Mountbatten however agreed with MacArthur and cautiously resisted all calls for an immediate deployment until after the formal Japanese surrender.[34] Mountbatten used the opportunity that the postponement presented for a brief vacation in Britain and talks with the British Government.[35] This Allied hold-up to liberation duties presented the Vietminh with an ideal window of opportunity to consolidate their power in Vietnam even further.

Nonetheless, the French attempted to circumnavigate MacArthur's impasse by covertly commencing limited reoccupation duties. Two teams of French officials were airdropped into Indo-China to reconnoitre the state of affairs on the ground and to prepare for a full French return. Pierre Messmer's unit was parachuted into Tonkin. Jean Cedile's group arrived in a similar fashion in Cochinchina in southern Indo-China. The Vietminh immediately arrested both of the French units.

Meanwhile, unimpeded by the Vietminh, the United States sent another Office of Strategic Services team to Hanoi. The United States now had two intelligence teams aiding the Vietminh. The Vietminh naturally interpreted this as a tacit indication of American support for the fledgling Vietnamese republic. Vo Nguyen Giap (a member of the Indo-Chinese Communist Party, the Leader of the Vietnamese Liberation Army and the Minister of the Interior) rapturously welcomed the second Office of Strategic Services unit. American officers regularly met and consulted with Ho Chi Minh. During the course of such discussions, the officers indicated the possibility of American support for Vietnamese self-government.[36] This directly contradicted official American government policy. Washington hastily told one of the team leaders, a Major Archimedes Patti, that the units should not become politically connected with either the Vietminh or the French. Jean Sainteny, the French Commissioner to northern French Indo-China, was more bellicose. In his eyes, Patti was 'a rabid anti-colonialist' who was trying to nudge American policy into supporting Ho Chi Minh against the return of the French colonial administration.[37]

On 2 September, MacArthur formally accepted the Japanese surrender. On the same day, the Vietminh declared an independent state of Vietnam using the American declaration of independence as their basis for doing so.[38] It was a clever move designed to impress the American officers in Hanoi and hopefully influence decision makers in Washington. Immediately, rioting broke out against the French citizens in Vietnam. Property was looted. A French officer in Saigon was killed and another wounded. A report circulated alleging that the Vietminh were molesting Europeans.[39]

The intense disturbances lasted for two days. All the while, Japanese troops in Indo-China did nothing to pacify the situation. They had formally surrendered control to the Allies and no longer regarded Indo-China as theirs to administer. As the former colonial power, it was only natural for Japan to be reluctant to intervene in the violence between the French and the Vietnamese. But at the same time, a large proportion of the Japanese forces in Indo-China was politically sympathetic to the Vietminh cause. Up to 3,000 Japanese military personnel voluntarily joined the nationalist struggle and aligned themselves with the Vietminh against the return of French colonialism. In addition, Japanese troops, who did not join the Vietnamese against the French, freely gave significant quantities of weapons and ammunition to the Vietminh.[40] It was left to Gracey, at that moment located in Burma, to issue a strongly worded long-distance communiqué to the Japanese High Command in Indo-China. In doing so, Gracey reminded them of President Harry S. Truman's order number one. Truman had foreseen that any delay to the arrival of the Allied liberation forces in the Far East could result in anarchy. He had therefore instructed the Japanese military to maintain law and order in the interim.[41]

It was into this cauldron of political violence that the initial deployment of Gracey's 20th Indian Division took place on 6 September. The British–Indian troops literally had no idea of the peace enforcement duties that awaited them in southern Indo-China. After the success of the Burma Campaign, liberation duties in French Indo-China (a Paris in the east) appeared an easy and welcome assignment. Indeed, Lt.-Colonel Jardine thought that it was better to take the pipe band rather than the three-inch mortar cannons to Saigon. After all, the war in the Far East was supposed to be over. But for the original 750 military personnel that accompanied Gracey to southern Indo-China, it was about to become rather more complex and dangerous.[42]

Gracey's intervention in Vietnam

The first British–Indian troops began to arrive in Saigon on 6 September.[43] Over the course of the next week, Britain transported just over a thousand men and 26 tons of supplies into Saigon. On 13 September, Gracey arrived in Saigon. Pham Van Bach, the Head of the Vietminh in the south, met him at the airport. Gracey, however, sidestepped the Vietnamese reception committee and set off at once for the city centre. Gracey had no orders to communicate with the Vietminh. His apparent snub to the Vietnamese delegation was in fact a convenient dodge to avoid a political ambush. Only the day before, fresh rioting had broken out in Saigon when freed French prisoners of war had conducted bitter reprisals against the local Vietnamese population. Gracey needed to ascertain a clearer picture of the security situation before he could risk talking to the Vietminh. On the way into Saigon, British officers briefed Gracey as to the local state of affairs. Upon arrival at British headquarters, Gracey's first action was to send British–Indian troops to evict the Vietminh from the French governor-general's residence. Japanese forces were ordered to begin disarming the Vietminh.[44]

The situation remained tense. The power vacuum of the previous month had put Saigon in a critical position. In the face of escalating political violence, Gracey was no longer merely administering liberation duties. He was also practising peace enforcement. In London, Ernest Bevin, the new Foreign Secretary, openly admitted that British–Indian forces were operating in extremely dangerous circumstances.[45] The British Government expected Gracey to disarm the Japanese, maintain law and order and permit the return of French colonialism. It was an unenviable position made all the more daunting by Mountbatten's personal assurance to Admiral Thierry D'Argenlieu, the French High Commissioner to Indo-China, that he would 'do my best as an Allied commander to look after French interests'.[46] D'Argenlieu therefore expected Gracey to deliver southern Indo-China into his hands.

The Chief Political Officer to SEAC, Maberly Esler Dening, warned the Foreign Office that Gracey would have to tread very carefully in French Indo-China. The danger was obvious for all to see. Britain needed to avoid accusations of interference in the affairs of another nation state – France.[47] India was already displaying signs of anxiety that Indian and Gurkha units were being deployed on the streets of Saigon against Asian nationalists.[48] It was therefore imperative for Gracey to pursue purely military objectives.

Yet Gracey still had to discover just how complicated the circumstances in southern French Indo-China had become. The delayed Allied deployment, the lack of Japanese control and the breakdown of traditional instruments of government had all added to the chaos in Vietnam. Ho Chi Minh had been able to form an embryonic government in Hanoi and establish himself as the nationalist alternative to the French and the Japanese.[49] In the north, the Vietminh was at its strongest and fully able to concentrate and consolidate its power as a realistic alternative to French colonialism. But in the south, the situation was very different.

In the south, a less cohesive movement of different nationalist groups had taken advantage of the power vacuum. In various districts in Saigon, a patchwork quilt of nationalist, communist, socialist, religious and criminal fraternities established separate strongholds.[50] None of these groups had the operational strength or the political skill to unite such disparate factions under the single banner of the Vietminh. In addition, the Vietminh in the south was weaker and less well organised than its northern counterpart. It also lacked a dependable method of communicating with Hanoi. By contrast, the indigenous Cao Dai and Hoa Hao religious communities had mass appeal in the south. They also possessed large quantities of arms and ammunition.[51] Likewise, Saigon also contained a large French population. It was therefore a difficult powder keg to manage with limited numbers of peace enforcers.

Washington and London had already approved of the return of Indo-China to French sovereignty.[52] But it was British–Indian peace enforcers who were being left in Saigon to manage law and order and avert a humanitarian disaster. During September, France was in no position to enact an immediate return to colonial rule. In the interim, Gracey had to prevent a slide towards anarchy. Should the French and Vietnamese populations have been left alone together, the political violence of the previous few days indicated the likely dire outcome of Franco-Vietnamese interactions in the south. In the north, Ho Chi Minh's dominance was more clear-cut.

Following Gracey's arrival in Saigon and the initial disarmament of the Vietnamese, the British enforced an uneasy peace. Yet this merely presented an opportunity for the Vietminh to reorganise and plan their next step. On 17 September, the Vietminh suddenly proclaimed a general strike. As the strike spread throughout Saigon, a Vietminh unit attempted to seize control of the power station. In this instance, they were easily turned away from the premises. But before long, all public services were in the hands of the Vietminh. On 19 September, the crisis escalated when Vietnamese demonstrations broke out against British–Indian troops.[53] Anarchy threatened.

Under the terms of the Hague Convention, Gracey was legally responsible for law and order, but this was rapidly slipping from his grasp.[54] Vietminh forces continued to seize control of strategic premises. Gracey sought an emergency conference with Brigadiers Hirst and Maunsell. In difficult and deteriorating circumstances, these three officers hurriedly fleshed out what subsequently became a highly controversial proclamation.[55] At the time of drafting the edict, the Vietminh were deliberately defying Allied peace enforcement duties. They were vigorously vying for the control of Saigon. Yet even in such a tense and highly charged situation, Gracey consciously attempted to preserve a degree of neutrality. He contacted the Vietminh in advance of his public announcement and informed them of both the general nature of the proclamation and the British obligation to maintain law and order.

Events came to a head on 21 September. With no sign of the political unrest diminishing, Gracey now attempted to lift Saigon out of lawlessness and impose British martial law. Gracey's emergency communiqué was formally displayed throughout the city. It represented a forceful crackdown on all paramilitary activity. The proclamation prohibited all public meetings, gatherings and protests. It permitted only Allied personnel to carry weapons. It imposed press censorship and a public curfew. At the same time, British–Indian forces seized control of the public services from the Vietminh. British–Indian troops also organised food distribution and other humanitarian aid. It was a comprehensive plan to re-establish British control in the city.

The decision to only allow Allied troops to carry arms also meant, however, that French forces in Saigon were able to openly maintain their weaponry. Vietnamese groups had two choices, either to surrender or to hide their arms. This discrepancy played into the hands of the French who, at this critical juncture on 23 September, began a counter-revolution against the Vietminh in southern French Indo-China. French troops reoccupied government buildings and took hold of all strategic infrastructure.[56] General Philippe Leclerc, the Commander in Chief of French forces in Indo-China, naturally found Gracey's emergency edict and subsequent actions appealing. He readily informed Paris: 'Gracey had in my opinion taken the best possible measures in the circumstances because if he had shown any weakness the situation might have become critical'.[57]

Leclerc's indebtedness to Gracey was unsurprising. But it also revealed how close circumstances in Saigon had become to a full breakdown of law and order. Depending upon the different city districts, it was a nervous and highly explosive state of affairs in which local conditions proved both highly fluid and dangerous. Decisive action was required to protect the lives of the British–Indian peace enforcers and also French and Vietnamese civilians. Gracey could not afford to lose control. The actions of the previous few days had demonstrated that the population in Saigon could easily turn upon the British–Indian troops as the political violence escalated. In this respect, Gracey had accurately assessed the current circumstances: 'no effective civilian government exist[ed]'. Vietminh claims otherwise were 'childish'. They simply did not possess the legal framework and administrative processes to form an effective civilian administration.[58]

Gracey moreover did have a legal responsibility to enact emergency powers under the terms of the Hague Convention: 'The authority of the power of the state having passed de facto into the hands of the occupant, the latter shall do all in his power to restore, and to ensure as far as possible, public order and safety'.[59] In addition, Gracey had no authority to negotiate with the Vietminh. At this stage, London and Washington fully supported the return of French sovereignty. If Gracey had stepped back at this juncture and left the situation solely in the hands of the French and the Vietnamese, the loss of life would have been horrific. In such circumstances, historians would have later crucified Gracey for failing to enforce the peace and abandoning his responsibilities under the terms of the Hague Convention.[60] Instead, Leclerc was initially able to report to Paris that following Gracey's proclamation 'no clashes have occurred'.[61]

Mountbatten was certainly troubled by Gracey's actions in Saigon. He urgently contacted Gracey to point out that the emergency proclamation exceeded Mountbatten's initial orders to the Allied liberation force in Saigon. By focusing upon the maintenance of law and order rather than the more-narrow remit of disarming the Japanese, Mountbatten stated that Gracey had assumed administrative jurisdiction over all of southern French Indo-China. Mountbatten was clearly anxious that Gracey's disaster management actions had actually broadened the scope of British liberation commitments. This was an understandable concern. But it also revealed that Mountbatten unrealistically expected Gracey to carry out his liberation duties in a power vacuum and in isolation from the political realities on the ground in Saigon. However, now that circumstances had changed and that the proclamation had been issued, Mountbatten was fully prepared to support Gracey as his 'man on the spot'.[62]

At a subsequent meeting between Cedile, Gracey, Mountbatten and General William Slim, the Commander in Chief of all Allied liberation forces in SEAC, Gracey accepted that Britain was restricted to using British–Indian troops in Saigon. He simply did not have the troop numbers for operations elsewhere. Thus, the rest of southern French Indo-China remained beyond his range of operations. But despite such limitations, Gracey also pointed out that this did not release him from his legal responsibility to maintain law and order. As Gracey argued, it was perfectly possible for Britain to maintain law and order in the rest of southern French Indo-China by using Japanese forces to police the peace. In fact, this was what Gracey had already ordered. In addition, this naturally aligned with Truman's order number one for Japanese forces to maintain law and order in the interval between the Japanese surrender and the return of the French administration.

When Mountbatten answered Gracey, however, he couched his reply in political rather than military terms. Mountbatten stated that the British Government did not want British–Indian casualties in non-British areas of responsibility (the return of French colonialism). Nor did London want to intervene in the management affairs of another country (France). This was a French concern and they needed to intervene with 'their own troops'.[63] It was an extraordinary response. Despite his previous commitment to support Gracey as his agent on the ground, Mountbatten again wanted to limit Gracey's operational purview. In the ongoing and increasing political violence between the French and the Vietminh, Mountbatten naïvely thought that it would be possible for Gracey merely to administer Japanese surrender duties and avoid any

British–Indian casualties. Yet this was the very same Mountbatten that had already promised his full assistance to D'Argenlieu. Now that the going was getting tough, Mountbatten undoubtedly wanted to ensure that it was only the French who were left with blood on their hands.

The British Government was likewise increasingly concerned about circumstances in Saigon. John Lawson, the Secretary of State for War, was dispatched on a fact-finding mission to Southeast Asia. Lawson met with Mountbatten, Slim and Gracey. It was agreed during their conference that Gracey would actively preserve law and order in southern Indo-China until the French administration was strong enough to take over. But Lawson also firmly stated that the British Government did not want to be drawn any further into an affair that it was only possible for France to resolve satisfactorily.[64] In the interim, Gracey's decision to maintain law and order appeared vindicated.

To alleviate the situation on the ground, SEAC now opened direct talks with the Vietminh.[65] Harry N. Brain, the Foreign Office representative in Saigon, met with various local Vietminh representatives. He poignantly stressed to the Vietminh that Britain was politically neutral in the Vietnamese dispute with France. Considering that London had already endorsed the return of French sovereignty, this was an interesting half-truth that Brain had uttered to downplay British involvement in Vietnamese affairs. Brain next pointed out to the Vietnamese representatives that although the United Nations did not recognise the loss of French dominion in Indo-China during the Second World War, the United Nations remained dedicated to the expansion of self-government for all colonial peoples. Brain had demonstrated Foreign Office public relations at their very best. He had treated Britain's position as unimportant while at the same time he had espoused that self-determination was a noble cause endorsed by the United Nations. Brain had stroked Vietminh egos, but at the same time he had not actually said anything of any substance or committed the British Government to any future course of action.[66]

The negotiations achieved their desired effect. On 1 October, a ceasefire was agreed between the French and the Vietminh. To boost British–Indian troop numbers and to ensure that law and order was fully maintained, Mountbatten gave formal approval for Japanese prisoners of war to be rearmed and to act as Allied peace enforcers.[67] Mountbatten then set about trying to skew the record about British activities in Saigon. In a personal correspondence with Tom Driberg, a radical Labour Member of Parliament and former journalist, Mountbatten, an aristocrat and member of the royal family, praised the equanimity of the Vietminh in accepting the terms of the ceasefire. At the same time, Mountbatten reserved his scorn for what he perceived as the true cause of the current crisis in Saigon, French obstinacy:

> If only the French will be reasonable, and come forward with an imaginative offer, the war in Indo-China can be over. If it is continued through French intransigence, I hope it will be made abundantly clear that it is nothing to do with South East Asia [Command].

Mountbatten was clearly preaching to the choir; he was drawing on the prejudices of the socialist Driberg. He went on to offer a blatant piece of self-serving propaganda. Mountbatten bemoaned to Driberg that if only he had been given a 'free hand' in Indo-China then the situation on the ground in Saigon would have been very different. In fact by now, the crisis would have been fully resolved.[68] Mountbatten had sacrificed both the British Government and Gracey in a grotesque act of hand-wringing and self-belief.

Gracey's summary of the circumstances in Saigon was characteristically more succinct. He reported that current state of affairs had not yet spun out of control but that the Vietminh represented a clear and present danger to the continued preservation of law and order.[69] Unlike Mountbatten, Gracey was not prepared to make political capital out of the situation in Saigon. The Vietminh, however, were not as self-restrained. A Vietminh broadcast accused the British forces operating in Saigon of being fully responsible for all casualties and loss of life. It claimed that Britain had pushed Vietnam towards war. If it had not been for Gracey's efforts then France would not have been able to launch its counteroffensive in the south. The broadcast thus firmly blamed Gracey and Britain for any future bloodshed.[70]

At the British War Office in London, the Joint Planning Staff agreed that Britain was legally responsible for the maintenance of law and order in southern French Indo-China. It also held that operations to preserve this should be kept to a minimum and transferred over from SEAC to the French administration in Indo-China as quickly as possible. Thought was given to whether Mountbatten should issue a public declaration in southern French Indo-China to clarify British–Indian operations. The Foreign Office pointed out that if Mountbatten made a statement along purely military lines concerning the British–Indian forces stationed in Indo-China, this could destabilise the circumstances on the ground even further as it would embolden the Vietminh into organising additional revolutionary activity. The Joint Planning Staff was in agreement with the Foreign Office assessment. The Foreign Office therefore concluded that Mountbatten should make a statement announcing that British–Indian forces would not put up with any activity that undermined the execution of their duties or security.[71] Bevin thought that such an announcement was critical as it both defined and clarified SEAC operations in southern French Indo-China.[72] The British Chiefs of Staff naturally agreed with the advice of the Foreign Office. This was because Britain needed French support elsewhere in the post-Second World War world for the maintenance of other security duties. Thus, the Chiefs of Staff believed that, regarding Indo-China, the French would be in favour of a more broadly defined remit for Gracey's British–Indian forces.[73]

On 9 October, Britain officially handed civilian affairs in southern French Indo-China over to France. The agreement, signed in London, formally passed all administrative responsibility for southern Indo-China from Gracey to D'Argenlieu.[74] The British Foreign Office anxiously held its collective breath.[75] In the light of the Franco-British treaty, Mountbatten called Gracey and Leclerc to an urgent summit in the Burmese capital, Rangoon. Mountbatten took personal charge of the meeting and worked out, with Gracey and Leclerc, what an appropriate British strategy should be regarding any further Vietminh attacks.[76] They did not have to wait long. The very next day, the Vietminh broke the terms of the ceasefire and resumed their struggle in the south. Once again, British–Indian forces were caught in the middle of violent clashes between the French and the Vietminh. As a new phase of political violence erupted in southern Indo-China, Slim ominously warned London that Gracey's directives only to be involved in the disarmament of Japanese forces were at present unworkable.[77]

The Vietminh were, unsurprisingly, aggrieved by the Franco-British treaty. They demanded that Britain immediately restore Vietminh power in Saigon. They also requested the disarmament of the French and the rearmament of their own units. Although Mountbatten politely forwarded the requests to London, he was not dismissing the Vietminh protests out of hand. Mountbatten remained highly sensitive to acts of negative Vietminh propaganda. He therefore purposefully asked Gracey to keep all British–Indian forces from creating the impression that they were using a full arsenal of sophisticated modern weaponry to brutally crush a technologically inferior opponent. Public opinion in Europe and the United States would not stand for such imagery. Mountbatten also ordered Gracey not to give any interviews to the media.[78] In the meantime, both Mountbatten and Slim frantically lobbied London for the swift Allied deployment of the 9th French Colonial Division to Saigon.[79]

On 10 October, the Vietminh ambushed a British–Indian patrol close to Saigon airport. As the political violence intensified, British–Indian patrols were also attacked in Saigon and other towns. Further British–Indian–Japanese operations were orchestrated to clear Saigon and all surrounding urban centres of Vietminh paramilitary activities.[80] Gracey's forces continued to operate in difficult circumstances. The power vacuum, the political violence, the limited numbers of British–Indian troops and the characteristics of the local population all conspired to make Gracey a reluctant peace enforcer. British–Indian troops openly engaged Vietminh forces in standard counter-insurgency warfare. Patrols were sent out. Premises were searched. Local inhabitants were questioned. Weapons were confiscated. Homes were burned.[81]

From 10 October 1945 to 27 January 1946, forty British, Indian and Gurkha troops were killed in the political violence. 106 French soldiers and 110 Japanese also died. 3,051 Vietnamese (including 25 Japanese deserters) lost their lives but no distinction was made in the British war report between civilians and enemy combatants. 576 Vietnamese were also reported as wounded and another 1,389 were missing or prisoners of war. The British war report did record that the French armed forces accounted for the most Vietnamese (not including Japanese deserters) deaths: 1,825 in total. British–Indian troops killed 651 Vietnamese. Japanese forces killed 550 Vietnamese.[82]

Gracey did not create the power vacuum. Nor was he to blame for the state of affairs that he inherited in southern French Indo-China. Gracey was attempting to administer the Allied liberation of southern Vietnam and Cambodia with limited numbers of British–Indian forces. Gracey did not actively seek a confrontation with Asian nationalism. Yet this was what greeted him in Saigon and dogged his liberation duties. And Gracey certainly sought to avoid any unnecessary violence. His reminder to the Japanese to maintain Truman's order number one, and Gracey's subsequent use of Japanese prisoners of war as Allied peace enforcers demonstrated his desire to prevent circumstances from slipping out of control and a humanitarian disaster engulfing the Franco-Vietnamese populations.

In spite of Leclerc's praise to Paris for Gracey's handling of the political violence in Saigon, Gracey was deeply troubled by the nature of the French counter-revolution in southern French Indo-China and the desperate way in which the French had re-established their colonial control. Pledges made by the French officials in Saigon, prior to their counter-revolution, to Gracey, to use the minimum amount of force necessary, had proven to be erroneous.[83] Indeed, Gracey was greatly disturbed by the general character of the French modus operandi in southern Indo-China. In correspondence to Slim, Gracey singled out Leclerc's command for withering criticism. In Gracey's opinion, Leclerc's operations against the Vietminh were being carried out with 'unnecessary brutality'. Gracey accurately predicted that the long-term consequences of Leclerc's operations would be disastrous for French policy in Indo-China and make further warfare inevitable:

> French troops are leaving a pretty good trail of destruction behind them, which will result in such resentment that it will become progressively more difficult for them to implement their new policy, and, I am convinced will result in guerrilla warfare, increased sabotage and arson as soon as we leave the country.

Gracey's letter to Slim without a doubt pulled no punches. He was clearly upset with the method of French operations against the Vietminh and the general attitude of French personnel towards the resurrection of French colonial control. These sentiments expressed to Slim contradict previous historical accusations that Gracey was a rabid colonialist eager to restore French imperial control.[84]

In addition, the Japanese prisoners of war, who were serving in the British–Indian–Japanese security operations, were equally upset as Gracey with the actions of the French armed forces in re-establishing French colonial control. The Japanese troops openly asked for British officers, rather than French officers, to issue them with their orders. The Japanese forces found it increasingly hard to implement French orders because of the 'schemeless' nature of the French military plans. Gracey concurred with the Japanese assessment against the French administration: 'the last is, alas, so true about the implementation of their plans'.[85]

Yet these attitudes greatly contrasted with those of Mountbatten. In spite of his previously expressed request to Gracey, in the presence of Slim, to leave all grisly reoccupation activities to the French, and his private attacks on French obstinacy and intransigence to Driberg, Mountbatten's assessment of French operations to D'Argenlieu was far more complimentary.[86] In one fawning communication, Mountbatten wrote to the French High Commissioner: 'our forces in SEAC are, I can assure you, honoured to serve in close co-operation with you and General Leclerc'.[87]

In October, the United States withdrew its participation in SEAC and closed the Office of Strategic Services missions to Hanoi.[88] The American involvement in French Indo-China had not progressed according to plan. In the north, the Office of Strategic Services missions to Hanoi had given tacit approval and ultimately false diplomatic expectation for American diplomatic support to the emergent Vietminh regime. In the south, the American Office of Strategic Services officer, Lt.-Colonel Peter Dewey had, to his great humiliation, been ordered out of Saigon by Gracey for seditious activities. But before Dewey managed to leave Saigon, the Vietminh assassinated him. The irony of Dewey's murder was that he held pro-Vietminh sentiments. Yet the Vietminh had still killed him. On the same day when Dewey was murdered, the Vietminh also attacked the Office of Strategic Services headquarters in Saigon.[89]

The Vietminh understood the direction of American foreign policy even if the Office of Strategic Services personnel did not. The Office of Strategic Services missions in Vietnam had persistently maintained strong anti-colonial undertones. But such an independent stance concerning American foreign policy was at odds with the decision-making process in Washington. It could not be permitted to endure. Thus, the United States removed its involvement in French imperial entanglements as it sought to reappraise its international predilections in the post-war world. French Indo-China was just not a priority. Instead, 50,000 American troops were sent to China to monitor the standoff between the Chinese nationalists and Chinese communists.[90] The Cold War was commencing.

However, as the build-up of French forces in southern Indo-China slowly gathered pace, the number of British–Indian operations started to diminish. France inevitably began to take a greater responsibility for security issues. In France doing so, Britain was not as reliant upon Japanese forces to maintain law and order. Gracey was therefore able to communicate to Mountbatten the news that British officers no longer actively commanded Japanese troops in the field. This would certainly have been welcome news in Whitehall. The British Ambassador to the United States, Lord Halifax, reported from Washington that the British use of Japanese troops had greatly angered American public opinion.[91] Gracey's operations against political violence in Saigon could hardly have been regarded as a textbook affair. But in London, members of the Labour Government justified Gracey's unusual methods because of the acute levels of violence enacted by the Vietminh.[92]

Mountbatten appeared content that Gracey's commitments in southern French Indo-China were gradually being scaled back. He duly informed Gracey that he would therefore inform Lord Alanbrooke, the Chief of the Imperial General Staff, about how dexterously and diplomatically Gracey had managed recent difficult events in Saigon.[93]

Within the British military circles, it looked as if Mountbatten was fully prepared to credit Gracey with any British achievements in French Indo-China. But in his continuing personal correspondence with Driberg, Mountbatten was far less willing to share any plaudits with others. He naturally expressed his pride at the way in which events in southern French Indo-China were progressing. But, as Mountbatten claimed, this was inevitable because: 'I have succeeded in carrying out the British commitment with more success than any of the prophets forecast'.[94]

On 25 December, Britain began to withdraw some of its forces from southern French Indo-China. A week later, Mountbatten and D'Argenlieu signed a formal statement passing all responsibility for the maintenance of law and order in the south over to the French.[95] France was extremely thankful for Britain's emergency management of the power vacuum and the political violence. The French administration in Saigon proposed that France should award full French military decorations to the British–Indian personnel involved in operations in Indo-China. However, E.W. Meiklereid, the British Consul-General in Saigon, cautioned that by accepting such trophies, Britain could be accused of actively pursuing a policy that had restored Indo-China to French control.[96] At SEAC headquarters, Mountbatten's secretary expressed greater revulsion at the French request. He bluntly stated: 'suspicion of our hypocrisy and possible dishonesty in this matter would be intensified by the acceptance of purely military decorations on the accomplishment of what has been stated to be purely pacific tasks here'.[97]

The international climate was certainly in line with such feelings. The President of the Indian Congress Party, Jawaharlal Nehru, compared the British performance in Indo-China to Nazi actions in Spain. Nehru was furious that Indian troops had been used against Asian nationalists.[98] In the context of the times, this was a powerful rebuke. The Indian National Assembly voted for a motion that complained at the sustained used of Indian troops in French Indo-China.[99] Meanwhile, Whitehall mandarins naturally agreed with the sentiments emanating from the British officials in Southeast Asia concerning the award of military decorations. The British Government therefore refused to permit the decorations, and it was left to a disgruntled and unwilling Mountbatten to notify D'Argenlieu of the British decision.[100]

Mountbatten later received the Grand Cross of the Legion of Honour, following another recommendation for a decoration from D'Argenlieu. After doing so, Mountbatten wrote to Gracey and pointed out that this award was for his wartime service in Southeast Asia rather than for Allied post-war operations in French Indo-China. What Mountbatten did not tell Gracey was that he had lobbied Sir Alan Lascelles, the Personal Secretary to King George VI, in order to receive his prize. The decoration may have officially been for his service as wartime Supreme Allied Commander, but it also looked as if Mountbatten had achieved a French award via a technical quibble. Either way, Mountbatten received a French decoration while the British–Indian forces who actually served in French Indo-China did not.[101]

Nonetheless, on the eve of the British–Indian withdrawal from southern French Indo-China, it was Mountbatten's management of SEAC, rather than Gracey's handling of liberation duties in Saigon, that was dramatically called into question. Dening, Mountbatten's Chief Political Officer, thoroughly denounced his Supreme Allied Commander to London. It was a strongly worded onslaught from a furious whistleblower. Dening's frustration with Mountbatten's self-serving conduct was clearly evident for all in the Foreign Office to see. He scornfully informed Bevin that Mountbatten only operated through a 'mixture of malice and fiction'. In doing so, Mountbatten had personally endangered SEAC liberation duties and the lives of the British–Indian personnel under his command. Dening offered London two highly critical but similar examples to support his attack: first, he made reference to SEAC operations in the Dutch East Indies; and second, he made a telling revelation about SEAC operations in southern French Indo-China.

In the Dutch East Indies, a limited number of British–Indian forces were operating in a post-war vacuum in very similar circumstances to Gracey and British–Indian forces in southern French Indo-China. In the Dutch East Indies, Dening revealed that Mountbatten had been openly supporting the indigenous population while at the same time he had been highly critical of the returning Dutch administration. This had greatly compromised the actions of the British–Indian liberation forces. British–Indian troops were thereby caught in violent clashes between the returning Dutch administration and Indonesian nationalists. In French Indo-China, Dening reported that Mountbatten had frequently ignored the advice of his Foreign Office advisers.

As a consequence of Mountbatten's actions, Dening witheringly concluded that SEAC no longer resembled an efficient Allied command. This was predominantly because Mountbatten constantly ignored the advice of those whom he commanded (Brain, Dening, Gracey etc.) while at the same time he ardently played up to persons of superior rank and status. Dening therefore recommended that the Foreign Office urgently needed to take over British policy in the region. A special commissioner was required to co-ordinate a consistent approach to the various crises in Southeast Asia. SEAC could not be trusted.[102]

During the Second World War in Europe, the British coalition government had already faced similar problems in Greece to those taking place in French Indo-China, concerning the arrival of Allied liberation forces and their reception by indigenous resistance groups. Despite the forewarning, after the war, the British Labour Government was repeating the mistakes of the immediate past. The British Government was simply overstretched by its post-war liberation commitments. Clement Attlee, the Prime Minister, Bevin and others were overwhelmed and disorientated by the terrible nature of the tasks that faced them. This scenario was not aided by Britain experiencing a financial Dunkirk, which ensured that adequate resources were not allocated to Gracey's mission to southern French Indo-China.[103] Britain's growing insolvency crisis should not be understated. This would eventually lead Britain into a state of quasi-permanent submission to its primary creditor – the United States.[104]

Even so, at times, leadership from London was found to be wanting. Attlee had already confused SEAC when he denied a statement from Lawson that British–Indian troops were being used to help the French in southern Indo-China.[105] Bevin had also managed to mislead parliament concerning the speed of the French deployment to French Indo-China.[106] And although he ultimately created the position of special commissioner for Southeast Asia, Bevin failed to take Mountbatten to task for his mismanagement of SEAC. Instead, Bevin unjustly chose to reward the whistleblower by telling Dening to personally resolve his dispute with Mountbatten amicably.[107] A serious complaint had thereby been met with indifference towards the key Foreign Office person concerned. London certainly revealed its ignorance at a time when Gracey and British–Indian peace enforcers needed their attention the most. As Slim had already pointed out to Whitehall, Gracey's directives to only administer the Japanese surrender were in the current context completely unworkable.

In the meantime, Gracey successfully handed over the containment of the Japanese prisoners of war to the French authorities. On 28 January, he left Indo-China.[108] As the main British–Indian force departed, France proceeded to re-exert its control over the rest of Indo-China. In Laos, French troops successfully engaged the nationalist Lao Issara militia and managed to seize control of the Lao capital – Vientiane. On 16 March, a large French task force arrived in Hanoi to re-establish colonial rule in northern Vietnam.[109] But these were entirely French orchestrated affairs. Vietnam had ceased to be part of Mountbatten's zone of operations. France had now embarked upon the myopic resurrection of colonial subjugation and French imperial grandeur.

As the First Vietnam War gathered pace, Mountbatten eagerly sought to polish his record in Southeast Asia. In the immediate aftermath of Gracey's emergency proclamation, Mountbatten had backed Gracey as his man on the spot. Later he had also informed Alanbrooke of Gracey's tact and dexterity in managing the difficult circumstances during the political violence in Saigon. But was this all merely false praise? As Dening had observed, Mountbatten was a highly skilled political operative who did not lack personal self-belief. Indeed, when things did not go his own way or at his desired speed, Mountbatten was not averse to using unofficial political channels (e.g. Driberg) in order to promote his own agenda – in other words himself.[110]

Thus, was Mountbatten truly content with Gracey's record in Saigon or solely concerned about his own? The final report that Mountbatten sent to the Anglo-American Combined Chiefs of Staff in June 1947 certainly praised Gracey's courage for operating British liberation tasks in difficult circumstances in Saigon. But the final report also savagely indicted Gracey for exceeding his orders from Mountbatten. Similarly, Gracey was scathingly blamed for supposedly giving France permission to enact the counter-revolution.[111] As the dust settled on Britain's modest involvement in French Indo-China, Mountbatten was eager to absolve himself of any liability for Gracey's alleged mismanagement of Allied duties in Saigon. Yet, as Mountbatten's correspondence with Driberg revealed, he was actually quite prepared to accept any paeans freely meted out about Gracey's operations. These were the actions of an obsequious sycophant who was desperate for British–Indian operations in southern French Indo-China not to tarnish his professional reputation or SEAC legacy.

In keeping with Mountbatten's character of playing up to persons of superior rank or status, two months after his damning report to the Combined Chiefs of Staff, Mountbatten performed a stunning volteface. He personally recommended Gracey to Mohammed Ali Jinnah as the ideal candidate to take over as the temporary Governor of Bengal. In Mountbatten's commendation, he perhaps surprisingly, given his recent report, highlighted to Jinnah Gracey's understanding and dexterity in working within indigenous nationalist melting pots. Above all, Mountbatten considered Gracey a highly appropriate candidate for the successful management of situations involving power vacuums and intense political violence. As Mountbatten observed, this was specifically because of Gracey's understanding and organisation during the crisis in southern French Indo-China.[112]

3
The Sideshow: Cambodia 1945

The Potsdam Conference in July 1945 had not only placed southern Vietnam within the sphere of British military operations against the Japanese, but it had also included the tip of southern Laos and all of the Kingdom of Cambodia. Allied military planners logically expected the war in the Far East to continue well into 1946. Military preparations and expectation were thus developed with this in mind. At this stage, there was no hint of a possible Japanese surrender. Furthermore, few in the Allied military establishment knew of the existence of an atomic weapon of mass destruction. All military strategy within SEAC dramatically changed in August. The two atomic bombs dropped upon Japan relegated existing plans for the continuation of the war to the wards of history.

The sudden Japanese capitulation caught London, Washington and SEAC completely unawares. SEAC had for a long time expected to have to fight its way into Indo-China rather than enact the long-range management of an immediate Japanese surrender. Its liberation plans were incomplete, and it lacked any accurate knowledge of the local situation on the ground.[1]

In addition, SEAC and the British War Office had been forced out of necessity to administer Japanese surrender duties, but they were ill equipped to deal with the political realities. The British Government initially attached Foreign Office representatives to SEAC until a separate Foreign Office infrastructure could be developed to represent Britain's geo-political and regional interests. In the meantime, the Foreign Office identified Thailand and Vietnam for urgent political analysis and deployed immediate but inadequate diplomatic missions to these areas. The Cambodian political situation was considered more of a diplomatic backwater to these main Foreign Office activities. It therefore remained solely within the purview of SEAC and military administrators, and consequently it became part of Gracey's area of responsibility.

Cambodia during the Second World War

Circumstances in Cambodia during the Second World War were similar to those in Vietnam. France had taken an initial interest in Cambodia with the establishment of a French protectorate in 1863, and it had gradually acquired a stronghold within the kingdom.[2] With the fall of France in 1940, the French authorities in Cambodia, as in the rest of French Indo-China, sided with the newly established regime of Vichy France. The Vichy Government had been established following the French armistice with Nazi Germany. Unoccupied France and its colonies, under the leadership of Field Marshal Henri Petain, henceforth became controversial collaborators with fascism.

During the autumn of 1940, Japanese armed forces entered northern Indo-China unopposed by the French military. By May 1941, two Japanese divisions had subjugated Cambodia.[3] Approximately 40,000 Japanese troops had taken over French Indo-Chinese airfields and naval bases. This occupation acquired vital rubber and tin supplies for the Japanese war effort. It also secured the region as a strategic staging location for further Japanese assaults upon China, as well as the Japanese expansion into the rest of Southeast Asia.[4] France was still the colonial power responsible for the day-to-day government of Indo-China. In the short term, the Japanese military establishment was prepared to coexist in an uneasy alliance alongside French colonialism and to conduct its work through the existing French colonial infrastructure. In the longer term (March 1945), Japan sought to remove its feeble European vassal and thus replace the French colonial management with Japanese imperial control.

In the meantime, Thailand fully exploited the frailty of the French Empire by requesting the return of Cambodia's western provinces to Thailand. The irony of this potential new conflict between Thailand and Vichy France was that both of the combatants had already entered into separate alliances with the only true imperial overlord in the region – the Japanese.[5] Thai opportunism concerning the Cambodian provinces was firmly rooted in the logic of Southeast Asian history. For almost six centuries, the Cambodians and the Thai had been engaged in constant warfare west of the river Mekong.[6] The powerlessness of the French colonial administration in Cambodia now provided Thailand, by the way of a little Japanese assistance, with a prime opportunity for the re-establishment of its regional authority.

In January 1941, Thai armed forces invaded western Cambodia and comprehensively defeated the French military. A French naval counter-attack proved to be more promising for Vichy France with about half of the Thai fleet destroyed without a single French loss. However, before any sustained escalation of the conflict, the Japanese intervened in the dispute in order to protect their wider war efforts against the Allies. Japan could ill afford for a Southeast Asian conflict located behind its front lines. This would disrupt its military logistics and resource management. Thus, the Japanese imposed a settlement whereby Thailand annexed the western Cambodian provinces of Battambang, Siem Reap and Stung Treng. Cambodian and French pride had been severely damaged by the incident. The Japanese intervention had directly benefited the Thai vis-à-vis its traditional Cambodian adversary. As a consequence, Cambodia had to forfeit its western rice-producing provinces, and it also lost a sacred religious icon, the Emerald Buddha, to Thailand.[7]

In reality, the Thai–Cambodian conflict was not the only episode of Thai opportunism concerning European discomfort in the region. Thailand, emboldened by the disquiet of the European colonial powers, excelled in its collaboration with the Japanese. The Thai Government permitted the Japanese armed forces to use the nation as a military staging post and logistical supply base for the invasion of Burma and Malaya. Coexistence with Japan for Thailand proved highly profitable. By doing so, when the chance arose, Thailand was able to annex the four most northerly of the British Malay States as a payment for their wartime assistance to the Japanese.[8]

In the short term, however, a callously undermined and damaged Cambodian nation simply had to accept Japanese supervision. After all, Japan controlled the region, and the Franco-Cambodian relationship remained intact despite the Allied liberation of metropolitan France in 1944. In this far-flung outpost of empire, Vichy-French authority had peculiarly survived the fall of Vichy France. Nevertheless, by early 1945, the Japanese had decided to resolve this anomaly. On 9 March, the Japanese armed forces in Indo-China enacted a coup against the Vichy administration. It was a blatant attempt to solidify Japanese imperial control in Southeast Asia and to prepare French Indo-China for a possible Allied invasion. The coup did not lead to the Japanese directly controlling Vietnam, Laos and Cambodia but rather to the establishment of three indigenous regimes sponsored by the Japanese.

In Cambodia, four days later, encouraged by the limitations of the French to resist the Japanese challenge to French colonial control and under the direct tutelage of the Japanese, the Cambodian King, Norodom Sihanouk, declared Cambodian independence. All previous

Franco-Cambodian treaties were revoked and replaced with an agreement to co-operate with Japan. Cambodia's newly established freedom was purely relative and largely symbolic. Japan had merely replaced France as the colonial power. At this stage in the Second World War, it was more pragmatic for Japan to exert its imperial ambitions than to use a weakened vassal such as the Vichy France colonial administration.

With the French removed from the political equation, Japan now had the opportunity to develop Cambodian nationalism along more favourable lines.[9] These circumstances made it possible for the Japanese to expedite the return to Cambodia of the nationalist leader Son Ngoc Thanh. Since 1943, Thanh, the former advisor to the Cambodian newspaper *Nagaravatta*, had been in political exile in Tokyo. Thanh now returned to Cambodia, with the blessing of his former hosts, where he was appointed as the Foreign Minister for Sihanouk's fledgling regime, and he also acted as an important conduit for continued Japanese control.[10]

Thanh was desperate to preserve Cambodian independence. He hurriedly organised the formation of a Cambodian militia, known as the Green Shirts, to defend the nation against the return of French colonial control. The Japanese, however, remained wary of concentrating too much power in the hands of one Cambodian. Thanh was ideal as a useful foil to Sihanouk. But demonstrating where the true power lay, the Japanese selected their own Cambodian candidate, Thioum Muong, to command the Green Shirts.[11]

In the meantime, the overly ambitious Thanh became rapidly disillusioned with Sihanouk's leadership. Sihanouk appeared reluctant to take the necessary steps to save Cambodian independence and prevent the return of French colonial control. Preparations needed to be made. The King's inactivity and Thanh's fervent desire to preserve Cambodia's immature independence led Thanh to take a drastic measure. On 9–10 August, he orchestrated an attempted coup against Sihanouk. The monarchy survived the coup attempt, but Thanh also benefited. The episode elevated Thanh from the position of foreign minister to the central post of prime minister in order that he should provide more dynamic leadership for the state.[12]

At the same time, on 10 August, Japan indicated its willingness to surrender to the Allies. Just as Thanh ascended to the premiership, his main sponsors teetered on the brink of capitulation. Seven days later, the Japanese southern armies surrendered in full.[13] As the Cambodian Prime Minister, Son Ngoc Thanh, was now best placed to take full advantage of the post-surrender power vacuum. The Japanese had already sidelined the French. Thanh controlled the government and the King appeared inactive. Nevertheless, in reality too much of Thanh's power depended on the Japanese. Sihanouk remained highly popular, and the Cambodian elite distrusted Thanh. Even members of the Cambodian Cabinet failed to support many of the new Prime Minister's policies.

Despite the fundamental instability of his own situation, Thanh embarked upon a dynamic attempt to shore up Cambodian independence and preserve his young administration. On 2 September, Thanh's government recognised Ho Chi Minh's regime in Vietnam. The Democratic Republic of Vietnam hastily established a diplomatic mission in the Cambodian capital Phnom Penh.[14] Regular contact between the two governments was maintained throughout September. This led to the Cambodian Prime Minister accepting a Vietnamese request for formal talks to begin to co-ordinate a pan-Indo-Chinese effort to resist the return of the French colonial state. The proposed consultation appeared promising. A Cambodian delegation was dispatched to negotiate with Vietnam. But the Cambodian pre-condition for the return of the historic provinces of Travinh and Soc Trang, now part of the Democratic Republic of Vietnam and previously held by French Cochinchina, prevented any meaningful progress.[15] The Democratic Republic of Vietnam had no desire to cede the provinces to Cambodia.

Thanh, however, was not prepared to put all of his faith for Cambodian independence into the hands of the Democratic Republic of Vietnam. He also sent out delegations to seek both diplomatic recognition and assistance from Thailand and Chiang Kai-Shek's nationalist China.[16] Considering that previous Thai involvement in Cambodian affairs had resulted in the liberation of three Cambodian provinces and caused an extremely offensive affront to Cambodian national pride, the request for Thai assistance was highly ironic.

On the home front, Thanh attempted to boost his political credentials and legitimacy. A nationalist demonstration in Phnom Penh in support of the Prime Minister attracted a crowd of 30,000 supporters. A swiftly arranged referendum on Cambodian independence resulted in 541,470 votes in favour with only two against.[17] Thanh naturally hoped to solidify the nation around his government and to demonstrate to the Allies that he commanded a popular mandate. At the same time, Green Shirt recruitment persisted.[18] Either by paramilitary force or by diplomacy, Thanh aimed to preserve Cambodian sovereignty.

In the meantime in southern Vietnam, a small British–Indian deployment had arrived to administer the Japanese surrender. However, the British–Indian forces quickly found themselves in the middle of a tense cauldron of political violence between various different Vietnamese nationalist groups and the local French population. In such circumstances, it was difficult to maintain law and order. In the midst of a rapidly deteriorating state of affairs in southern Vietnam and with no first-hand political knowledge of the situation on the ground in Cambodia, the British liberation force commander Major-General Gracey gambled that 'Cambodia has no strong militant anti-French element at the moment and appears passive'.[19]

Gracey's intervention in Cambodia

Gracey had indeed taken a calculated risk that the situation in Cambodia was much quieter than what he was experiencing in southern Vietnam. But compared to the sporadic outbursts of intense urban violence in Saigon, the prospect of a markedly different scenario in the traditionally more tranquil climes of Cambodia must have been quite appealing. That said, Gracey had not taken leave of his senses. Instead Gracey was quite prepared to learn from the chaotic situation in southern Vietnam and attempt a radically different approach towards his liberation duties in Cambodia.

On 28 September, Gracey met with Admiral Lord Louis Mountbatten, the Supreme Allied Commander for Southeast Asia, for an urgent conference concerning British liberation duties in French Indo-China. Against the backdrop of further political violence in southern Vietnam, Gracey outlined his plans for administering the Japanese surrender in Cambodia. At the forefront of his mind was the growing apprehension that any British intervention in Cambodia would reap similar consequences to the British involvement in Vietnam. He therefore proposed a radically different solution for Cambodia. This demonstrated both Gracey's ability to learn from the mistakes of his Vietnam deployment and his deep-seated anxiety at the prospect of further political violence in Indo-China. Gracey proposed to Mountbatten that the most affective way to handle Allied duties in Cambodia and preserve law and order was 'to condone the past actions of the PM [Thanh] and to enlist his support; in fact to treat him in the same manner that we had dealt with Aung San in Burma'.[20]

Gracey's far-reaching proposal was for Britain to endorse Thanh's Cambodian nationalist movement. It was a watershed statement that actually went symbolically much further than the British accommodation of Aung San. In Burma, Aung San had established a national army under Japanese tutelage, but he had then crucially switched sides in 1943.[21] Thanh however had always collaborated with the Japanese, and he had then worked with the Vietminh to prevent the return of the French colonial administration. These were the very same Vietminh that Gracey had been forced to deal with concerning the outbreak of political violence in southern Vietnam.

Yet, surprisingly, Gracey regarded Thanh as the natural solution to the Cambodian question. Gracey was even prepared to base British policy upon the legitimacy of Thanh's government. Gracey's sentiments were remarkable and were certainly not in harmony with the highly negative comments made by numerous critical and often pusillanimous historians concerning British–Indian operations in southern Vietnam.[22] The dichotomy between Gracey's approaches to Cambodia and Vietnam demonstrated how flexible his approach to peace enforcement had become by developing differing diplomatic, military and political solutions to crisis situations. But it also showed how far-sighted he was in anticipating that it was possible for the European powers to cultivate co-operative nationalist politicians while at the same time enforcing more draconian measures against the extremists. This strategy eventually became the mainstay of British imperial policy.

Hence the key to Gracey's pitch was that Britain should give its support to Thanh and work alongside the Cambodian nationalist movement rather than against it. It was an attractive proposition. Gracey's limited resources were already overstretched through attempting to maintain law and order in southern Vietnam. Britain had neither the means nor the appetite for a second enforcement campaign in Cambodia. Mountbatten accepted the inducement and therefore agreed with Gracey's political resolution for Cambodia. Together they decided that the French should impose the proposed settlement. They envisaged a scenario whereby Colonel Jean Cedile, the French Commissioner in southern Indo-China, would be sent to Phnom Penh to work out the necessary details with Thanh. French troops would then take over from the Japanese armed forces and Britain's limited resources would be spared from any involvement in Cambodian affairs.[23]

The plan was not without its faults. It heavily relied upon Cedile imposing a British political solution upon Cambodia, a French colony, rather than reimposing full French colonial control in whatever fashion France deemed appropriate. It also assumed that Thanh would accept negotiations with Cedile that a compromise could be reached and that the Green Shirt militia would permit the return of the French armed forces. Above all, Gracey's plan was to be achieved with little British oversight. The chief architect willingly supposed that co-ordination could be maintained at arms' length from Saigon.

In the end, Gracey's plan to work alongside Thanh and Cambodian nationalism was not tested on the ground. Mountbatten and Gracey, pleased with their Cambodian solution, immediately took the plan into a meeting with John Lawson, the British Secretary of State for War. Lawson fully comprehended the difficult situation that the British–Indian forces currently faced in French Indo-China. But he emphasised that it was not the place of the British military establishment to impose a political settlement on to an allied sovereign power. London understood the risks that it was asking Gracey to take but 'it was fundamental of His Majesty's Government not to interfere in the internal affairs of non-British territories'.[24] Georges Bidault, the French Foreign Minister, had already visited Washington and achieved American support for a return of France's Indo-Chinese colonies. The British Embassy in Washington confirmed that the American State Department policy did 'not recognise any territorial changes which have been made under duress during war'.[25] Cambodia, Vietnam and Laos were the sole responsibility of the French.

Lawson naturally attempted to reassure Gracey and Mountbatten that the British Government had taken into account the tough circumstances in which British–Indian forces had been deployed in French Indo-China. Furthermore, he 'appreciated that the instructions from London made this extremely difficult in Indo-China; a single slip might well have grave repercussions'.[26] But in reality, Lawson condemned Gracey's plan to work alongside Cambodian nationalism to the annals of history. The French were now responsible for Thanh and British–Indian forces would have to go to Phnom Penh to disarm the Japanese. Gracey was in effect being asked to maintain a position of neutrality, neither to endorse Thanh nor to turn him over to the French but at the same time to enforce the Allied peace settlement and liberation duties.

Nonetheless, while Gracey and Mountbatten deliberated with Lawson, the situation in Cambodia changed once more. This reflected Britain's impotence and its inability to dictate events rather than to react to them. Thanh's own relationship with the Cambodian elite and members of his cabinet had deteriorated even further. In seeking to ally an independent Cambodia with Vietnam to the east and Thailand to the west, Thanh had ignored the logic of Cambodian history. In his ardent nationalist fervour to prevent a French return, he had allied Cambodia with its traditional regional foes. In doing so, the Prime Minister had inadvertently undermined his political powerbase and estranged himself from the bulk of the Cambodian population. These foreign enemies had previously used Cambodia's weaknesses to seize Cambodian provinces or install their own puppet regimes to exploit Cambodia's natural resources.

The Cambodian elite had long feared full colonisation by one or more of its powerful Southeast Asian neighbours. Before the advent of French colonial control, their lands had suffered at the hands of Thai and Vietnamese incursions. By connecting Cambodian independence to Thailand and the Democratic Republic of Vietnam, Thanh had invoked powerful images of a weak Cambodia being controlled by its larger and more authoritative neighbours. The Cambodian elite could not ignore these warnings from history. Thanh's naïve overtures to the Democratic Republic of Vietnam caused particular anxiety and hostility from within his own cabinet. Three senior government ministers: Khim Tit, the Minister for Defence; Nhek Tioulong, the Minister for Education; and Sum Hieng, the Minister for the Interior, all crucially withdrew their support for the Prime Minister.

This political disagreement isolated Thanh from the rest of the Cambodian elite. Annoyed at the diplomacy with Thailand and Vietnam, fears emerged within elite circles about the growing power of Thanh. Cambodia was traditionally a very conservative society based around the monarchy. An alliance with the Democratic Republic of Vietnam evoked fears of republican proselytism. Similarly, the cabinet dissenters believed that in the short term a return to French colonialism was better for Cambodia's long-term national interests. First, France, a victorious Allied power, would be better placed to advocate for the return of the provinces lost to Thailand during the Second World War. Second, Cambodia suffered from a dearth of indigenous professional and technically skilled workers. Thus, any potential exodus of the current resident French population could critically weaken the embryonic nation internally and at the same time vis-à-vis its stronger regional neighbours.[27] But above all, Thanh's dynamic leadership and national zeal just did not have the same attraction as Sihanouk's divine status. In a deeply conservative and religious society, only the king could enact the spiritual appeal needed to create the homogenous political momentum required for sustainable independence.

Mountbatten, as Supreme Allied Commander for Southeast Asia, was responsible for multiple British liberation operations within the region. One of these, the removal of Japanese forces from Thailand, naturally raised further problems for British duties in Cambodia because of the dubious status of the three provinces seized by Thailand during the Second World War.[28] It therefore appeared prudent for the Foreign Office official Maberly Esler Dening, who was serving as the Chief Political Officer to Mountbatten, to counsel the Thai Government that Britain did not acknowledge any territorial changes obtained under duress during the Second World War. In addition, Dening informed the Thai authorities that the border changes remained solely a bilateral issue between France and Thailand.[29]

The emphasis upon bilateral negotiations was a shrewd political manoeuvre. British Malaya had also lost territory to Thailand during the war and Britain hoped to establish the bilateral precedent as the appropriate avenue for its safe return. London thereby reiterated the importance of this position with a direct communiqué to Mountbatten. The War Cabinet instructed Mountbatten that the three Cambodian provinces held by the Thai could only be returned to Cambodia after an appropriate settlement between France and Thailand. The Cabinet also warned Mountbatten that if the French tried to retake the lost territory by a military endeavour then he should immediately contact London for further direction. Mountbatten did not have the authority to act unilaterally on this matter. If fighting broke out, he was specifically ordered that he could not assume that SEAC should intervene and establish Allied military control over the provinces.[30]

London had every right to be both suspicious and jittery. Mountbatten's planning staff had already drawn up a procedure to 'institute martial law in Siam [Thailand] and French Indo-China with or without reference to the Siamese [the Thai] or French authorities'.[31] In this context, Gracey's declaration of martial law in Saigon on 21 September should not be taken in isolation from the prevailing mood within the planning staff at SEAC headquarters which was to execute emergency measures where needed.[32]

On 26 September, Dening met with Pierre Clarac, the French negotiator for the return of the lost Cambodian provinces, and Prince Viwat, the Thai counterpart. Dening hoped to be able to play the role of an honest broker. But in a classic scenario of the occupier holding the trump card, the Thai Government showed little inclination to begin any meaningful negotiations with France.[33] London, however, wanted the clash to be concluded as soon as possible. Thailand had been identified by Whitehall as the strategic lynchpin for post-war co-operation in the defence of Burma, India, Indo-China, Malaya and the southwest Pacific.[34] The British Government had learned the vital lesson of the Second World War. British interests became vulnerable when Thailand was occupied by a hostile foreign power.

As it was, the internal situation in Cambodian politics returned to the forefront of Allied liberation activities. Thanh's regional diplomacy had already lost the support of his cabinet. Now Khim Tit, the Minister of Defence, took affairs into his own hands. Khim Tit flew to Saigon for urgent talks with the British and the French. During the course of the discussions, Khim Tit formally requested the return of French colonial control.[35] The stage was therefore set for an uncertain reception for British–Indian forces when they actually arrived in Phnom Penh.

On 9 October, the headquarters staff of the British liberation force for Cambodia began to arrive in Phnom Penh. Gracey placed all of his operations in Cambodia under the command of Lt.-Colonel E.D. Murray. Senior Japanese officers were immediately arrested by the British and flown out of the city to Saigon.[36]

The situation was tense. Murray operated under similarly vague instructions and with similarly restricted resources to his commanding officer in Saigon. Murray was therefore ordered to enforce liberation duties by: maintaining law and order; protecting Allied nationals; disarming Vietnamese agents; and preventing Vietnamese weapons from being secretively brought into Phnom Penh. In addition, he was also asked to 'ensure the stability of the Cambodian Government'. This was an interesting stricture. How should Murray define 'government'? The King had left the day-to-day affairs of the Cambodian state in the hands of a prime minister – Thanh. But Thanh's own cabinet had rebelled against him. The paramilitary Green Shirts naturally supported Thanh. Yet Khim Tit had already visited Saigon on behalf of the unhappy Cambodian elite and invited the French colonial regime to return to power. From the British Government perspective, Lawson had specifically squashed Gracey's suggestion that the British could operate alongside Thanh.

It therefore appeared that Murray was being ordered to work with the Cambodian Cabinet for the day-to-day administration of the nation. This would ensure the effective operation of the government, but not under the leadership of a pro-Japanese nationalist prime minister.[37] Indeed, two companies of French commandos under the command of Lt.-Colonel Houard accompanied Murray to Phnom Penh with the specific purpose of arresting Thanh. But, curiously, upon arrival Houard merely added to the confusion in the city by failing to apprehend the Prime Minister.[38]

At this stage, Murray possessed an eclectic array of military personnel with whom to uphold the peace. Allied military forces at his disposal were limited to one platoon of the 1st Battalion of Gurkha Rifles (30 men), two companies of French commandos under the command of

Houard and released Allied prisoners of war. Attached to these Allied personnel were the 55th Japanese Division, Japanese Air Force personnel and the Japanese Police Force. As in southern Vietnam, components of the defeated Japanese armed forces were re-equipped and expected to enforce Allied liberation duties (against the Japanese and other groups). In addition Murray also used the indigenous Cambodian police service.[39]

The French failure to arrest Thanh certainly made Murray's position more problematic. For a week, Murray was now forced to work with Thanh alongside Cambodian nationalism. Houard would not take the Prime Minister into custody, and General Philippe Leclerc – the Commander in Chief of French forces in Indo-China – had to fly to Phnom Penh and arrest Thanh himself. Murray's failure to arrest Thanh aligned with Mountbatten's perspective. Mountbatten believed that only the French should adequately resolve such unsavoury tasks.[40] In the meantime, Murray needed to carry out his Cambodian duties. Fortunately Khim Tit decided to return to Phnom Penh. His arrival demonstrated where the true power in the Cambodian Government lay. On 10 October, Murray visited Khim Tit and brokered all the necessary logistical arrangements for the effective co-operation between the Allied liberation forces and the Cambodian Government.[41]

Two days later, Khim Tit attended Murray's headquarters in Phnom Penh for further discussions. In tri-lateral talks between Khim Tit, Murray and Houard, it was decided that it would be prudent to remove Vietnamese workers from the Cambodian railways.[42] These workers along with a large Vietnamese civilian population could offer support to the communist Vietminh or the Cambodian nationalist group, the Khmer Issarak, and thereby destabilise an already delicate situation.[43]

Upon securing the railway infrastructure, Murray next turned his attention towards the police service. An hour after meeting Houard and Khim Tit, Murray called upon Thanh to discuss the disarmament of Vietnamese members of the Cambodian police force.[44] This demonstrated that the Prime Minister still held considerable power. If Thanh was merely a lame duck then Murray could have achieved all of the necessary arrangements an hour earlier from Khim Tit.

Murray's conference with Thanh went well. The Prime Minister readily confirmed to Murray that all of the Vietnamese elements within the Cambodian police service had already been disarmed. With Murray's request dealt with and with his fears allayed, Thanh then used the meeting as an opportunity to explain to Murray his popular mandate for Cambodian self-government.[45] A rapprochement appeared to have been made. The next day Thanh reciprocated Murray's calling of the previous day and visited British headquarters in Phnom Penh. He was invited to confer with Murray and his staff.

Once the social delicacies had been dealt with, Thanh used the conference to put Murray on the spot. The Prime Minister questioned Murray about the most dubious section in his instructions from Gracey. Thanh assertively announced to the British staff that a clearer definition was required concerning Murray's order to 'ensure the stability of the Cambodian Government'. Murray deftly responded to the Prime Minister that he possessed no civilian authority. This was purely a British military mission with very specific Allied liberation duties to accomplish. Therefore, Murray ambiguously stated that the order should be taken to mean that he (Murray) ought to make certain 'that the lawful government of Cambodia was not [to be] interfered with by subversive influences or force'.

Murray had conveniently sidestepped the problem. He had chosen not to define 'lawful', nor did anyone present ask him for further clarification. Above all, Thanh appeared content with the response. The bluff had worked. Thanh no doubt believed that he was the head of the lawful government that Murray had been instructed to protect. This was definitely aided by the subtext for the rest of the meeting, which continued to infer that the full civilian government within Cambodia rested with Thanh and his ministerial cabinet. Thanh therefore concluded the conference with temperate assurances to Murray about the British military mission receiving the complete co-operation of the Cambodian Government. In addition, Thanh dutifully arranged for an audience to take place between Murray and the King on 18 October. This could not have taken place any earlier because Sihanouk had wisely decided to absent himself from Phnom Penh on a four-day pilgrimage while the political settlement between the British, the French, Thanh and the Cambodian elite was worked out. Without a doubt, the Prime Minister left the British headquarters pleased with his negotiations.

Khim Tit, however, now resolved to move decisively against the Prime Minister. On the same evening as Thanh's visit to the British military headquarters, Khim Tit dined with Murray to fortify his position with the Allied commander. The uneasy truce between all of the political constituents in Phnom Penh was shattered the following day. Officially the Japanese armed forces had been placed under the command of Murray and the British military mission. But reflecting that a deal must have been struck during dinner the previous evening, Khim Tit now gave the orders for a number of rearmed Japanese military units to seize control of the Cambodian rail network. The pretence for this decisive action was to prevent Vietnamese workers from pilfering railway implements or destroying rail equipment. Murray hurriedly flew from Phnom Penh to Saigon to confer with Gracey. To begin with, his briefing in Saigon presented Gracey with the latest state of affairs in Cambodia but then it transitioned into a more specific parley concerning the delicate details pertaining to the arrest of Son Ngoc Thanh.[46]

Murray had been compelled to work with Thanh due to the spectacular failure of Houard and his French commandos to arrest the Prime Minister. French incompetence had clouded an already difficult scenario. The French still wanted to get rid of Thanh, while the British Government remained adamant that all domestic affairs should be left to the French to deal with. If Murray continued to work alongside Thanh, then the Prime Minister's position as the de facto head of a Cambodian nationalist government would be solidified. However, the re-establishment of French colonialism was connected to the resurrection of France as a great power.[47] It eradicated the stain of defeat and the guilt of Vichy France. The French therefore naturally preferred to regard Thanh as an opportunist and a Japanese collaborator.

At the same time, although Thanh commanded the support of the Green Shirts, his mutual collaboration with the Democratic Republic of Vietnam and the open rebellion of his cabinet colleagues hardly painted the scene of a stable situation for the Allied liberation forces to operate in. Murray had observed at first hand the difficult state of affairs and operating circumstances that the British–Indian forces faced in Saigon. Neither he nor Gracey had the resources to deal with the outbreak of simultaneous power vacuums in Saigon and Phnom Penh. In such conditions, Murray feared the Vietnamese population in Phnom Penh above the Cambodian nationalists. Yes, Thanh's supporters – especially the Green Shirts – were dangerous. But the large Vietnamese populace in Phnom Penh could easily turn against Murray's limited British–Indian forces and enact violent acts of revenge as compensation for British military actions in southern Vietnam.

The deliberations between Gracey and Murray were complex. But the Cambodian instability could not be permitted to persist indefinitely. It had to be rectified. Murray believed that the most logical solution was for Thanh to be detained as soon as possible in order to prevent any further slide towards a more serious breakdown in Cambodian law and order.[48]

As the commanding officer on the ground, Murray's convictions prevailed. The following day, General Leclerc, the French Commander in

Chief in French Indo-China, flew from Saigon to Phnom Penh. Thanh was cordially invited to attend a meeting at British military headquarters where, without a word being uttered, Leclerc promptly arrested the Prime Minister and accompanied him back to Saigon.[49] Murray instantly acted to prevent a nationalist backlash in Phnom Penh. He already had jurisdiction over the Cambodian police service, and it was now deployed to arrest anti-French subversives. A new government was hastily formed in Phnom Penh under the auspices of a new prime minister.[50] Prince Monireth, the Prime Minister, was King Sihanouk's older brother. The counter offensive to Thanh's premiership continued. Later the same day, three more Cambodian nationalist leaders were arrested. Two officers of the Green Shirt militia were also detained.[51]

Nevertheless, the position in the Cambodian capital was still not secure. The day following Thanh's confinement in Saigon, numerous disturbances broke out in Cambodia. The railway workers reacted to the news of Thanh's arrest by promptly going on strike. Elements of the Japanese armed forces were once again rapidly drafted into the railway yards. This time, it was to operate the rail network. The Green Shirts were still openly carrying weapons and freely roamed Phnom Penh. An intense standoff persisted. Cambodia stood on the edge of the precipice. But at this crucial juncture, Sihanouk returned to Phnom Penh. Large crowds jubilantly came out to welcome the King home from his pilgrimage. This prevented any more action by Thanh's supporters. Mountbatten would later inform the Anglo-American Combined Chiefs of Staff that it had been necessary to preserve the King's neutrality while Thanh was arrested. Therefore, Sihanouk had undertaken a four-day pilgrimage away from the capital city, and he had been conveniently absent from Phnom Penh when Leclerc had enacted the unsavoury deed.[52] The day following Sihanouk's rapturous return, the Green Shirts had their weapons successfully removed by the Japanese. A conference was held to co-ordinate the actions of the British, the Cambodian police and the leaders of the Cambodian National Guard. The momentum at this point had turned against Thanh's supporters. A further ten Vietnamese agitators were detained.

On 18 October, Murray met with Sihanouk. The irony was evident. Thanh, who was now imprisoned in Saigon, had originally brokered this audience with the King. At the same time, as Murray's meeting, Khim Tit effectively convened with the disgruntled railway workers to negotiate for a return to work. Within three days, the opposition to Thanh's arrest had petered out. Stability had been restored, and by 22 October the French armed forces were successfully carrying out security duties in their colony. The next day, Sihanouk satisfactorily reinstated all Franco-Cambodian agreements. France had effectively resumed its status as colonial master. Limited opposition to the return of the French administration did persist. But in the main, the remnant of Thanh's nationalist supporters had fled to either Thailand or southern Vietnam. There they joined a number of disparate anti-French groups such as the Free Cambodia Party, the Indo-Chinese Communist Party, the Vietminh and the Khmer Issarak.[53]

The political situation in Phnom Penh had at first been erratic. But in the end, it was more effectively resolved than the crisis in Saigon. Life in the Cambodian capital now returned to normal. Murray was rewarded for his part in enforcing the peace settlement and preventing a descent into greater political violence. Britain promoted Murray to the rank of brigadier.[54] In addition, Sihanouk later rewarded Murray with investiture into the Royal Order of Cambodia.[55]

Murray now deemed the circumstances in Phnom Penh stable enough for the British military mission to begin to co-ordinate food convoys for the relief of Saigon. Cambodia, a relative sideshow to the political violence in southern Vietnam, was now a crucial Allied element in a strategy to relieve the Vietminh embargo around Saigon.[56] At the same time, Cambodia's constancy compared to southern Vietnam was corroborated by Allied reconnaissance into other parts of the kingdom. For the most part, the country appeared tranquil and the people affable towards the French.[57] There remained certain regions susceptible to violence and conflict, but these tended to be predominantly along the Cambodian border with southern Vietnam. For example, on 20 November, Lt.-Colonel Wenham, a British officer, and 300 Japanese troops successfully pushed Vietnamese forces out of Ha Tien on the Vietnamese-Cambodian border.

Stability in Cambodia continued to improve. As a result, Murray was now able to enact his main Allied liberation duties. On 25 November, Murray implemented the official Allied surrender measures towards the Japanese. General Sakumay and the Japanese 55th Divisional Headquarters in Phnom Penh were directed to lay down their armaments.[58] Britain no longer needed Japanese assistance for peace enforcement in Cambodia. British investigators subsequently arrived in Phnom Penh to look into Japanese war crimes committed during the Second World War. Normal Allied occupation duties were now underway. By 19 December, 8,372 Japanese troops had been disarmed and evacuated from Cambodia.[59]

Nonetheless, despite the winding down of Allied surrender duties, British (and Gracey's) involvement in Cambodian affairs had not yet ceased. The Cambodian–Thai border dispute remained unresolved. Admiral Thierry D'Argenlieu, the French High Commissioner for Indo-China and a former Carmelite monk, unsurprisingly wished for the provinces to be returned to French control as soon as possible. He therefore dispatched French observers into Thai-controlled Battambang (one of the disputed provinces) without prior discussion with either the British or the Thai authorities. Mountbatten logically feared a new international dispute. As a result, D'Argenlieu was ordered to attach his observers to Lt.-General Evans' Allied liberation force that was operating in Thailand. The ever-impatient D'Argenlieu then petitioned to have Battambang removed from Evans' zone for liberation activities and placed within Gracey's jurisdiction, thereby metaphorically reuniting the province with the rest of Cambodia.[60]

The deployment of French observers should have been handled in a more diplomatic fashion. Yet the French instructions to their observers were issued in the most inflammatory of terms. The officers were expected: to uphold the 'spirit of France' and counter any Thai misinformation; to demonstrate that France maintained its claim to the provinces on behalf of Cambodia; to appraise D'Argenlieu of all Thai activities in the provinces; and to develop liaisons with the Allied liberation forces.[61] As soon as Evans became aware of the orders, he hurriedly arranged to confer with Gracey and Hugh Bird, the British Consul-General in the Thai capital – Bangkok. Evans wanted the first two clauses in the French instructions removed from their orders. Any French actions to preserve the spirit of France, to oppose Thai propaganda and to sustain French rights to the provinces could have grave repercussions. The orders were simply too broad. The situation was not auspicious, and it was made even worse because Evans, like Gracey, had exceedingly limited resources to police the disputed territories. He could only spare two officers to act as Allied observers in Battambang.

Evans therefore cabled Major-General Harold Pyman, the Chief of Staff to the Allied liberation forces in SEAC, with the stark warning that any British troops left in the disputed provinces would inevitably become drawn into the Franco-Thai conflict. Evans wanted SEAC to give him an entitlement to withdraw any French observers from the area that he deemed to have exceeded their orders. He also sought specific permission to remove one French officer who had already made himself deeply unpopular.[62]

The French appreciated the weakness of Britain's position in the region. They therefore agreed with Evans' request to reduce the terms of reference for their observers in the provinces and to the removal of their most ostracised officer. But at the same time, they also informed the British that Evans had already approved plans for French observers to remain in Battambang to prevent the Thai from achieving a moral victory.[63] The French were unhelpfully pushing their luck. Gracey urgently cabled Evans and ominously warned him that the French would now advocate for more observers to be sent into the disputed provinces.[64] The mood within Thai Government circles could not have been positive. Evans responded to Gracey with an austere note of caution that unless Mountbatten specifically supported this latest stroke by the French that Gracey should intervene to avert any such French actions. The Thai Government would surely detain any French aircraft or personnel who foolishly embarked upon such endeavours.[65]

Not to be prevented from taking further action, the French now resorted to a propaganda offensive against Thailand through radio broadcasts made from Saigon.[66] Britain was unable to prevent the transmissions, but the transcripts were shown to British personnel before each broadcast was made. The local British Foreign Office and Publicity Office staff deemed such transmissions useful propaganda in order to preserve British authority in the region. However, this turned out to be a serious mistake. The broadcasts naturally provoked a hostile reaction towards France from the Thai media. Pierre Clarac, the French negotiator with Thailand, consequently arranged that no further broadcasts would be made that referred to the contentious provinces.[67]

In the meantime, Thailand remained content to drag its feet concerning any form of negotiated settlement.[68] After all Thailand already possessed the three disputed provinces. It was not in its national interest to implement an urgent transfer. France, as expected, found this unacceptable. Gallic pride had to be restored in the region. But in reality, both Thailand and France were guilty of displaying an ardent reluctance to negotiate positively for a diplomatic resolution to the quarrel. Thus, the omens did not appear positive. Dening, the Chief Political Officer to SEAC, observed the stalemate with some trepidation. He particularly feared that D'Argenlieu would attempt to undertake further direct action against Thailand rather than any form of diplomatic settlement. Dening unpromisingly warned the Foreign Office in London that 'I am afraid that I can think of nothing that I could say or do to improve the situation'.[69]

Clarac readily confirmed Dening's suspicions about D'Argenlieu. The highly reactionary High Commissioner was capable of provoking the ire of both the British and the French within the region. Clarac believed that D'Argenlieu wanted to develop a more antagonistic policy of propaganda towards the Thai. Clarac understood that D'Argenlieu was working towards, in due course, the goal of grabbing hold of the provinces by the deployment of French troops. In order to prevent this reckless scenario from developing any further, Clarac requested that British pressure be applied to Thailand for the resumption of diplomacy.[70] This time, however, Clarac was not hampered by a Thai unwillingness to attend the talks but rather by his political superior, the French High Commissioner. D'Argenlieu had evolved a suspicious opinion towards Clarac's more proactive stance in connection with the deliberations. This reflected the different divisions within the French establishment in Indo-China with reference to how best to settle the confrontation with Thailand.[71]

As SEAC Allied liberation duties diminished during early 1946, the British Foreign Office began to assume a greater responsibility for the negotiated agreement between the French and the Thai.[72] London hoped that France and Thailand could be persuaded to resolve bilaterally the border argument and thus untangle Britain from the fate of the three disputed provinces.[73] But the situation was complex and ultimately, because of a failure to rectify this issue, France remained technically at war with Thailand.[74]

The internal situation in Thailand following the Second World War certainly did not help Franco-Thai negotiations. The Thai governments were weak and any damage to their national pride in the negotiations with the French could hinder internal political stability.[75] The Thai parleying position thereby proved intractable. The Thai strategy in the negotiations centred upon three hard-line solutions. First, they advocated referring the argument to the United Nations. Second, they suggested that a referendum should be undertaken in the disputed provinces concerning succession to either Cambodia or Thailand. Third, the Thai offered to purchase the three provinces from Cambodia. Unsurprisingly all of these remedies were unacceptable to the French.[76] Both sides in the discord were gambling for high stakes. The three disputed provinces were the most profitable rice-producing areas within French Indo-China.[77] The ultimate prize of either continued Thai occupation or French reacquisition was evident to all of the players involved in the conflict.

In the meantime, with vastly reduced SEAC forces in the region, raids across the border between Cambodia and Thailand hindered any serious political resolution. On 24 May and again on 26 May, large numbers of French military personnel crossed the river Mekong and attacked the Thai Army. The French also sporadically bombarded Thai territory.[78] The French attempted to justify the incursions to Lord Killearn, the British Special Commissioner in Singapore, as little more than 'a small police matter'.[79] Thus, Dening's fears pertaining to a French escalation at this point looked as if they had been fully justified. Faults had clearly existed on both sides of the debate. But now, in order to prevent an escalation of the conflict, British and American observers were sent to the French side of the border.[80] To add injury to insult, France also increased its diplomatic pressure upon Thailand by threatening to block Thai membership of the United Nations.[81]

The Thai counter-attack to the French raids arrived on 9 and 10 August. Despite the presence of the international observers, 500 Cambodian and Vietnamese rebels accompanied by a small detachment of the Thai military attacked Siem Reap. The rebels occupied the ancient Cambodian temple complex of Angkor Wat. The premier symbol of Cambodian national pride, sovereignty and civilisation had been attacked. French paratroopers were hastily deployed to the temple complex and a ferocious battle developed.[82]

As a direct result of the offensive, the French Government immediately suspended all talks with Thailand.[83] Again Thailand and France stood on the edge of the precipice. It looked like direct confrontation was at this point unavoidable. British intelligence informed London that France now appeared to be on the verge of using its full military might to take back the three disputed areas.[84] As if to confirm the preparations for a large French assault, D'Argenlieu asked for the removal of all of the international observers.[85] Britain assumed that a French attack would swiftly occur as soon as the rainy season was over. The intense bitterness on both sides of the debate had led the British to conclude that France would not be content merely to regain the three Cambodian provinces and that additional Thai territory would now be seized by the French in righteous indignation as compensation for the territorial clash.[86]

In November, however, France backed down from a direct military confrontation, and it proposed that Britain should leave all of its observers along the Thai–Cambodian border even after the remaining Allied liberation troops had been withdrawn from the rest of Thailand (Gracey's Allied liberation force had left Indo-China earlier in 1946).[87] The British Chiefs of Staff held no objections to the French request, but the Foreign Office was more reticent.[88] The Franco-Thai border had not proved to be a safe arena in which to deploy international observers.

In addition, the resolution of the disputed provinces looked unlikely to be resolved in the near future. SEAC therefore decided to withdraw all of their observers, as their safety could not be guaranteed.[89] The observers however were not removed. In an extreme volt-face, a Franco-Thai treaty was successfully concluded on 17 November. SEAC and the United States now urgently agreed to send additional officers to act as witnesses to the territorial transfers despite there being no Allied troops on hand to provide the required additional security protection. In one of the last acts of SEAC liberation duties, British officers successfully monitored the territorial transfers.[90]

Despite the successful conclusion of the Franco-Thai treaty, Thailand continued to meddle in Cambodian affairs. At the same time as British officers were supervising the return of Battambang, Siem Reap and Stung Treng, in December 1946 the Vietminh commenced a general insurrection against the French colonial control of Indo-China. Guided by the devout communist leader Ho Chi Minh, the Vietminh embraced the Maoist tactic of initially occupying and maintaining rural areas before moving into the towns and the more difficult conundrums of urban warfare.[91] Thailand was best placed to take full advantage of this latest Indo-Chinese development. The Vietminh needed to be able to fund their military undertakings against the French.

In these circumstances, Thailand became the natural receiver of Vietminh agricultural products. The Vietminh exported animal pelts, coffee, rice, salt and sugar to Thailand to finance their war effort. A sophisticated trading network was established across Indo-China (including Cambodia) centred upon Bangkok.[92] The quantity of goods involved was not insignificant. By 1947, the Vietminh had achieved supply parity with French Indo-Chinese rice exports.[93] Thus, as a new regional geo-political fracas erupted, Thailand became an important financier and profiteer in Indo-Chinese affairs. Britain though was absolved of handling this new outbreak of political violence. By this time Britain had completed its Allied liberation duties and ended all British obligations concerning the administration of the Japanese surrender within Cambodia.[94]

4
The Enforcement: Indo-China 1945–1946

British liberation activities in French Indo-China were not solely orientated around the political resurrection of French colonial control. Britain's obligations under international law were far more complex. The Hague Convention of 1907, to which Britain was a signatory, decreed that

> The authority of the power of the state having passed de facto into the hands of the occupant, the latter shall do all in his power to restore, and to ensure as far as possible, public order and safety.

Gracey, as the Commander in Chief of the Allied liberation forces in southern Indo-China, had therefore taken on 'the authority of the power of the state', and in doing so he became fully responsible for 'public order and safety'.[1] This encompassed more than just the political return of the French colonial administration to southern Vietnam and Cambodia. In a dangerous power vacuum, the breadth of such a legal responsibility meant that Gracey had a duty of care towards the indigenous civilian populations (Cambodian, French and Vietnamese) within his zone of Allied operation. In order to uphold such a responsibility, Gracey plainly had to ensure some kind of adequate humanitarian aid and military infrastructure. But how far he could realistically do so, and for how long, would be ultimately shaped by bigger policy decisions elsewhere. In this respect, Gracey's ability to act was controlled by others. He was trapped between politicians and revolutionaries. This was a crude attempt by SEAC at peace enforcement, and external constraints did much to limit Gracey's methods.

From the perspective of both Washington and London, once the Japanese had surrendered, French sovereignty had automatically returned to Indo-China. But France was simply unable to establish, let alone maintain, an adequate security infrastructure. Indeed, it was left to Britain and Gracey's limited military resources to form an emergency interim administration in southern Indo-China. This ad hoc measure was not a desire to create a temporary British government agency, but rather an impromptu holding pattern until an adequate French organisation could be established. What this meant for Britain was that, if Gracey was going to be able to extricate rapidly his forces from southern Vietnam and Cambodia, Allied military assistance would have to be provided to the returning French colonial administration. This, however, proved incredibly frustrating and complex.

In addition, Britain had first-hand experience with the Bengal famine (1942–1943) of how insecure food supplies could threaten local colonial administrations. The Allied wartime bombardment of French Indo-Chinese ports and railway yards had destroyed almost all logistical infrastructure. At the same time, meteorological conditions in Vietnam had resulted in a poor rice harvest. In Cambodia, the most profitable rice-producing provinces had been seized by Thailand. These circumstances, when combined with the effective disintegration of the civilian administration in August 1945, created a humanitarian crisis. Such a human catastrophe threatened any semblance of continued law and order.[2] Humanitarian aid for the civilian population of French Indo-China was therefore a vital component of the state-security infrastructure.

Protecting the peace: Military aid

Gracey possessed very limited military resources and comparatively small troop numbers for Allied liberation operations in southern French Indo-China. Under these circumstances, the key to the maintenance of any internal state-security infrastructure would be just how quickly Britain and the United States could transport adequate numbers of French troops and equipment into Saigon. However, because of his limited resources, Gracey could barely enact initial emergency measures to preserve public order. The sheer size of southern Vietnam and Cambodia meant that large numbers of troops would be required to bring full internal stability to the French territories. The maximum number of personnel allocated to Gracey by SEAC for operations in southern Indo-China and Cambodia was 25,748 (consisting of a mixture of British, French, Indian and Gurkha, air force, naval and army personnel).[3] It would naturally take time for them all to arrive in Saigon and reach their optimal operational efficiency. But the reality in September 1945 was very different. Only 750 men were initially sent into southern Vietnam and well into October Gracey had only 1,800 men at his disposal.[4] Thus, even if Britain had the political will, it was in no position to provide the necessary quantity of armed forces needed to pacify the situation. At the end of the Second World War, Britain was financially bankrupt and its resources were severely overstretched. Therefore, a logistical delay concerning the supply of military aid to the French appeared unavoidable. But any postponement in military aid inevitably placed the small numbers of Gracey's forces deployed in Indo-China in grave danger.

In the same way in which Gracey's political actions in French Indo-China have proved historically controversial, so too has been the procurement of military aid from the British by the returning French administration. Some of the same historians that have sought to criticise Gracey for taking sides in southern Vietnam have also attempted to attribute provision of military aid, for the returning French regime, predominantly to Britain.[5] In this light, the blood-spattered return of the French Empire in Indo-China rested more comfortably with the old world colonial powers – Britain and France – than the enlightened values of the new world liberator – the United States.

In reality, by the end of the Second World War, the United States had already assumed hegemony over the new world order.[6] Britain had by now declined in its status from an equal partner in an uxorious relationship with the United States to a humiliating position of dependency. This meant that any successful French return to Indo-China could only be possible with specific American assistance. The French clearly understood the geopolitical shift. Desperate to enact a triumphant French military return to Indo-China, France readily began to purchase both the equipment and the necessary shipping from the United States.[7] Despite SEAC liberation operations being mostly a British concern, Britain was equally keen for the French to develop military assistance from the United States.[8] Britain simply did not possess the military aid quantities that the French desired. In addition, any attempts by Britain to provide transportation for the French armed forces would directly compete with Britain's electoral commitment under Operation Python to demobilise British and colonial troops.[9]

Nevertheless, the political violence in southern Vietnam continued. This placed an added burden upon SEAC. In order to safely remove Gracey's limited forces as quickly as possible, Mountbatten therefore had to ask London for extra French troops and shipping to be sent to Indo-China.[10] But immediate policing concerns plainly could not be resolved by long-range requests to London for assistance. It simply took too long to acquire even an adequate verbal, let alone a physical, response. The situation on the ground was critical. Civilian lives were at risk and Britain was legally responsible for public safety. As a result, Mountbatten arranged for Gracey to rearm a number of Japanese prisoners of war with the aim of Japanese military units supplementing the limited numbers of British–Indian armed forces available in southern Indo-China. These Japanese units would be specifically engaged by Britain in the preservation of law and order.[11]

The deployment of Japanese prisoners of war as Allied peace enforcers was not an ideal solution for policing the power vacuum. The situation in southern Indo-China was regarded from London with a high degree of anxiety. Mountbatten naturally found common cause with the Joint Planning Staff at the War Office in Whitehall. The Joint Planning Staff were unrelenting in their advocacy for additional British–Indian forces to be attached to Gracey's command. But controversially, the Joint Planning Staff also naïvely believed that Gracey's forces should be concentrated in Saigon. The rest of Indo-China ought to be left for the French to administer. Yet at this juncture, French governmental apparatus and personnel were non-existent. The resurrection of French infrastructure would require a sustained period of peace enforcement.

In the confines of London, over 6,000 miles away from Saigon, the Joint Planning Staff solution to the Indo-Chinese conundrum no doubt appeared logical. Gracey would concentrate his limited resources in the area of greatest need and highest population density – Saigon – and he would only intervene elsewhere in southern Indo-China if it proved absolutely necessary.[12] In reality, such plans were obsolete, as Gracey's headquarters had already assumed the role of the state under the terms of the Hague Convention. In doing so, Gracey was at that very moment attempting, with inadequate resources, to police political violence in both southern Vietnam and Cambodia. London meanwhile continued to deliberate.

At the same time, another issue that Gracey faced concerning military aid also came to the fore. As SEAC was responsible for all Allied operations and infrastructure within Southeast Asia, any French troop deployments by Britain in French Indo-China would have to be resupplied through SEAC. For the moment, it would be logistically impossible to do otherwise. This proved to be the case until adequate French logistical support could be developed. The easiest way for SEAC to resupply French forces was to issue them with compatible equipment from the

British military stores in the region. Thus, when the French forces ran out of bullets, they would receive alternative British substitutes.

But a French proposal to send the 9th Colonial Division to southern Indo-China threatened this local logistical arrangement. The French 9th Colonial Division was organised according to the standards of an American, rather than a British, military division.[13] If the division was successfully conveyed to French Indo-China, once it had exhausted its initial quantities of American ammunition, it would be impossible for Britain to assist with making further resources available unless the United States agreed that Britain could directly issue American lend-lease equipment to the French armed forces.[14] The American situation concerning military supplies was complicated by a plethora of contradictory orders emanating from different parts of the Washington political apparatus. The sudden termination of the war had thrust American leadership into the global spotlight. At the State Department, the European and Far Eastern offices pursued competing and often conflicting policies regarding the future of French Indo-China.[15]

Mountbatten remained optimistic that with sufficient military supplies Leclerc would be able to take over security duties from Gracey on 2 October. It initially appeared that Gracey's mission to Saigon would be terminated in a little under a month from the first British–Indian troop arrivals. Staff at SEAC had estimated that by 2 October an initial upsurge of 2,245 French troops would have been deployed against the political violence in southern Indo-China. As a worst-case scenario, Mountbatten calculated that it would be possible to let the French takeover slide until the 20 October, thereby creating a logistical window for another 2,150 French troops to arrive.[16] The delay had the natural advantage of permitting a more potent French return. This would allow for more French resources to be allocated to preserving public safety, and thereby diminish the opportunity for continued political violence. Nevertheless, Mountbatten was desperate for France to assume military responsibility for French Indo-China as soon as possible. Any delay beyond 20 October could have grave repercussions elsewhere within SEAC. Mountbatten faced multiple difficult liberation duties across Southeast Asia, and he urgently needed to be able to use British–Indian troops currently on active service in southern Indo-China to police surrender duties in Borneo and elsewhere.[17]

SEAC therefore continued to lobby London concerning the logistical crisis that it faced in southern Indo-China. Mountbatten urgently needed large numbers of additional French troops to be sent to Saigon.[18] The use of Japanese prisoners of war as Allied peace enforcers was far from ideal. The circumstances that the British–Indian forces faced in French Indo-China were not auspicious. In Saigon, the political violence continued with Gracey's international peace enforcers pincered between a general Vietnamese insurrection and the return of the French colonial regime. In Phnom Penh a nationalist regime against French colonial rule had been established. The pro-Japanese collaborator Son Ngoc Thanh led this.

By 28 September, events in Saigon were deemed serious enough to be brought to the attention of Clement Attlee, the British Prime Minister. Attlee immediately made a request for an up-to-date briefing to be prepared concerning the violent situation in French Indo-China by the British War Cabinet secretariat.[19] But although Attlee considered the British position in Indo-China sufficiently thought-provoking to bring before the full Cabinet Defence Committee, he curiously requested for all French Indo-Chinese business to be scheduled for discussion in one week's time.[20] Considering that British–Indian troops were operating in severely dangerous circumstances in Saigon, the delay was surprising. Attlee clearly did not fully comprehend the gravity of Gracey's situation, British obligations for the maintenance of law and order or the necessity of handing such responsibilities over to the French as soon as possible. If he had truly understood the situation on the ground in French Indo-China, the duplicity of the Prime Minister would have been staggering. Attlee would have broken the ethical bond (a duty of care) between the British state and its armed forces. He would have needlessly delayed a cabinet debate about British military personnel serving in violent conditions to enforce the Allied post-war peace settlement in a non-British territory.

In the meantime, Attlee asked the War Cabinet secretariat for additional details concerning the possible movement of French troops scheduled for transportation to Indo-China. Despite the presence of British–Indian troops on the ground in southern French Indo-China, Attlee obviously regarded the Indo-Chinese power vacuum as a French priority rather than a British one. Gracey's forces were being asked to provide a temporary holding pattern until a more permanent French resolution was possible. The longer this scenario continued, the greater was the danger for Gracey that British military personnel, rather than French, would be entangled in political violence.

At the War Office in Whitehall, the British Chiefs of Staff indicated to the Prime Minister that it was physically possible for Britain to expedite the deployment of the 9th French Colonial Division to Indo-China by up to one month. But this acceleration would come at a political price. The cost for Attlee was that any action to speed up the delivery of French military resources and personnel to relieve Gracey and British–Indian forces in Indo-China would result in an unacceptable political delay to British post-war demobilisation plans. Under the terms of Operation Python, Attlee had already made a political commitment to discharge British forces personnel stationed in Britain, India and the Mediterranean. The ships allocated to Operation Python were the same vessels needed to hasten the employment of the 9th Colonial Division to Indo-China. Thus, it was not the intensity of the political violence in southern Indo-China that put an upper limit on Britain's troop numbers and logistical commitment in Indo-China. Sufficient numbers of British troops and ships existed. But domestic political considerations surrounding the necessity to complete Operation Python confined Gracey's operations in French Indo-China to a political backwater.[21]

On the other hand, British deliberations concerning military aid for French Indo-China were about to take another unexpected turn. When the full Cabinet Defence Committee assembled in London on 5 October, an extraordinary argument played out. In the course of its regular business agenda, the committee considered Mountbatten's request to accelerate the movement of French troops to Indo-China in order to relieve Gracey's involvement. Lord Alanbrooke, the Chief of the Imperial General Staff – the head of the British armed forces, believed that the circumstances on the ground in French Indo-China were 'not at present sufficiently serious' to justify the expense of speeding up the delivery of the French armed forces. SEAC had continually pleaded for the opposite. Alanbrooke had made a bizarre statement. The most senior military commander in the British armed forces, in an open cabinet meeting, had advocated for government financial savings over the lives of British, Indian and Gurkha personnel serving in a peace-enforcement capacity in a non-British colonial territory.

Oliver Harvey, the Foreign Office representative on the committee, immediately challenged Alanbrooke's position. The Foreign Office presented a stark warning. The longer Gracey's enforcement activities lasted, the greater the potential damage to Britain's international reputation. Harvey reasoned that it was therefore a geopolitical necessity for Britain to speed up the transfer of law and order responsibilities in Indo-China to France. This naturally required accelerating the delivery of the French armed forces. Attlee, however, sided with Alanbrooke. In doing so, the Prime Minister's decision condemned Gracey to another period of uncertainty until adequate French resources could be sent to French Indo-China. It was an absurd breach of trust by the Cabinet Defence

Committee. British military forces were being expected to police Allied liberation duties in the midst of ardent political violence for the sake of budgetary issues. This was a French colonial territory, but Britain would not speed up the arrival of additional French military forces by one month because of the miserly attitude of the nation's most senior military commander. Transportation costs thus outweighed the potential financial and human outlay associated with increased political violence or a delayed British–Indian departure from French Indo-China.

To add insult to injury, the Joint Planning Staff at the War Office had prepared in advance a detailed briefing for the Cabinet Defence Committee. This highlighted the fact that Gracey still remained legally responsible for the maintenance of law and order within his area of command. But, again reflecting the gulf between London and Saigon, the Joint Planning Staff also advised the Cabinet that Gracey should keep such law and order duties to an absolute minimum. In the midst of highly volatile, mobile and sporadic political violence, Gracey was expected to keep public-order duties to a bare minimum.

Even though in cabinet debate Attlee had prevented the acceleration of French military forces, the Joint Planning Staff briefing had also recommended for Gracey to hand over all security tasks to the French as soon as possible.[22] The Joint Planning Staff briefing clearly exposed a number of government contradictions. First, Gracey had a legal responsibility to maintain law and order, but he was also unrealistically expected to keep such activities to a minimum. Second, Gracey was expected to hand over security duties to the French without delay, but the Cabinet had refused to accelerate the French military deployment that would enable this to happen.

The Cabinet Defence Committee had demonstrated the depth of disconnect between policy and operational necessities. London, without a doubt, misunderstood the gravity of Gracey's circumstances. Yet, in spite of the logistical machinations in Whitehall, limited French military aid did materialise in Indo-China. The French battleship, the *Richlieu*, arrived in Saigon with further military supplies, but this hardly represented the decisive arrival of the massive volume of military resources required to sustain a new French administration and public safety.[23]

Nevertheless, despite a defeat in the Cabinet Defence Committee, the Foreign Office remained frantic to speed up the employment of any French troops to Indo-China. It wanted to return civilian administration to French control and remove British–Indian forces as quickly as possible. Ernest Bevin, the Foreign Secretary, therefore swung his full political support behind the need to supply warships to hasten French military deployments.[24] The irony of the situation was that the British diplomatic corps was more interested in extricating British military personnel from danger than was the War Office. The ruling of the Cabinet Defence Committee made the Foreign Office position appear forlorn. But Bevin possessed an important ally in General Slim, the Commander in Chief of all Allied land forces in Southeast Asia.

Slim now communicated to Alanbrooke his misgivings concerning Gracey's involvement in French Indo-China. In doing so, he highlighted how critical military aid had become to the success of Gracey's mission. Sufficient quantities of French troops within the region simply did not exist. British–Indian forces were therefore forced to maintain essential services and prevent the slaughter of the civilian population. If the current political violence in southern Vietnam escalated into a full-scale Vietnamese uprising against French colonial control, as had already happened in northern Vietnam, then the safety of the civilian population could be placed in dire jeopardy. In such circumstances, Gracey's limited military resources would be simply overwhelmed and unable to enforce either their legal or moral obligations.

Slim therefore emphasised how treacherous the logistical stalemate had become. Military aid was imperative. Gracey's forces were deeply unpopular with the local Vietnamese population. In addition, elements of the local French population had begun to take security issues into their own hands. British military personnel needed to be extracted as soon as possible.[25] This was made even more apparent on 9 October when France formally resumed administrative control for southern Indo-China and Cambodia from Britain. Thus, with Slim's ominous warning from Southeast Asia and in London Bevin's push for greater logistical co-ordination, the eight ships provided by the United States to transport 7,700 troops from France to Indo-China during October were joined by another flotilla for the conveyance of an additional 14,000 French troops.[26] The Foreign Office had prevailed over the Cabinet Defence Committee. On 24 October, Bevin confirmed to the House of Commons that every effort was now being made to transport French troops and military equipment to Saigon.[27]

Despite the best efforts of Slim and Bevin, both Mountbatten and Gracey still faced unprecedented turmoil and political violence in southern Indo-China. In November, almost two months after the first British–Indian troops had arrived in Saigon, Mountbatten was still frantically cabling the British War Office for adequate resources to relieve Gracey of Allied liberation duties in French Indo-China. The size of southern Indo-China and the intensity of the political violence against the French administration repeatedly swallowed up French military resources as soon as they arrived in Saigon. But it still remained necessary for SEAC to free Gracey's forces from Indo-Chinese operations, as they urgently needed to be redeployed to the Dutch East Indies. The disastrous state of SEAC operations in the Dutch East Indies necessitated the French resuming control of Indo-China as quickly as possible.[28]

Nevertheless, as French troop numbers steadily increased in Indo-China, so too did French operational capabilities. However, Leclerc still could not commit to the large-scale military operations that he desired without sufficient aerial support. Ever weary of further military entanglement, Britain would not allow British pilots to support French military operations. France did not have any aircraft of its own available. Thus, questions concerning military aid surfaced once again. Leclerc eagerly requested that Mountbatten should supply a squadron of Royal Air Force Spitfires for French pilots to use on security operations in Indo-China. Mountbatten readily agreed with the request. He was desperate to speed up the French military capacity to carry out any large-scale security operations and thereby remove Gracey's forces from Indo-China. Hence, Mountbatten advised the British Chiefs of Staff not only to supply one squadron of Mark IV Spitfires but also to supply the necessary spares for their ongoing maintenance to Leclerc.[29]

By now, it was very clear that the potency of the French military return to Indo-China was fully dependent upon Britain and the United States. France simply could not transport sufficient numbers of troops or furnish them with adequate equipment without British and American assistance. But this situation also exposed Britain's geopolitical weakness within the new world order. At the Cabinet Defence Committee, Attlee's political myopia lacked a broader strategic vision. His inability to see French Indo-China as a priority, in conjunction with SEAC military overstretch, revealed Britain's powerlessness and the extent of its imperial decline. Britain was struggling to carry out simultaneous peace-enforcement campaigns in Indo-China, Thailand, the East Indies and elsewhere. The days of independent military action and gunboat diplomacy were over. Britain could no longer afford to act in isolation from its American financial master. Hence, a sizeable part of the correspondence between SEAC and London concerning military aid for French Indo-China was also copied to the Joint Service Mission in Washington.

The United States was therefore made fully aware of military supply issues concerning French Indo-China. Washington was kept fully abreast of the latest French requests to London and the subsequent paucity of French military capabilities in Indo-China. Likewise, via the same channel, Britain was perfectly conscious of Washington's fears that American lend-lease equipment within SEAC would be automatically handed over to the French by the British without prior American approval. Britain could not just dispose of American equipment however it saw fit. The French were free to purchase American military supplies. But now that the Second World War was over, the American sourced lend-lease equipment could not be donated by Britain without causing a diplomatic incident.

A growing British paranoia and subservience to American military management therefore came to dominate Anglo-French discussions concerning military aid. For example, when the French requested that the British Admiralty supply landing craft to French forces in Indo-China, the First Sea Lord could not reply in a bold and positive fashion. Most of the landing craft located within SEAC were of an American lend-lease origin. There were only two British vessels that were available for immediate transfer. The First sea lord, however, informed the French that if they secured American approval, then more landing craft could be immediately dispatched for them to use.[30] Thus, the United States was in the ascendancy and Britain clearly did not want to upset its stronger Allied partner. The downside to this new relationship was that the failure to secure rapid resupply no doubt added to the longevity of Gracey's sojourn in French Indo-China.

Britain was overly zealous about being seen by the United States to be following the correct protocol with regard to its lend-lease equipment. Yet the United States was perfectly happy to directly supply the French with military aid whenever possible. This was especially the case when France was prepared to pay the United States for such services. In December 1945, for example, 279 American military vehicles were purchased by France from the United States and stored in Calcutta awaiting shipment to Saigon.[31] Despite such inconsistencies, Britain remained wary of merely handing American lend-lease equipment directly to the French. American approval had to be obtained first. Where possible, Britain would substitute British supplies for American lend-lease equipment.[32] But although Britain was in far better shape than post-war France, Britain was in many respects as equally dependent as France upon the United States for military aid.

Any residual American anti-colonial sentiment in Washington was also compromised by its own actions. At the Potsdam Conference, the American military establishment had approved plans for the French armed forces to be used in the war against Japan.[33] America had already donated equipment to French Indo-China. Subsequently, it had sold aid to French Indo-China. It had provided the ships to transport French troops to Indo-China. Finally, it continued to rebuild the material capacity of French forces in metropolitan France despite such equipment then being used by French forces in Indo-China.

Conflicting signals emanated from Washington. It was perfectly acceptable for Allied powers to purchase American military aid. Yet it was improper for Britain to donate American sourced equipment to the same European allies. But France, like Britain, was bankrupt. When possible, the French bought American military aid. But at the same time, the French also sought to supplement these supplies with donations from other sources. Britain could not afford to ignore such requests. The rehabilitation of France was considered vital by Britain for the defence of Western Europe.[34] The logic of recent history indicated that British post-war security depended upon it. A strong democratic France was geographically important to buffer Britain from totalitarian regimes. The resurrection of the French Empire was a vital component in any French restoration project. France would simply cease to be a great power without the colonial resources needed for post-war reconstruction.

Britain clearly could not keep away from lend-lease questions. It was in Britain's national interest to see France rehabilitated as quickly as possible. To this end, it was plainly easier to transfer lend-lease supplies within SEAC to French control rather than face the logistical problems associated with transportation from Britain. The Cabinet Defence Committee discussions had revealed that Attlee did not possess an adequate number of vessels to move French troops let alone the additional equipment needed to employ them in Indo-China.

Meanwhile, France continued to rebuild its armed forces. In doing so, it inevitably desired further support from Britain to re-equip the French 3rd Colonial Division. Ever mindful of the American attitude towards such requests, the British War Office attempted to achieve this with solely British supplies. No American lend-lease equipment was to be used.[35] However, the War Office quickly discovered that if it followed this policy then only 900 British sourced vehicles would be transferred into French hands. Whereas, if American lend-lease equipment could also be offered then a further 1,300 vehicles would be provided as well. The added bonus was that all of these vehicles were currently attached to British–Indian forces in Southeast Asia. Indeed some were already in French Indo-China being used by Gracey's 20th Indian Division.[36]

The logical solution was for Britain to transfer such vehicles to the French armed forces in Indo-China. It made no sense for the War Office to seek to resupply French colonial forces in Indo-China from Europe.

It was thus left to Major F.H. Weaver to remind Mountbatten that SEAC needed to obtain adequate American approval for the handing over of lend-lease materials.[37] Weaver also contacted the United States to double check that permission had actually been granted.[38] Weaver's cautiousness illustrated how paranoid Britain had become concerning lend-lease issues. It also demonstrated how subservient Britain had become to American wishes. Hidden beneath the surface of Weaver's correspondence was Britain's imperial decline. Britain's great power status was waning. This was accelerated with the advent of the Cold War and finally brought into stark reality during the 1956 Suez Crisis.[39]

Nonetheless, British military aid to French Indo-China did not just include material conveyances. Britain also sent military instructors to French Indo-China to train the French forces in how to use their newly acquired equipment. The French, however, were desperate to reacquire Indo-China. They were, in simple terms, too impatient to put their new equipment to work. Thus, the British training teams found themselves underemployed by the French. The dearth of French military supplies proved so severe that as soon as any material arrived in Indo-China, it was hurriedly shipped to whichever front-line unit needed it the most. Little training was deemed necessary. Despite the tropical climate, no attempt was made by the French to inspect the equipment transfers or check its general working order.[40]

During the course of its initial deployment in French Indo-China, SEAC had been unprepared to define the extent of British maintenance for the French armed forces. Gracey's Allied liberation duties possessed no fixed date for a withdrawal. SEAC did not anticipate a prolonged Indo-Chinese venture. However, as the months ticked by, with the outbreak of political violence and continued logistical problems, SEAC could no longer afford to sustain an open-ended commitment towards maintaining French weaponry. In the spring of 1946, this dilemma came to a head. From 15 February onwards, Britain decided to limit this perpetual drain on its resources by charging France for all maintenance costs.[41] This was merely an interim measure. As an early indication of future British intent, it was designed to prepare the French for what was to follow. Six weeks later, all British liability for the upkeep of the French armed forces in Indo-China came to an end.[42]

Britain had successfully supplied military equipment to French forces in Indo-China. It had been prepared to train French forces in Indo-China in how to use this equipment. It had maintained and serviced French military equipment. It had also transported supplies of a more general nature to French Indo-China. Yet the physical shipment of such resources also posed problems for Britain. The sheer distance of Indo-China and also the Dutch East Indies from Europe meant that it was not easy to send large quantities of supplies without employing provision for resting and refuelling services in India. Ceylon was currently out of the question due to political unrest. The Singapore dockyards were simply located too far away for most ships to reach them in a single trip from Europe.

India therefore agreed to act as a staging post for two to three French ships each month. But this did not sit comfortably with the Indian civilian population and labour strikes were threatened. Indian sympathy for Asian national movements did not endear the local population to the restoration of French colonialism. A solution was required to dampen Indian political fervour. Lord Wavell, the British Viceroy, accepted that it was absolutely impractical for ships bearing the French flag to be rested in Indian ports. He therefore agreed for British or American flag vessels to be used instead. With the limited quantities of post-war shipping available, it appears illogical that these alternative flag vessels were newly supplied from different Allied shipping stocks. It was more likely that the French flags on the original ships were merely substituted with American and British ones as soon as the vessels entered Indian territorial waters.

Despite Wavell's ploy of swapping the flags, the ships were still transporting French troops and their final destination was still Indo-China. To further dilute the potential for political unrest, Wavell instructed that at any one time only two to three British and American vessels bound for Indo-China could be rested together in Indian ports. He also instructed that such breaks could only last for the duration of two to three days. During that time, the French troops were forbidden from taking shore leave and their presence was to be hidden from the Indian population. This meant that the troops were confined to quarters beneath the decks. To prevent any mishaps, no provisions were made available. Wavell's plans represented a massive and highly dangerous top-secret public relations operation to expedite resources to French Indo-China. If any word leaked out about the true nature of the bunkering amenities, the subsequent political disturbances would prevent any future vessels bound for French Indo-China or the Dutch East Indies from making use of Indian port facilities.[43]

By January 1946, Washington had become acutely sensitive to the criticism of French military operations in Indo-China and Dutch activities in the East Indies. The violent rebirth of old world colonialism did not sit well with new world American values. Washington therefore sought to dissociate itself from all military activity in Southeast Asia.[44] The timing was not ideal. In southern French Indo-China, political violence had delayed the successful completion of Japanese surrender duties. Washington therefore resolved that SEAC was to remain in Indo-China until all of the Japanese prisoners of war had been repatriated back to Japan. The chaos of the last few months had gone on long enough. But in order to soften the blow, the United States argued that Britain could also separate itself from all Indo-Chinese affairs by delegating its SEAC surrender responsibilities to the French colonial authorities.[45]

In the circumstances, this represented an extraordinary attempt by the United States to cut and run. The United States did not want to hand over operational authority from SEAC to the French. But at the same time, the Americans wished to delegate all SEAC responsibilities onto the French. With the continuing political violence, the new American directive did not bode well. Lord Alanbrooke, who in October had resisted the warnings of British diplomats concerning British entanglement in French Indo-China, now sided with the Foreign Office. Alanbrooke considered it inauspicious for British–Indian operations in southern Indo-China to continue. Anticipating further danger, he advised that Mountbatten should give up all SEAC Indo-Chinese operations as quickly as possible.[46] Without American support, the British Chiefs of Staff did not want French Indo-China to remain within SEAC. If circumstances deteriorated even further, Britain could not afford to be left on its own with the responsibility for resolving the Indo-Chinese conundrum. The British Chiefs of Staff therefore argued that Leclerc should act as the Allied liaison agent in French Indo-China while the final Japanese surrender duties were completed.[47]

At last, Alanbrooke had demonstrated some foresight. At that time, France was readying a military taskforce in southern Vietnam to invade the north and dispose of the independent Vietminh administration. As a result, Alanbrooke hurriedly referred the future structure for the Allied command in Indo-China to the Joint Service Mission in Washington. With the anticipated widening of political violence in Vietnam, neither Britain nor the United States wanted to be responsible for military affairs in Indo-China.[48] The United States therefore agreed for Leclerc to act as the sole Allied liaison agent. Britain and the United States used the decision to immediately distance themselves from French military activities in Indo-China.[49]

A British military mission was temporarily attached to the British consulate in Saigon to manage the Allied reassignment of southern Vietnam from SEAC to full French control. Britain hoped that by facilitating such a measure it would be rewarded by being able to establish an aircraft staging post in Saigon for the air traffic route to Japan and Hong Kong.[50] In such circumstances, not all of Gracey's Allied liberation forces could be withdrawn immediately. Indian transportation units stayed in Saigon until April to help the French with dockyard operations and maintenance. But in effect, all British military assistance was petering out. At last, an effective French administration was in place. The French were now responsible for all public order. The British military mission was therefore gradually scaled down. 330 Royal Air Force personnel remained in Saigon to oversee the operation of the staging post.[51]

Protecting the peace: Humanitarian aid

The food crisis that Gracey faced in French Indo-China in 1945 was part of a wider humanitarian conundrum. The sudden termination of the global conflict had made large numbers of civilians dependent upon the Allied liberation forces in Europe and Asia for basic food supplies. But the famine in Indo-China started long before the cessation of the Second World War and the arrival of the British. During what proved to be the final few months of the war, civil unrest had affected rice supplies. With the removal of the Vichy France administration in Indo-China, in March 1945, uncertainty concerning the political future of Indo-China gathered momentum. In such circumstances, the already small wartime investment in the general economy weakened even further. Irrigation levees were not adequately maintained, crops were not planted and general food production diminished. The Japanese responded by stockpiling rice supplies. Yet these were solely for their use. Thus, civilian administrative dislocation coupled with the wartime destruction of port and rail infrastructure presented a severe challenge to the Allied liberation forces. This difficult scenario was also combined with natural disasters caused by drought and erosion, especially in the north. In consequence, a grisly emergency situation was created for the arriving Allied liberation forces in French Indo-China to manage.

The north of Indo-China was particularly badly hit by the famine conditions. The power vacuum after the Japanese surrender in August 1945 accelerated civilian unrest. The famine was a dangerous political weapon. It traversed political ideologies. It could unite the masses in a common cause against the returning French regime. Cambodia and Vietnam possessed vast rice-growing areas. Yet these also needed to be stable in order to remain productive. Cambodian and Vietnamese rice production was not just necessary to feed the Indo-Chinese population, but other parts of the French Empire depended upon the rice produced from these areas as well. It was also required to assist with food supplies in the British colonies of Hong Kong, India and Singapore. Indo-Chinese rice production was therefore considered vital to global food supply.

Emergency food relief in Indo-China therefore became a law and order concern for SEAC. But any potential resolution was hampered by Allied theatre geography. The famine conditions in Vietnam crossed the boundary between two very different Allied military theatres. It had been an American decision at the Potsdam Conference in July 1945 to permit two Allied theatres to operate within Indo-China. This wartime arrangement had now effectively split Vietnam into two. In northern French Indo-China, above the 16 parallel, nationalist China was accountable for all Allied liberation duties. In southern French Indo-China, beneath the 16 parallel, SEAC was similarly responsible for all Allied liberation duties. Circumstances in the north were not auspicious. The north had been badly affected by the famine. However, the Chinese nationalist forces in the north did not possess the logistical equipment required to alleviate this situation for them. Thus on 28 August, Chiang Kai-Shek, the Chinese nationalist leader, asked Mountbatten if he could purchase 5,000 tons of rice from Saigon. Chiang Kai-Shek intended to use the rice purchase from southern French Indo-China as a method of feeding his troops in the north. This request was not intended to aid the general food situation in the north. It was merely made to ensure that the Chinese deployment did not damage northern food supplies any further. The Chinese not placing any additional demands upon the limited civilian food stocks available would thereby achieve this.[52]

Nevertheless, British–Indian troops had not yet arrived in Saigon and Mountbatten had no way of assessing the position in southern Indo-China. For all that he knew, the rice supplies in the south could be in just as dire a condition as the situation in the north. Mountbatten advised Chiang Kai-Shek to take the issue up with the newly established United Nations Food Commission. This was not a political snub. At that very moment, neither Gracey nor Mountbatten had any method for assessing or assisting the Chinese with rice supplies. The logical solution was therefore for the Chinese to make a referral to the fledgling United Nations.[53]

In London, the British Government remained fully updated about the growing food crisis in Southeast Asia. To prevent a humanitarian disaster and ardent criminal profiteering, the War Cabinet planned for Britain to co-ordinate rice prices in the three big rice-producing deltas of Southeast Asia – Burma, Indo-China and Thailand. The dearth of rice production raised the spectre of rampant inflation, black market speculation and civilian unrest.[54] It played into the hands of the Asian nationalists and communists. Thus, the humanitarian crisis threatened regional economic meltdown and political instability. Indo-China was of particular concern to the mandarins in Whitehall. It was regarded as a geopolitical fulcrum for Southeast Asia. If the situation in Indo-China could be urgently addressed, then this would aid greater regional stability and security.

The British War Office, the Ministry of Production and the Board of Trade all hastily combined resources to establish an Indo-Chinese relief scheme.[55] In September 1945, Britain was able to offer France an emergency aid programme for Indo-China with the twin aims of preventing disease and civilian unrest. The disaster management scheme was a relatively small affair. Britain had few resources of its own, and it had a large number of post-war duties to administer. Whitehall therefore made it very clear to France that the emergency programme for Indo-China had a limited scope. France would clearly have to attain supplies from other sources, as it could not depend upon sustained British relief (Table 4.1).[56]

The French heeded the British advice. In doing so, they gratefully accepted Britain's limited aid package. But the French were also able

Table 4.1 British minimum French Indo-China programme September 1945.[57]

Textiles	
Raw Cotton (lbs)	6,720,000
Cotton Yarn (lbs)	560,000
Mosquito Netting (lbs)	360,000
Bleached Sheeting (square yards)	40,000,000
Satinade (square yards)	10,000,000
Print Cloth (yards)	5,000,000
Cloth, dyed in the piece (yards)	50,000
Vehicles	
Trucks (units)	3,000
Passenger Cars (units)	750
Automotive Replacement Parts (units)	134,000
Motor Cycles (units)	100
Wagons and Drags (units)	100
Bicycle Spare Parts (tons)	250
Bicycles (units)	500
Sewing Needles	
Hand Sewing Needles (needles)	1,000,000
Medical Supplies	
Medical Supplies (tons)	100

to purchase emergency food and other humanitarian supplies from the United States. In San Francisco, France assembled stores containing 15,000 tons of cement, chemicals, condensed milk, flour, iron, paper and steel for transportation to French Indo-China. Two vessels were arranged to ship the emergency aid. The first vessel was dispatched to northern Indo-China while the second vessel was sent off to southern Indo-China. However, by this time the French authorities in Indo-China had managed to develop a tempestuous relationship with the Chinese nationalists administering Allied liberation duties in the north. This ultimately resulted in both ships being received in Saigon.[58]

France regarded American procurement as a vital component in addressing the humanitarian crisis in Indo-China. Indeed, this proved to be particularly appealing to the French. By freely purchasing the supplies, France was able to obtain the aid without any political strings being attached to the shipments. The United States also favoured this arrangement as long as the French were prepared to pay for their resources. American old world anti-colonialism was not scrupulous enough to resist taking money from French imperialists. Hence, the two vessels that initially left San Francisco for Saigon set a precedent for future aid supplies. Between September and December, a further five shipments were arranged by France from the United States. These consignments were needed to transport an additional 60,000 tons of purchased materials to Indo-China by the end of 1945.[59]

Meanwhile British–Indian troops had by now arrived in Saigon. They faced a plethora of liberation duties with limited resources. The nature of the political violence in the south meant that in the early stages of the British deployment, law and order duties took precedence over initial food supplies. Gracey's troops were not equipped to deal with simultaneous humanitarian relief and peace-enforcement duties. In the interim, the local population had to make do with existing food supplies. In southern Indo-China this was much less of a problem than in the north. Furthermore, in fairness to Gracey, SEAC was fully aware that supplies purchased by France in the United States were already en route to Saigon. As the Allied commander on the ground, Gracey must have known about this arrangement.

Nevertheless, it was imperative that the administrative control of the south should revert to the French as quickly as possible. France would then be able to use what remained of its antiquated colonial infrastructure and knowledge to alleviate food supply issues. Despite their colonial organisation being blighted by Vichy France and eventually disbanded by the Japanese, the French nonetheless possessed the resources to reach a far greater proportion of the civilian population with emergency aid than the limited British–Indian forces at Gracey's disposal.

On 9 October, France resumed its administration of southern French Indo-China. Gracey had been in charge for merely a month and three days. Despite the resumption of French colonial control, food shortages continued. But with the French supposedly overseeing relief efforts, British attempts to relieve the crisis became progressively more fruitless and observational. The return of the French colonial administration meant that for Gracey humanitarian aid and public-order issues became a secondary issue. Primary importance was the completion of the Japanese surrender and associated security duties. Britain was no longer the 'occupant' under the terms of the Hague Convention.[60] France now bore this legal responsibility.

Therefore, with administrative issues restored to France, Whitehall hoped that Indo-Chinese food supplies could be utilised in other parts of Southeast Asia to relieve famine conditions in the wider region.[61] This again demonstrated the policy disconnect between London and Saigon. In the spheres of military aid and humanitarian assistance, London readily demonstrated its detachment from Saigon. France certainly did not help with this disconnection. The French were desperate to prove that they controlled Indo-China. A successful resumption of colonial control symbolised the restoration of France as a great power. This was definitely a distortion from the facts on the ground. Hence, on the surface the French had resumed their management of southern Indo-China, but in reality the humanitarian crisis continued. French Indo-China was in no way ready to assist in the relief of any other Southeast Asian areas. Indeed northern French Indo-China still experienced severe humanitarian aid shortages. SEAC thereby arranged to fly six Japanese aircraft into northern Indo-China with emergency supplies on board. But the venture did not proceed according to plan. Immediately upon landing at Tourane, Chinese Allied liberation forces seized control of the aircraft making further shipments impossible.[62] Gracey's command may not have now been officially responsible for public safety, but where possible they continued to intervene on humanitarian grounds.

Britain had no control over the administration of northern Indo-China. All northern issues had to be settled bilaterally between France and China – the Allied liberation power. Yet the situation in the north represented a patchwork quilt of humanitarian issues. In the areas controlled by the Chinese, British reports confirmed that food and medicine supplies for the European population were stable. But at the same time, prices were escalating, thus reflecting increased civilian stockpiling and pessimism. In the areas controlled by the Democratic Republic of Vietnam, famine conditions persisted. The civilian population was especially restless in these areas. The imposition of a poll tax to fund the Democratic Republic of Vietnam's administration had not been well received at all. Food supplies remained critical and regional flooding now threatened any new agricultural ventures in the north to alleviate the situation.

Gracey found that, to a degree, he was able to intervene in the tense circumstances facing northern Indo-China. The French administration in southern Vietnam desperately needed coal to fire the power station in Saigon and provide electricity for the city. The French therefore loaded 2,000 tons of rice onto a ship in Saigon harbour and sent it off to northern Indo-China.[63] In the port of Haiphong, an exchange took place under British supervision. The rice was unloaded from the French vessel and replaced with coal for the power station in Saigon.[64] Once again British–Indian peace enforcers had intervened in a small way to ensure a degree of civilian stability.

The unremitting political violence in the south provided other opportunities for Gracey's peace enforcers to administer further supplies of humanitarian aid. One Vietnamese offensive against the return of French colonial control involved the organisation of a food blockade in the combined metropolitan areas of Cholon and Saigon. Although the blockade did not directly affect British–Indian duties in administering the Japanese surrender, British–Indian armed forces did intervene to ensure that adequate food supplies reached the civilian populations. With the political situation in Phnom Penh adequately resolved by the British, Brigadier Murray, Gracey's Commander in Chief in Phnom Penh, organised the movement of relief supplies from the Cambodian capital into Saigon area. The Vietnamese blockade was thereby broken by Murray's relief efforts.[65]

In the midst of continuing political violence, the British staff in Saigon continued to monitor food supplies. In December, a fresh British appraisal of humanitarian problems in Indo-China again highlighted the gravity of the situation. Britain estimated that, at that moment, French Indo-China was facing a food deficit of about 35,000 tons. Security in Indo-China prevented the sufficient sowing, harvesting and transportation of food supplies to market. In addition, the French had reserved 200,000 tons from the next harvest to improve conditions in the north.[66] This would naturally restrict supplies in the south. To assist the French administration, Britain resolved to enact an aerial survey of rice production in Indo-China. An aerial survey could act as an important gauge of the total acreage under cultivation and thereby assist France in predicting more accurately the total tonnage for the 1946 harvest.[67] In theory, by being forewarned France would be better placed to prepare emergency measures.

The state of affairs in northern Indo-China continued to remain outside of Britain's remit. Nevertheless, Britain sent Colonel Walker-Chapman on a fact-finding mission to the Democratic Republic of Vietnam's capital – Hanoi. Walker-Chapman was able to confirm that circumstances in the north remained dire. The Vietnamese were unwilling to sell food supplies to the French and the black market was thriving. With coal production in the north at 100 tons a day, the Chinese again wanted to enact the bartering of northern coal reserves for southern rice supplies. This time, however, a shortage of adequate shipping prevented a successful exchange.[68]

By January 1946, market prices in the south started to decrease.[69] Economic conditions appeared to be stabilising. Gracey met with Meiklereid to reappraise the humanitarian situation and to discuss the possibility of exporting French Indo-Chinese rice supplies to other parts of Southeast Asia. This, however, proved to be a forlorn hope. The need to relieve northern Indo-China prevented any exports from the south to the rest of the region. The other SEAC humanitarian crises were therefore referred for assistance to the newly established United Nations Relief and Rehabilitation Administration.[70]

In the meantime, D'Argenlieu, the French High Commissioner in Indo-China, had also applied for assistance to the United Nations Relief and Rehabilitation Administration. He wanted United Nations resources to lend a hand with shipping rice and medical supplies into northern Indo-China. D'Argenlieu was naturally suspicious of the new United Nations Relief and Rehabilitation Administration's remit. Any successful appeal by D'Argenlieu could result in American observers being sent into northern Indo-China. The French inevitably feared any American attempts to meddle in the running of their colonies. Nevertheless, Denning observed that D'Argenlieu appeared determined to proceed with an application to the United Nations Relief and Rehabilitation Administration. The apparent dichotomy between D'Argenlieu's fears and his actions was readily apparent to Dening. The application was a duplicitous public relations exercise. When the severity of the Indo-Chinese food crisis became more generally recognised, a French approach to the United Nations Relief and Rehabilitation Administration would safeguard French actions in Indo-China against any anticipated global censure.[71]

However, by January 1946, United Nations Relief and Rehabilitation Administration personnel were already present in Saigon to monitor evacuees and to study the food crisis in southern French Indo-China. But a far greater crisis was brewing in the north than the south. In the north, Britain still had no Allied jurisdiction and could only observe China, the Democratic Republic of Vietnam and France continually sidestep each other and their humanitarian responsibilities for the establishment of a successful relief programme. The political stakes were simply too high to be abandoned. Meiklereid continued to warn the Foreign Office about the dearth of future rice supplies from the north. He gravely predicted that the only logical outcome of the current impasse was a humanitarian disaster: 'unless very drastic and immediate measures are taken, the death toll in Tonkin [northern French Indo-China] from famine is likely to be measured in millions rather than the thousands'.[72]

Hence, the state of affairs in the north incessantly weighed heavily upon circumstances in the south. The Chinese Allied liberation force was supposed to maintain a position of neutrality towards the Democratic Republic of Vietnam. Yet in many instances, the Chinese nationalists preferred to assist Vietminh officials in preference to their French counterparts.[73] This greatly added to the crisis in the north. The patchwork quilt of turmoil persisted. The Hague Convention clearly transferred public order to the Chinese in northern Indo-China. But as Meiklereid observed from Saigon, in many cases the Chinese appeared to have merely abandoned all responsibility for such measures. He continued to warn the Foreign Office that impending 'disorder, anarchy, ruin and famine' would be the sole outcome. Only great power involvement could now save the situation. A failure to act, Meiklereid grimly forecast, would result in hundreds of thousands of needless Vietnamese deaths.[74]

The gravity of the humanitarian crisis was evident for all in London and SEAC to see. But by early January 1946, the British role in Indo-China was changing. With the resumption of full French administrative control in southern Indo-China and Cambodia, Gracey's mission to Indo-China was coming to a conclusion. Washington and London were both keen to dissociate themselves from the conditions on the ground.[75] This meant that Leclerc would have to administer the final phases of British surrender duties vis-à-vis the evacuation of Japanese prisoners of war.[76]

Mountbatten proposed that British humanitarian interests should be left in the hands of both the Foreign Office consulate and the inter-service military mission in Saigon. SEAC was packing its bags. It was for this joint consulate and inter-service team to keep Britain informed of future French humanitarian and rice-production strategies.[77] This was a clear attempt by Mountbatten to cut and run. Britain had tried to do what it could with limited resources to avert a humanitarian disaster. But at the end of the day, only the French and the Vietnamese could satisfactorily resolve the situation on the ground.

With the Japanese disarmament completed, neither a British nor a nationalist Chinese presence served any meaningful purpose.[78] As far as humanitarian aid was concerned, the little assistance that Britain had initially offered had by now dwindled to next to nothing. British activity was impotent and Mountbatten's influence over D'Argenlieu ineffective. Serious famine conditions continued in the north. A lack of adequate vessels still persisted in preventing the transportation of humanitarian relief. The French continued to distrust the Chinese to effectively administer any aid. At the same time, the 1946 harvest conditions were not encouraging. The dislocation of the consumer markets had resulted in fewer crops being sown.[79] The outlook appeared bleak.

In such circumstances, SEAC attempted once more to orchestrate rice supply from southern Indo-China to the north in return for coal shipments to the south. In order to make the proposal more appealing, Britain offered France the use of a British vessel solely for this purpose.[80] The proposition seemed genuine, but in reality it was half-hearted and belated final attempt by SEAC to cleanse itself of guilt regarding the ongoing disaster in the north.

Not to be deterred by the gravity of the crisis or the powerlessness of SEAC policy within French Indo-China, Mountbatten sent a glowing report of his Indo-Chinese mission to the British Chiefs of Staff in Whitehall. He surprisingly claimed that the British position in respect to the French colonies had never been stronger. In fact, Britain would almost immediately be able to 'cash in' on the benevolence of the general Indo-Chinese populace in order to profit British trade and stature. Indo-China was a valuable regional partner that would soon be able to export coal and rice, which would naturally benefit Britain's other interests.[81] It was an incredibly optimistic and naïve assessment of the circumstances in Indo-China. Mountbatten had minimised any negative news and portrayed his mission in the most positive of terms. In Whitehall, wiser heads than Mountbatten at the War Office and the Foreign Office chose not to follow up with Mountbatten's glowing endorsement.[82] The reality of the dire state of Indo-Chinese affairs was evident to all concerned. The situation made a mockery of Mountbatten's analysis and boundless self-belief.

Nevertheless, Britain persisted in taking an interest in Indo-Chinese food supplies even after Gracey, and the main SEAC force departed French Indo-China. An Indian transportation unit remained in Saigon to assist the French with operating and maintaining the main dockyards until April. A Royal Air Force staging post was also established at Saigon to help with expediting communications to Hong Kong and Japan.[83] Despite concerns as to how much rice could be realistically harvested, collected and transported within French Indo-China, Britain still desperately needed to secure a reliable source of food to alleviate other famine conditions in the region.[84]

On 11 February, the United Nations General Assembly asked for all member states to assist with a massive act of humanitarian intervention to address worldwide food deficits.[85] As SEAC continued to wind down its Indo-Chinese commitments, the Foreign Office made the appropriate arrangements to establish a special commissioner in Southeast Asia to co-ordinate a more definitive British policy response. The dislocation of London from Southeast Asia was addressed by the creation of the post. Based in Singapore, the Special Commissioner carried the rank of a full British ambassador. One of the main elements of the position was to act as a humanitarian tsar and assist with intra-Allied humanitarian crises in the region. On 21 February, Bevin announced to the House of Commons that Lord Killearn had been appointed as the Special Commissioner.[86] The appointment of Killearn, however nebulous, indicated that at the very least Britain had learnt from its earlier mistakes.[87] SEAC and the War Office therefore continued to downsize their commitment to the human crisis in French Indo-China while in parallel the new Foreign Office-led mission under Killearn was established in Singapore. Foreign Office ascendancy in British Government policy indicated a new and more vigorous commitment to the supervision of humanitarian aid in the region. But by May 1946, SEAC had ceased all direct military involvement in French Indo-Chinese affairs.

5
The Aftermath: Bengal and Kashmir 1946–1951

In 1939, one simple act had demonstrated that Britain's relationship with India remained highly paternalistic, heavy handed and imperially minded. London had informed India that because Britain was at war with Nazi Germany, India too was at war. Indian views on whether the colony should go to war were not sought; Indian participation was merely assumed by London. Britain was at war and therefore the dependent empire was also at war. India had thereby been confirmed as a lowly member of the colonial empire. This supposition by Britain undermined the pre-1939 Anglo-Indian political process. In the period leading up to the Second World War, Britain had made a number of positive overtures towards Indian politicians that India would eventually achieve Dominion status (similar to Australia, Canada, New Zealand and South Africa). Hints of political evolution had appeased the aspirations of the Indian political establishment and blunted the demands of the nationalists for an independent India. Now, in 1939, Britain had issued a unilateral declaration of war and conclusively proved that India lingered as just another part of the dependent empire. When the going got tough, political evolution had become non-existent. In reality, Britain had demonstrated that autocratic imperial management persisted, and Britain had confirmed that consultation and partnership remained but an illusion. This crushed the hopes of Indian nationalists, especially the Indian National Congress Party. Congress immediately reacted to Britain's political betrayal by demanding a key role in India's wartime central government. This was automatically denied by Britain.

The Second World War proved that political power in India rested, for the moment, with the British colonial administration. Although this power enabled Britain to maximise India's war effort, the mistrust that it generated was both far-reaching and long lasting. Subsequent British political gestures during the Second World War were rejected by both of the main Indian political parties – the Hindu dominated Congress Party and the Muslim League. In the meantime, the deeply dissatisfied Congress Party quickly introduced a popular call for civil disobedience against the British authorities. This was followed in 1942 by the larger and more dangerous Quit India campaign. The Quit India movement was a serious act of political violence against colonial control. The timing of the campaign was critical. It managed to threaten the very fabric of British rule in India just as the Japanese military made significant gains against the British armed forces in Burma. Forces from both within and outside of its jurisdiction endangered British control of South Asia. Britain naturally responded by detaining the leaders of the Congress Party.

Although the Quit India campaign was eventually suppressed by Britain, the detention of the Congress Party leadership created a dangerous political vacuum in India. This void enabled Jinnah and the Muslim League to press for a separate homeland for Muslims – Pakistan. In the absence of the senior members of the Congress Party leadership, Jinnah successfully took an internal issue and transformed it into an international one. Half of the Indian Army was Muslim. Thus, with Britain desperately needing to defeat Japanese imperialism, the Muslim League became a powerful political voice at the crucial moment when the Congress Party leadership faltered. Nevertheless, the Second World War destroyed Britain's ability to evolve India towards some distant form of self-government. In the short term, Britain had resisted the Congress challenge. But in the longer term, Britain had lost control of the political process and the eventual timing of Indian independence.

The Second World War therefore eroded Britain's colonial authority in India. Britain had become estranged from the Congress Party during the war. When the war finished in 1945, Congress put renewed pressure upon Britain for immediate Indian independence. Even as Gracey and elements of the 20th Indian Division were being deployed in southern French Indo-China, the Indian question, concerning the political destiny of India, became the most important problem within the British Empire. Yet the wartime political deadlock between the Congress Party and the Muslim League continued with Jinnah demanding a separate state for Indian Muslims. At the same time, violence broke out between the Hindu and Muslim communities.

In August 1946, Jinnah launched a campaign of direct action to press for the creation of Pakistan. Severe rioting broke out across northern India. Thousands of people died during the political violence. Britain could no longer maintain effective law and order in India. The very fabric of British rule was breaking down. The Viceroy, Lord Wavell, therefore proposed that Britain should enact a staged retreat from India. It was a grave admission of defeat. In London, Attlee and the British Government were horrified with Wavell's frankness and his open advocacy of a British withdrawal. Wavell was swiftly dismissed by Attlee and replaced as Viceroy by Mountbatten.[1] Events in southern French Indo-China had not as yet prejudiced the British Government against Mountbatten. For the moment, despite the warnings from the Foreign Office, Mountbatten was still regarded as a relatively safe and diligent pair of hands to oversee Asian crisis management duties.[2] Mountbatten's subsequent supervision of the transfer of power from Britain to India and Pakistan would cast fresh light upon his political and diplomatic ineptitude.[3] In the meantime, following the completion of its mission in southern French Indo-China, the 20th Indian Division was disbanded in early 1946. Gracey, for the time being, became the General Officer Commanding and Commander in Chief of the Northern Command in India. In 1947, he was made the Chief of Staff of the newly formed Pakistan Army.[4]

Following the Second World War, the political stance that the British Government took on India was certainly shaped by a financial crisis at home. Britain emerged from the war bankrupt and in the middle of a financial Dunkirk.[5] It was unable to develop any plans for a sustained domestic economic recovery. Britain's financial fragility should not be understated. Britain had come out from the Second World War as the world's largest debtor nation. It owed around 4.7 billion pounds sterling. In addition, it needed a huge American loan to remain solvent. In 1947, things deteriorated even further when severe winter weather resulted in a fuel crisis. Industrial production consequently fell. This resulted in further financial chaos. It prompted a convertibility problem for exchanging British pounds into American dollars. This meant that Britain experienced acute monetary difficulties in servicing its American loan repayments.

In the immediate post-war period, Britain also had to grapple with increased military spending and the cessation of American lend-lease supplies. Britain, as a victorious Allied power, was expected to disarm the belligerent nations (Germany and Japan) and to enforce the United Nations peace settlement. The contrast in the geopolitical attitude between Britain and France could not be more striking. Immediately after the Second World War, France wanted naïvely to enact a glorious return to French Indo-China in order to erase the stain of wartime collaboration with fascism and prove its continued great power status. But unlike France, Britain was forced to make a series of grim pragmatic readjustments to its imperial priorities. At the same time that Britain had to come to grips with a domestic financial crisis and the external situation in India, it was also attempting to resolve an escalating conflict between the Arab and Jewish populations in Palestine. This proved, like the First Kashmir War, to be an issue that Britain was simply unable to resolve adequately of its own accord. Both Kashmir and Palestine reflected Britain's maturity as a great power. Britain was becoming increasingly impotent and unable to answer difficult and complex questions concerning decolonisation. Britain's frailties were evident for all to see when eventually the crises in Kashmir and Palestine had to be referred by Britain for resolution at the United Nations. Thus, certain parts of the British Empire had become a burden, and Britain was no longer able to draw any strength from keeping them. In fact, India and Palestine were rapidly wearing Britain out. The fear of how to navigate decolonisation and preserve British interests haunted Whitehall policymakers. As the crises escalated, Britain was staring into the political unknown.

Against this background, Attlee decided that Britain should withdraw from India no later than June 1948. The British Cabinet confirmed the Prime Minister's decision in February 1947. The Government hoped that setting a definite timetable for a British withdrawal from India would encourage the Muslim League and the Hindu Congress Party to co-operate with one another.[6] Unfortunately, Britain flinched first. Neither Congress nor the Muslim League was prepared to negotiate with each other. The stakes were too high. At the same time, the British negotiating position had been dramatically undermined by the announcement of a specific date for the British departure. British control over events in India rapidly began to unwind. Circumstances on the ground in India made a British retreat in June 1948 seem too far away. The newly arrived Viceroy, Mountbatten, quickly concluded that India was in fact on the verge of massive civil war. The only alternative to the indigenous political intransigence appeared to be the partition of British India into two separate nations – India and Pakistan – followed by a hasty British retreat from South Asia. In many respects, this was very similar to Wavell's breakdown plan, which had previously been dismissed by the British Labour Government, but Mountbatten's plan achieved this in a less controlled and orderly fashion.

On 14 August 1947, Pakistan became an independent nation state. India gained its independence on 15 August.[7] Two centuries of British rule had been swept away. Britain had lost the most important part of the British Empire. Yet the partition of Indian territory into two separate nations satisfied no one. Pakistan encompassed two territorial units – West Pakistan (modern Pakistan) and East Pakistan (East Bengal, otherwise now known as Bangladesh). These two halves of the new state were separated by India. To make matters even worse, Pakistan was a single nation state. Therefore, East Pakistan was governed from 1,100 miles away in West Pakistan. In addition, the partition of British India into India and Pakistan had divided British India along religious lines. But British India had been a large patchwork quilt of religious entities. After partition, millions of Muslims remained in India and large numbers of Hindus now lived in Pakistan. Independence was therefore followed by an intense period of political and religious violence.[8]

The true number of deaths in the period surrounding the partition of British India into India and Pakistan will never be known. Some historians have estimated that the total number of people killed in Bengal and the Punjab ranges from 200,000 to three million, while others have suggested more conservative but still horrific figures of 500,000 to one million people.[9] What is certain is that in the chaos that followed partition, Muslims tried to flee India for the safety of Pakistan and Hindus fled Pakistan for the refuge of India. Britain had not wanted to partition India into two separate nation states. But Britain was left with no other choice because the Congress Party and the Muslim League simply could not agree to anything else.[10] The direct result of this British colonial denouement and indigenous political intransigence was a colossal refugee crisis and a massive amount of political violence. In June 1947, for example, 300,000 Hindus and Sikhs lived in the city of Lahore in Pakistan but by 30 August 1947 only 1,000 remained.[11]

Gracey and the crises in Bengal and Kashmir

The political violence that Gracey had previously faced in Vietnam and Cambodia was in relation to the future of the French Empire. When, in August 1947, India and Pakistan separated from the British Empire, this was met with violence and turmoil in South Asia. Gracey was now faced with political violence in a former British colony. Although Gracey was not directly involved in the crisis in Bengal, his professional reputation, integrity and his modus operandi in southern French Indo-China was brought into question during a high-level discussion between Mountbatten and Jinnah. Given how sensitive the situation in Bengal had become during the partition of British India, it was revealing that

Gracey was considered worthy of a significant role in the province; circumstances certainly dictated that an exceptional person was required to manage a highly volatile state of affairs. Likewise, Gracey did play a significant role in the subsequent Kashmir war, the most important of the unresolved issues following the independence of India and Pakistan.[12] These episodes – in Bengal and Kashmir – reveal not only how misrepresented Gracey had been as an old-style British imperialist but also how his previous experiences in Vietnam and Cambodia shaped both his understanding and his subsequent crisis management activities during another challenging period of political violence. Finally, it was inconceivable that Gracey's familiarity with circumstances in Vietnam, Cambodia and Kashmir did not influence his firmly held belief in 1950 that the continuing and extremely capricious situation in Bengal should be referred to the United Nations.[13] This again demonstrated how readily Gracey had learned vital lessons in one situation and then used them to influence his thinking in a later arena of political violence. These were not the actions of an old-fashioned dyed in the wool imperialist, as his detractors concerning Vietnam have often claimed, but rather, far-sighted attempts to learn from the mistakes of the immediate past.

The crisis in Bengal in 1947 reflected the chaos of decolonisation in the rest of British India. British rule had come to a sudden halt. In the aftermath of independence, political violence in some regions intensified. One such area was Bengal. Independence divided Bengal in half. West Bengal became part of an independent India. East Bengal developed into East Pakistan. With the partition of Bengal, millions of Hindus sought to move west out of East Pakistan to escape from their ongoing maltreatment by the Pakistan police.[14]

Even before Britain handed control in East Bengal over to Pakistan, Mountbatten had been deeply worried about events in the province. A political power vacuum was just beginning which looked likely to mature at a critical juncture, i.e. the weeks either side of the official transfer of power. It had originally been intended that Sir Archibald Rowlands would be installed as the Governor of the province, in Dacca the capital of East Bengal, just before East Bengal was transferred from British to Pakistan control. The Governor would first of all be responsible for the ceremonial handover of power from Britain to Pakistan. He would then assist the new government in East Bengal with the successful establishment of a civilian administration. Nine days before independence, however, Rowlands was still in Europe. A similar situation had already arisen in the United Provinces of northern India where the Governor, Mr Roy, had been delayed in his arrival from Britain.

It was thought that Roy would arrive in the United Provinces about a month later than expected. In the case of the United Provinces, the Indian Government had willingly accepted Mountbatten's advice and appointed an interim Governor to ensure political stability and continuity. Mountbatten therefore urged Jinnah and Pakistan to do the same for East Bengal.

The appointment of an interim Governor in an emergency situation was no easy business. This required an unusual person with acute sensitivity, tact and diplomacy. It would also be an advantage if the ideal candidate also possessed previous crisis management experience from having worked in the intense cauldron of decolonisation and the rise of Asian nationalism, especially if they had first-hand experience of an Asian power vacuum and political violence scenario. Mountbatten naturally recommended Gracey to Jinnah as the perfect interim Governor. After all, as Mountbatten communicated to Jinnah, the General had successfully demonstrated his 'great experience as an administrator in French Indo-China'.

When the chips were down and Mountbatten needed a safe pair of hands to administer a crisis, Mountbatten turned to the current Chief of Staff of the Pakistan Army to step into the breach – Lt.-General Sir Douglas Gracey. The mere fact that Mountbatten had chosen a military man as the ideal temporary governor rather than a civilian indicated the intensity of the circumstances on the ground and the dire state of affairs that obviously existed in East Bengal.[15] Despite a wealth of other senior military officers available to Mountbatten, Gracey's recent actions in French Indo-China made him the ideal candidate for the position.

On the other hand, the Viceroy's recommendation certainly contradicted the tone of his 30 June report to the Anglo-American Combined Chiefs of Staff. Mountbatten had sent the report only two months previously as a way of concluding his Allied liberation duties and Supreme Allied Command activities in Southeast Asia. In Mountbatten's extensive report, Gracey was accused of having blatantly exceeded his orders. This hardly demonstrated the characteristics of a level-headed commander who possessed the necessary safe pair of hands needed for the administration of East Bengal.[16] Indeed, Mountbatten's criticisms in the report were particularly damning. Gracey was blamed for all of the failures incurred during the British deployment in southern French Indo-China, while Mountbatten took full and sole credit for all of the successes. Gracey was fully aware of the comments made by Mountbatten in the report. Gracey penned his own firm rebuttal to the Anglo-American Combined Chiefs. In his defence, he highlighted the errors in Mountbatten's appraisal – Mountbatten's confusion of Saigon (Vietnam) with Surabaya (East Java) – and he set out a very clear chronology of his Indo-China excursions concerning the nature of his orders, his pre-arrival knowledge of events on the ground and his subsequent management of the political violence and the power vacuum in Saigon.[17] The Mountbatten–Gracey relationship did not appear to be the most auspicious upon which to base crisis management in East Bengal. Nonetheless, Mountbatten believed that Gracey was the most suitable candidate for the task at hand.

Jinnah, however, decided that Gracey was better suited to remain as the Chief of Staff to the Pakistan Army. Frederick Bourne was appointed as the Governor of East Bengal.[18] This was just as well, as at the same time, the future of Kashmir had not as yet been resolved. Events moved quickly. Within two months of independence, the future of Kashmir had become the cause of the first major conflict between India and Pakistan. In these circumstances, all of Gracey's skills honed in southern French Indo-China were needed to avoid a more brutal and prolonged South Asian conflict than the stalemate that eventually emerged in Kashmir.

Hence Kashmir proved to be the most difficult issue for Mountbatten to resolve concerning the partition of India and Pakistan. Indeed the K in the spelling of Pakistan represented the region of Kashmir.[19] Kashmir was a princely state in which the majority of the population was Muslim. But a Hindu Maharaja, Hari Singh, ruled Kashmir. The princely state was also Nehru's tribal home and he had even honeymooned in the area.[20] At independence in August 1947, Hari Singh signed a standstill agreement with Pakistan to continue trade and economic activity. The standstill agreement bought Kashmir political breathing space. Singh faced the same choice as the other princely states in India. Singh could sign a treaty to accede with either India or Pakistan. The problem was that Singh hesitated. He just could not make up his mind as to whether he would side with India or Pakistan.[21] Singh even suggested that Kashmir should continue as an independent nation state, but given the circumstances this was highly problematic.

In the meantime, internal dissent against Singh's rule developed in the west of Kashmir, close to the border with Pakistan. Field Marshal Claude Auchinleck, the Supreme Army Commander for both India and Pakistan, had already arranged with Mountbatten that if warfare broke out between India and Pakistan, British personnel attached to either set of armed forces would immediately be stood down to prevent British personnel from fighting against one another.[22] During September, the standstill agreement between Kashmir and Pakistan began to break down. Whether this constituted an economic blockade by Pakistan is open to debate. But the flow of trade between the two states became increasingly obstructed.

In early October, peasants in the town of Poonch revolted against their Hindu landlords. In London, *The Times* newspaper reported that when Singh's troops retook the town 1,700 Muslims where brutally slaughtered. As news of the massacre spread, 100,000 refugees fled the province of Jammu. This provoked Pakistan, who regarded the Muslim majority Kashmir state as an appropriate area to merge with Pakistan, to arm the peasants in Poonch. Both India and Pakistan began to be involved in secret operations in Kashmir.

On 22 October, Pathan tribesmen invaded Kashmir in support of the residents of Poonch. In Poonch, the local population hastily organised their own militia to defend themselves against Singh's forces. On 24 October, the residents of Poonch formed their own government of Azad Kashmir and declared their independence from the rest of Kashmir. Despite the rapidly escalating situation, at this stage, senior members of the Pakistan Government were divided about how to react to the increasing crisis involving Kashmir. However, in India, Nehru preferred to see the events that were unfolding in Kashmir as part of an orchestrated Pakistan plot to seize control of the princely state.[23]

India and Pakistan may have achieved independence in August 1947, but the Pakistan and Indian armed forces were still led by British generals. Gracey thus received an intelligence report on 24 October detailing the numbers, weaponry and movements of the Pathan tribesmen. He immediately telephoned Lt.-General Sir Rob Lockhart, the British Commander in Chief of the Indian Army. It was a bizarre scenario. As Pakistan and India slid towards open warfare over Kashmir, the senior British commanders in both independent nation states were able to simply telephone one another to circumnavigate their respective political masters.[24] This was not the first time that Gracey had contacted Lockhart with concerns about the tribesmen.[25] But the practice of negotiating behind the back of the civilian authorities would have surely troubled Gracey who was a principled soldier and very sympathetic to Pakistan.[26]

Nevertheless, on 24 October Lockhart took Gracey's report and urgently briefed Mountbatten and Auchinleck. If Gracey and Lockhart had been placed in an ambiguous situation, Auchinleck's position was far more dubious. The British Field Marshal was the Supreme Commander of the armies of both India and Pakistan. Gracey, Lockhart and Auchinleck had been placed in an horrendous ethical quandary. They desperately wanted to prevent the political violence in Kashmir from spreading any further. But at the same time, they were answerable for their actions to Indian and Pakistan politicians who were playing for a highly intoxicating prize.[27]

The circumstances appeared grave, and Gracey was not prepared to leave anything to chance or misinterpretation. He immediately followed up on his telephone call to Lockhart with a written statement. In a detailed telegram, Gracey reported to Lockhart that on 22 October about 5,000 Pathan tribesmen had entered Kashmir and seized control of the city of Muzaffarabad and the town of Domel. Gracey also revealed that his intelligence source had every reason to believe that the tribesmen were about to attack the town of Kohala. But in this regard, Gracey's telegram to Lockhart on 24 October was by now obsolete. Events had moved more quickly than many had anticipated. and the Pathan forces were now in the town of Uri, which was about half way to the summer capital of Kashmir – Srinagar.[28]

Events now accelerated even more rapidly. With the Pathan tribesmen swiftly advancing upon Srinagar, on 25 October Hari Singh fled the city. The very next day he signed an act of accession between Kashmir and India. A day later, on 27 October, India began to fly troops into Srinagar to protect the city from the Pathan forces.[29] These actions naturally enraged Jinnah who regarded Kashmir, with its majority Muslim population, as a region that should merge with Pakistan rather than India.[30]

Jinnah decided to act. He resolved to order Gracey to send two brigades of the Pakistan Army into Kashmir.[31] It was an ambitious plan. The two brigades were to take control of the strategic Banihal pass, the town of Baramula, the Mirpur district of Jammu and the capital of Kashmir – Srinagar.[32] Jinnah did not inform Gracey in person. He instead arranged for his political acolyte Sir Robert Mudie, the Scottish Governor of West Punjab, to telephone Gracey with his instructions for a Pakistan military intervention.

Gracey, however, did not want to send the Pakistan Army into Kashmir. During his telephone conversation with Mudie, Gracey actively sought to delay any immediate action. He told Mudie that before he could act that he would obviously need to consult with Auchinleck, who was the Supreme Commander for both India and Pakistan. In requesting a dialogue with Auchinleck, Gracey had directly refused to obey Jinnah's order to send the brigade stationed at the city of Attotabad and the brigade quartered at the city of Sialkot into Kashmir. At this point in the conversation, Mudie became greatly irritated and responded to Gracey in a most robust manner.[33] Gracey was shaken by both Jinnah's order and Mudie's method of delivery. He telephoned Auchinleck at 1 am on 28 October to confer with the most senior British military officer in the region.[34]

Auchinleck fully supported Gracey's decision not to send two brigades from the regular Pakistan Army into Kashmir.[35] The Chair of the United Nations Committee on India and Pakistan, Josef Korbel, subsequently described Gracey's decision not to carry out Jinnah's order as 'wise'. Gracey clearly understood the grave consequences that would have resulted from acting upon Jinnah's rash demand.[36] Any escalation of the conflict would have simply overwhelmed the embryonic Pakistan armed forces. It would have also threatened the very existence of the nation that Jinnah had so painstakingly laboured to create – Pakistan. Jinnah was gambling with the future not only of Kashmir but also of a Muslim homeland in South Asia. These were high stakes; Jinnah sought to risk everything by engaging in an immediate conflict with India for the sake of Kashmir. But for the moment, the new sovereign state of Pakistan was not in a strong enough position to withstand a major war with its larger and more powerful Indian neighbour. This reality and Gracey's refusal to enact Jinnah's order prevented a grotesque escalation of political violence in an already dire geopolitical situation.

Jinnah's anger at the current state of affairs in Kashmir was genuine.[37] But his order to Gracey was clearly intentional and planned well in advance. The two brigades that he wanted to send into Kashmir were already fully trained, briefed, equipped and waiting to go. When Singh acceded Kashmir to India, Jinnah merely brought forward his plan for Pakistan to act. As Chief of Staff to the Pakistan Army, Gracey must have known that the brigades had been readied for war. Even if Gracey had not been officially told where Jinnah intended to use the brigades, the events of the past week ought to have made their intended destination very clear. Yet Gracey had been strictly ordered by the British Government to prevent a larger war developing between India and Pakistan. Thus, as soon as it appeared that the brigades were to be used by Jinnah against India, for offensive rather than for either humanitarian purposes or to preserve law and order, Gracey chose to act against Jinnah. He thereby prevented the brigades from being sent into Kashmir.[38] This was consistent with Gracey's modus operandi to maintain law and order in southern French Indo-China.

Gracey's response to Jinnah's highly emotional and controversial order was both rational and logical. In his defence at the time, Gracey emphasised Pakistan's military weakness compared to that of India. The

Pakistan Army had a dearth of reliable indigenous officers. In addition, the few nationalised members of the officer corps that it did possess had very little combat experience. Gracey attributed the lack of Muslim officers to Muslim students performing poorly in competitive exams compared to their Hindu counterparts. In August 1947, the Pakistan Army only possessed four Lt.-Colonels.[39] Similarly, economic realities also tied Jinnah's hands at this crucial moment. Pakistan did not have the financial security required for large defence-related operations. It certainly did not possess adequate military stores for a major and elongated conflict. But India did.[40]

Furthermore, Gracey fully understood the consequences of Auchinleck's stand down order. But in the heat of the moment, with Indian troops arriving in Srinagar, did Jinnah? Gracey's defiance of Jinnah's order was later controversially described as 'a lost opportunity' for Pakistan by the author Alastair Lamb.[41] He stated that it was certainly highly questionable whether or not Jinnah completely understood the characteristics of the stand down order. Lamb's key argument in this regard was that if the stand down order was actually activated then the British personnel in both the Pakistan and the Indian armed forces would have to stand aside as the conflict developed. In such circumstances, this would equally impact both belligerent nations, although India clearly possessed stronger armed forces than Pakistan. In addition, Lamb also questioned whether or not Auchinleck's stand down order was even a realistic threat. If the stand down order had been issued, the resultant loss of British influence in both the Indian and Pakistan governments would have resulted in grave foreign and defence policy denouements for British influence in the region just as the Cold War intensified.[42] Without a doubt, Jinnah had serious reservations about Gracey not risking a wider war. He openly stated as much to Mudie and Sir George Cunningham, the Scottish Governor of the North-West Frontier Province, during a meeting at Ali Khan Liaquat's house.[43] Liaquat was the Prime Minister of Pakistan. From the Pakistan perspective, swift intervention at this stage in the conflict could reap unforeseen rewards.

It was therefore left to Auchinleck, on 28 October, to explain to Jinnah that because Singh had already signed to accede Kashmir to India, the dispatch of Indian troops to Srinagar had been entirely legal. Auchinleck openly used the occasion to threaten Jinnah with his stand down order. If Jinnah decided to send the Pakistan Army into Kashmir then all of the British personnel in Pakistan would be withdrawn from assisting the Government of Pakistan. This brutal restatement of Gracey's position from the chief architect of the stand down order forced Jinnah to back down immediately.[44] Jinnah was naturally suspicious of Auchinleck. After all, Auchinleck was the Supreme Commander for both the Indian and the Pakistan armed forces.[45] Nevertheless, because both India and Pakistan continued to use large numbers of British personnel as advisers after independence, Britain was able to exert a large amount of political and military leverage upon both Pakistan and India. Pakistan required the assistance of more British personnel than did India. Therefore, Britain was naturally able to bring more pressure to bear upon Pakistan than upon India. In this instance, on 28 October, Auchinleck's threat of the stand down order being issued severely restricted Pakistan military activity in Kashmir.[46] But had the order actually been activated it would, in fact, have left the Pakistan Army completely leaderless.[47]

As the Chief of Staff to the Pakistan Army, Gracey was responsible for building up the operational strength of the military. Gracey was certainly conscious of the pitfalls of rushing this process. He purposely slowed down the nationalisation of the army and elongated Pakistan's military dependence upon British assistance. This gave British personnel more time to train the armed forces and senior Pakistan officers greatly benefitted from being able to attend the Imperial Defence College in London. Liaquat and other Pakistan politicians were most unhappy with the slow evolution of Pakistan military leadership and they instructed Gracey to speed up the nationalisation process. Gracey was subsequently ordered to have completed the full process of nationalisation by 1950. In the meantime, Gracey used the window of opportunity afforded to him to promote openly pro-British Pakistan officers. These officers were less militant than those with stronger political tendencies. They naturally agreed, for example, with Gracey concerning the cautious Pakistan Army response to the situation in Kashmir. These officers also tended to be militarily strong but politically weak. Furthermore, they were certainly more moderate than Liaquat and other Pakistan politicians desired. The Pakistan political class wanted to actively promote younger officers who had a propensity to be more rash and certainly more in favour of immediate military action – whatever the final consequences.[48]

Jinnah, Liaquat, Mudie and Cunningham met with Gracey on 28 October. Gracey had refused to obey Jinnah's order only the day before. This new meeting was also on the same day as Auchinleck's frank exchange with Jinnah concerning the stand down order. The meeting was a preamble by the Pakistan delegation to a wider conference involving Mountbatten, Nehru and Singh concerning the deteriorating situation in Kashmir. The Pakistan delegation used the briefing session to consider the possibility of helping the Muslim population in Azad Kashmir with manpower, weapons and ammunition. But they stopped short of debating the need to send in regular Pakistan troop units. Auchinleck and Gracey's position had been respected. In any event, further discussion was cut short by the arrival of Mountbatten, Nehru and Singh.[49] This changed the dynamic of the conference. Not only were the Pakistan delegation faced with Nehru and Singh, in their opinion the chief protagonists in the crisis, but Liaquat also did not trust Mountbatten whom he believed to be a puppet of the Indian Government. In such circumstances, Liaquat regarded the Kashmir war as an Indian orchestrated conspiracy against Pakistan.[50]

On the same day, Earl Alexander of Hillsborough, the British Defence Minister, contacted both Auchinleck and Gracey to praise them for their swift and diligent management of the crisis. Alexander was pleased that Auchinleck and Gracey had avoided the escalation of a wider and more bitter conflict. The reaction of the Pakistan Government to Kashmir accession had for the moment been curtailed. The men on the spot, rather than in London, were actively crafting British policy.[51] Such a fluid situation required an immediate and pragmatic response in the region. In doing this, Auchinleck and Gracey never deviated from the broader British objective. Above all, at this stage, London wanted to avoid a direct conflict between India and Pakistan. The political violence in Kashmir threatened this outlook. This was reinforced when on the same day as Alexander's message, the Pathan tribesmen brutally massacred all of the priests, nuns and Europeans who had taken refuge at St Joseph's convent in Kashmir. The massacre confirmed the intensity of the rapidly escalating political violence and the prospect of a greater humanitarian disaster if the situation continued to spiral out of control.

Against the backdrop of the worsening situation in Kashmir, on 30 October Attlee contacted Jinnah and suggested that the Kashmir question should be settled by a referendum. This was the first time that Britain had offered this democratic solution as a means to resolve the crisis. Britain continued to push for a democratic resolution from this point on. Thus, the idea of a plebiscite in Kashmir became the mainstay of British policy concerning the dispute. Two days later, for example, Mountbatten visited Jinnah in Lahore to again propose a Kashmir plebiscite. Jinnah though was unmoved.[52] Meanwhile, Auchinleck and Gracey with the assistance of Philip Noel-Baker, the British Secretary of State for Commonwealth Relations, ensured that the Kashmir crisis was not ignored at the United Nations.[53]

The British call for a referendum appeared to Jinnah to be a political sideshow when the Indian Army was daily consolidating its position in Kashmir. On 8 November, the Indian military reoccupied the city of Baramula. As they entered the city, the Indian Army discovered that the Azad Kashmir forces had massacred large numbers of the civilian population. Estimates of the casualties range from 500 to 13,000. What was clear was that political violence enacted by the Azad Kashmir forces had lost them some local support. In addition, the Indian occupation of Baramula was a turning point in the crisis for Nehru. Above all, it persuaded Nehru that an Indian victory in Kashmir was ultimately possible. It also convinced Nehru that justice was on India's side and that in the end the United Nations would support India rather than Pakistan.

Heavy snow in Kashmir during the winter months brought most military operations by either side to a standstill.[54] The winter lull provided a valuable breathing space. In December, with the pause in physical operations on the ground, the Pakistan general staff began to offer greater strategic assistance for future irregular operations in Kashmir.[55] In January 1948, allegations emerged that Pakistan soldiers were helping the Pathan forces in Kashmir.[56] The outlook appeared bleak. On 17 January, the United Nations Security Council called on both India and Pakistan not to escalate the conflict any further.[57] Yet Kashmir was a world away from the United Nations. In February, further reports circulated of Pakistan troops operating inside Kashmir on behalf of the Pathan tribesmen and the Azad Kashmir forces.[58] On the Indian side of the border, the Indian Army began to ready its forces for a renewed offensive in the spring. On 15 March, the Indian Defence Minister announced in the Indian Assembly that a plan had been drawn up to clear the 'so called raiders' from Kashmir within two to three months.[59] The stage was therefore set for further confrontation and violence.

Behind the scenes, British officers on either side of the dispute continued to maintain secret contact with one another. On 19 March, Gracey went to New Delhi for a two-day meeting with the Joint Defence Council. He also held detailed informal talks with Major-General Roy Bucher, who had replaced Lockhart as the Commander in Chief of the Indian Army. The finer details of the Bucher–Gracey discussions would have far-reaching consequences. Bucher hoped to be able to use these discussions to create an informal truce with Gracey that would pave the way for firstly a formal ceasefire and secondly a United Nations resolution of the dispute. On 19 March, the first Bucher–Gracey consultations began. Sir Lawrence Grafftey-Smith, the British High Commissioner to Pakistan, kept London fully up to date with the talks as they progressed.

Bucher was not best pleased with the Indian stance towards the Kashmir war. He was personally against the idea of the Indian Army taking over the control of Azad Kashmir. Bucher therefore agreed to use the talks to negotiate a de-escalation of the Kashmir war with Gracey.

Before arriving in New Delhi, Gracey had already brokered a deal with the Azad Kashmir leadership for the Indian troops besieged at Poonch to withdraw from the town. Bucher now agreed that, as the beleaguered Indian forces withdrew, they should not damage the town. Bucher also agreed that he would stop the Indian Air Force from bombing Azad Kashmir positions. In return, Gracey would prevent Azad Kashmir troops from shelling the departing Indian troops. Gracey would also endeavour to discourage Azad Kashmir forces from undertaking raids on the town of Uri, which was currently located behind the Indian front line. Interestingly, Bucher told Gracey during the course of their discussions that he thought that the Indian Army had no actual intention of advancing any further. Despite all evidence to the contrary, in Bucher's opinion there was no planned Indian spring offensive.

Grafftey-Smith and Sir Terrence Shone, the British High Commissioner to India, kept London fully briefed on the Bucher–Gracey talks. But their accounts to London significantly differed. It was also clear from Bucher's subsequent reaction to Gracey's decision to send units of the regular Pakistan Army into Kashmir that Gracey and Bucher had different ideas about what their discussions had essentially achieved. What was certain, however, was that Bucher was utterly convinced that India would not launch a spring offensive and that Indian troops would withdraw from the town of Poonch. The major difference between Shone and Grafftey-Smith's accounts was over the deployment of the Pakistan Army in Kashmir and the implementation of the British-sponsored plebiscite to resolve the crisis. The Indian diplomat and writer Chandrashekhar Dasgupta has argued that Gracey did not fully understand how vulnerable Bucher was making himself by negotiating this forcefully behind the back of the Indian Government. In misunderstanding the weakness of Bucher's position, Dasgupta claimed that Gracey had put Bucher in a tight spot. But in reality, both generals were in a bind. They were both engaged in detailed operational negotiations behind the backs of their respective governments.

Nevertheless, on this occasion the talks had gone further than Bucher had expected. Following Gracey's departure, Bucher was clearly worried about what had actually been agreed upon. Ronald Brockman, Mountbatten's secretary, and Shone both told an overly anxious Bucher to inform the Indian Government about the talks with Gracey. The

Indian Government unsurprisingly rejected all aspects of the talks. It also banned any future prospect of further informal discussions between Bucher and Gracey. The Indian reaction was to be expected. The Indian Defence Minister had already announced that there would be a spring offensive. The Bucher–Gracey talks had also included discussions about the introduction of the Pakistan Army into Kashmir. This was something that the Indian Army would not have welcomed. Especially, as it was something that Noel-Baker had already begun to push for at the United Nations.[60] Britain clearly did not want India to gain the upper hand in the dispute. A stalemate appeared most favourable to British interests.

On 12 April, the Indian Army captured the town of Rajouri. The Indian offensive, which Bucher had denied to Gracey, was commencing. As the Indian Army attempted to gain the upper hand villages were burned and the civilian population was massacred.[61] Gracey was greatly concerned about the nature of the Indian Army's spring offensive.[62] He informed the Pakistan Government that unless regular units of the Pakistan Army were hastily sent into Kashmir, the entire princely state would fall to the Indian advance. The Pakistan Government naturally backed Gracey's assessment.[63] Gracey, the general who had prevented two brigades from being sent into Kashmir the previous October, was now openly advocating the swift employment of the Pakistan Army into the Kashmir war.

On 20 April 1948, Gracey reported to Mountbatten that he expected that the main thrust of the Indian offensive would soon begin. As units of the Pakistan armed forces were being rushed for deployment into Kashmir, Gracey now lobbied for the British stand down order not to be issued. Mountbatten was certainly privy to information concerning both the Pakistan offensive and to Gracey's request for suspending the stand down order.[64] But Bucher may have misread the Pakistan response to any Indian Army spring advance. Later, during August 1948, Bucher complained to Gracey that he had in effect been kept in the dark about the introduction of regular units of the Pakistan Army into Kashmir. But if this had been the case, why was Bucher so fearful following his March discussions with Gracey? His decision to confide his uneasiness to both Brockman and Shone indicated that on this occasion something highly unusual had been discussed with Gracey compared to other informal liaisons. In addition, the Indian reaction to the talks and Noel-Baker's positive stance at the United Nations, for the introduction of regular Pakistan military units into Kashmir, appeared to contradict Bucher's protestations of innocence. Nevertheless, in fairness to Bucher, communication between Gracey and Bucher had to be ambiguous. The two British officers were representing opposite sides of the conflict. At times, both Bucher and Gracey had to hint and insinuate their true feelings lest the Indian and Pakistan governments took offence with the ongoing and often extensive informal dialogue between British officers on either side of the dispute. This naturally led to communication problems. In this instance, Gracey had told Mountbatten that he had indeed suggested to Bucher that the Pakistan Army would be deployed in Kashmir. Only Bucher had misread the suggestion and did not guess that the repercussions that Gracey had hinted at during their consultations involved the ultimate response – a regular Pakistan troop deployment.[65]

India introduced economic warfare in response to the deployment of the Pakistan Army into Kashmir. The Indian Army prevented any supplies from reaching the town of Madhopur and the city of Ferozepur.[66] On 2 May, Gracey returned to New Delhi to consult with Mountbatten. Gracey's assessment of the situation in Kashmir was not positive. He feared that the Pakistan Government was fighting for a lost cause and that, if the Pakistan Army openly engaged the Indian Army in Kashmir, it would soon run out of ammunition. Gracey firmly believed that India would be the only victor in either the Kashmir war or a wider war between India and Pakistan. But at the same time, Gracey noted the nature of the exceedingly difficult situation that currently prevailed. The Pakistan position was hopeless if it sent the regular army into Kashmir. But the Pakistan Army was also fully aware that, because of the Indian offensive, the Azad Kashmir forces would collapse very quickly without further Pakistan military assistance. Pakistan was already sending regular troops into Kashmir as irregulars.[67] But the circumstances had dictated that these efforts were not enough to prevent the slide towards a military disaster. A turning point had been reached. Two days later, Grafftey-Smith reported that the Pakistan Army was now fighting alongside the Azad Kashmir forces in Kashmir.

Noel-Baker immediately sought confirmation that the Pakistan Army was actively engaged in the Kashmir war.[68] On 10 May, Grafftey-Smith confirmed to Noel-Baker that Gracey had indeed reported to him that a number of Pakistan Army battalions were currently operating inside Kashmir. The deployment was along exactly the same lines as the secret Bucher–Gracey talks in New Delhi during March. There was considerable evidence that this Pakistan Army deployment did not take Bucher or the Indian Government completely by surprise. First, it followed the same path as the secret March discussions, which India already knew about. Second, Bucher delayed the Indian counteroffensive, thus purchasing

The Aftermath: Bengal and Kashmir 1946–1951   121

valuable time for the Pakistan troops to secure their primary objectives. Third, Noel-Baker, without Cabinet approval, fully backed the Pakistan decision to move the regular army into Kashmir. Fourth, Gracey had already informed London of the planned Pakistan deployment. Fifth, the British failure to enact the stand down order once the Pakistan Army had been sent into Kashmir indicated London's tacit approval of events on the ground.[69] Finally, neither Pakistan nor India informed the United Nations Security Council of either the Indian Army's April offensive or the Pakistan deployment of regular troops into Kashmir. This was a curious omission by both nations as India and Pakistan were often overly emphatic in bitterly complaining about each other to the United Nations Security Council during the Kashmir war. This certainly indicated that neither India nor Pakistan were surprised or even worried by the escalation of the conflict during April and May 1948.[70] Britain, on the other hand, was deeply troubled by the Indian offensive and the Pakistan decision to deploy regular troop units in Kashmir. This intensification of the conflict seemed to suggest that the worst-case scenario for British interests in the region had now materialised. Pakistan and India were beginning to engage in a fully blown intra-dominion conflict over the future of Kashmir.

In May 1948, Pakistan initially deployed three regular battalions of the Pakistan Army into Kashmir. They were sent to locations close to Mirpur, the west of Poonch and the strategic mountain of Pandu. Pakistan would later increase its military presence in Kashmir from three to 12 army battalions.[71] Thus, upon Gracey's advice to the Pakistan Government regular units of the Pakistan Army had been sent into Kashmir. This escalation of the conflict was to protect Pakistan's boundaries from being overrun by the Indian spring offensive. Despite Indian denials, the Pakistan Government was deeply concerned that the Indian Army would not limit its advance to operations to Kashmir but that it would now seize the initiative by attacking Pakistan as well. If the Indian advance succeeded then India would have gained unilateral control of Kashmir. In addition, 2,750,000 Muslim refugees would have been driven out, ahead of the Indian advance into Pakistan. Gracey was no doubt conscious of the local repercussions that would follow in the wake of such a humanitarian disaster. He was fully aware of the logic of recent history and the horrendous communal violence that had been enacted by the Muslim and Hindu populations upon each other during the partition of India and Pakistan. Gracey's decision to send the Pakistan Army into Kashmir therefore represented a pragmatic attempt to prevent an escalation of political violence. His decision to ignore the British stand down order indicated that in the current dire state of affairs, Gracey's crisis management skills were highly fluid, flexible and adaptable. He would not pedantically see the order issued if it threatened greater chaos and anarchy. Gracey's decision to send the Pakistan Army into Kashmir was thus a considered attempt to create a stalemate as the least worst-case option for all concerned.

Likewise, Gracey was also concerned about the effect that a successful Indian advance would have upon the Pathan tribesmen. A decisive Indian victory against the Pathan forces could turn the Pathan tribesmen against their Pakistan paymasters. In such circumstances, the Pathan tribesmen could be particularly aggrieved that Pakistan had failed to provide them with greater support against the Indian Army. The leaders of the Pathan tribes in Swat, Chitral and Afghanistan could rise up with Indian support and thereby threaten future Pakistan security.[72] Gracey obviously considered the Pathan tribesmen to be fickle military allies.

As the conflict intensified, Mountbatten left South Asia on 21 June.[73] Several skirmishes now occurred between the Indian and Pakistan armed forces. The British Foreign Office revealed to its delegation at the United Nations that Britain was fully aware, thanks to Gracey, that Pakistan had three brigades of the regular Pakistan Army currently operating in Kashmir. Nevertheless, despite the presence of 10,000 Pakistan troops in Kashmir, Britain chose not to reveal this development to the United Nations Security Council.[74] It was therefore with irony that on 14 July the United Nations Security Council called upon both India and Pakistan not to escalate the conflict further.[75] Meanwhile, the United Nations Committee on India and Pakistan arrived on a fact-finding mission in Kashmir.[76]

At the same time, during July, 200 policemen in Dacca had gone on strike. This had been provoked by communist elements in East Bengal. Pakistan therefore faced two crises simultaneously. In the west, Pakistan was engaged in a war with India over Kashmir. In the east, Pakistan was facing renewed political violence in East Bengal. Separating the two emergencies was 1,100 miles of Indian territory. Pakistan did not have the resources to resist crises on two fronts. Gracey therefore made a strategic decision to focus his military attention upon the situation in the West Punjab. Pakistan simply could not defend Pakistan and deal with crises in Kashmir and East Bengal at the same time. Gracey had to give greater priority to the war in the west.[77]

By the end of July, the Indian Army had advanced well beyond the line that the Bucher–Gracey talks had envisaged for the creation of a truce in Kashmir. Bucher had previously denied all knowledge that Pakistan troops would be deployed in Kashmir. But Whitehall was content that Gracey had indeed kept Bucher fully up to date with such developments. The problem was that because the talks had been an informal affair that communication issues were bound to arise. For example, it was highly conceivable that, because of informal nature of the talks, Bucher might not have told the Indian Government of everything that had been discussed. In such circumstances, Bucher's later protestations of his ignorance as to Gracey's true intentions could have been solely intended as a face-saving exercise for Bucher vis-à-vis the Indian Government rather than a deliberate attempt to smear Gracey. Both generals were working in highly unusual and difficult conditions.

Nevertheless by the end of July, the worsening state of affairs in Kashmir meant that Gracey was becoming increasingly desperate. As the Indian offensive continued, Gracey became more outspoken. He even resorted to using the media as propaganda weapon in an attempt to balance the conflict. Gracey also increased the number of regular Pakistan Army battalions operating in Kashmir from three to four. Regular units of the Pakistan Army were openly operating in Kashmir and still no British stand down order had been issued. On 27 July, Gracey confirmed to Bucher that regular units of the Pakistan Army were operating in Kashmir. He also told Bucher that the British Government knew about the deployments well in advance. This concurred with what Liaquat had said to Gracey in May, when Liaquat had revealed that the presence of the Pakistan Army in Kashmir was already well known. The Pakistan Government had certainly told Noel-Baker in advance of such a deployment. But by failing to issue the stand down order, the British Government appeared to be turning a blind eye to events on the ground.[78]

In August 1948, Gracey was called to testify before the United Nations Committee on India and Pakistan. At that moment, the committee was taking evidence concerning the crisis in Kashmir. Gracey presented his testimony to Josef Korbel, the Czechoslovakian chairman of the committee. Gracey explained to Korbel in great detail the current military situation and his thinking behind sending the regular Pakistan Army into Kashmir.[79] Even in August 1948, both the Indian and Pakistan armed forces remained heavily dependent upon the assistance of British military personnel. The Pakistan armed forces employed 801 British personnel and the Indian armed forces engaged a further 499 British advisers.[80] Therefore, Bucher and Gracey still managed to exert a considerable amount of influence over and receive valuable information about the military resources of both of the belligerent nations.

Jinnah died on 11 September.[81] With the passing of the father of the nation, Bucher pushed for a United Nations administered ceasefire agreement.[82] The stalemate that Bucher and Gracey hoped to insure appeared to be at last within their grasp. Both Bucher and Gracey were convinced that neither side could win a decisive victory in the Kashmir war. But they both feared that Indian and Pakistan obstinacy would ensure that the war was not currently seen as unwinnable by either of the main protagonists. This belligerent attitude could lead to grave political consequences in the region and create greater levels of political militancy in both India and Pakistan. The actions of the last few months had already significantly altered the political landscape. In stunning volte-face from October 1947, Gracey was now highly respected by Liaquat. In comparison, Nehru had become highly suspicious of Bucher. Nevertheless, both British officers wanted the war to end swiftly and above all to avoid any further escalation of the conflict. The United Nations Committee on India and Pakistan and the United Nations Security Council both agreed with Bucher and Gracey's outlook.[83]

On 4 November, the Indian Air Force attacked a Pakistan supply flight bound for the town of Gilgit. India had been able to attack the flight due to the fact that Air Vice-Marshal Thomas Elmhirst, the British officer acting as the Commander in Chief of the Indian Air Force, was away on tour. The Pakistan Government decided to continue with the supply flights despite the risk of further Indian attacks. Air Vice-Marshal Allan Perry-Keene, the Air Commander of the Pakistan Air Force, and Gracey had both been present during the Cabinet meeting discussions. Upon finishing the meeting, they immediately went to see Grafftey-Smith, the High Commissioner in Pakistan, to discuss the issue further. Fortunately neither India nor Pakistan sought to widen the war to include aerial combat. In this instance, both nations enacted a rapid retreat and played down the possibility of an air war concerning the destination of military supply aircraft.[84]

Nevertheless, the Indian offensive continued. By the middle of November, the unremitting nature of the Indian advance had caused panic within the Pakistan Government. The Indian Army was on the verge of threatening the Jhelum boundary between Kashmir and Pakistan. The Kashmir war had now reached the border with Pakistan. Fearing for the security of the independent Muslim nation state, the Pakistan Government ordered Gracey to protect the border at all costs.

The veracity of the Indian advance forced Shone, the British High Commissioner in India, to warn Noel-Baker that in order to protect the boundary Gracey would have to throw all of the remaining elements of the entire Pakistan Army into the conflict.[85]

Gracey was therefore left with no other choice but to send all of the residual units of the Pakistan armed forces to the Jhelum border to prevent the Indian advance.[86] By now the British stand down order had been proven to be obsolete. It was widely held that if the British personnel were now withdrawn from the dispute then this would result in an even larger regional conflict.[87] Ironically, Grafftey-Smith thought that Gracey had on this occasion overstated the strategic significance of the Indian advance and that the Pakistan border was not in as much danger as Gracey had claimed.[88] Grafftey-Smith was also able to reveal to Noel-Baker that Nehru was downplaying the strategic significance of the latest phase of the Indian offensive.[89]

Nevertheless, the latest Indian advance and the Pakistan counter-reaction raised more geopolitical anxieties surrounding the Kashmir war. Both Grafftey-Smith and Shone hoped that a new Bucher–Gracey meeting would provide some way to decelerate the crisis and 'relieve the existing tension'.[90] At the same time, Noel-Baker penned an urgent brief to Attlee about the crisis. He proposed that Sir Alexander Cadogan, the Permanent British Representative to the United Nations Security Council, should try to use his influence to involve the United States in finding a solution to the dispute.[91]

On 25 November, Bucher arrived in Karachi for two days of discussions with Gracey. Yet again the British generals were exploring the possibilities for establishing a truce behind the backs of their regional masters. During the course of the talks, Bucher revealed to Gracey that India had not as yet planned any further large-scale Indian Army offensives.[92] This revelation, therefore, set Gracey's mind at ease about the possibility of a future Indian northern offensive. It also confirmed Grafftey-Smith's assessment that Nehru had indeed downplayed the significance of the latest Indian advance. The circumstances surrounding the Indian advance thereby appeared less pessimistic than had first been thought.

Despite Bucher's disclosures, Gracey naturally remained wary of Lt.-General K.M. Cariappa's, the General Officer and the Commander in Chief of Delhi and the East Punjab, modus operandi. Was Cariappa, really to be trusted? Bucher freely admitted to Gracey that he had experienced a number of problems while working alongside Cariappa. In Bucher's opinion, at times Cariappa acted completely outside of

Bucher's control. But on this occasion, Bucher faithfully told Gracey that there would be not be an Indian Army attack on the town of Kotli and that he was perfectly happy to inform Gracey if India changed its mind and betrayed him.

The nature of the latest Bucher–Gracey talks revealed that Britain still wanted to create a military stalemate in Kashmir as this could eventually lead to a truce and a subsequent ceasefire. The Bucher–Gracey discussions favoured Pakistan only so far as to produce the possibility of the stalemate. Furthermore, there would be no reciprocal offer by Gracey to Bucher to inform him of any planned Pakistan Army offensives. The situation on the ground meant that Pakistan was not in the military ascendancy and therefore did not require its plans to be shared with Bucher. In the meantime, Gracey considered that the Indian armed forces partaking in the advance were highly vulnerable to shelling from the Pakistan Army. This could assist the Pakistan Army in shoring up the Jhelum border.[93]

Gracey now decided that, given the current state of affairs, a limited Pakistan Army offensive might push Nehru closer towards negotiating table.[94] If Pakistan could blunt Nehru's military confidence then he might be more willing to negotiate. It was a dangerous bluff. But just as Gracey began to contemplate such an action, his previous fears concerning Cariappa were fully realised as India initiated another Indian Army advance.[95] The renewed Indian offensive forced Attlee to discuss the Kashmir crisis at a meeting of the British Cabinet in London. Alexander, Bevin and Noel-Baker were all in attendance. The Indian Government insisted that the latest advance was in fact of a very limited nature in order to reinforce existing Indian positions. The Pakistan Government protested the opposite.[96] Attlee considered the current situation to be 'very grave'. Alexander, the Minister of Defence, ominously informed his colleagues that it was exceedingly difficult to establish what exactly India intended to achieve during the offensive. Alexander considered that the recent change of command in the Indian Army was not helpful to the current circumstances.[97] His comments revealed that Whitehall, as well Gracey, was equally wary of Cariappa. The comments also suggested that Bucher, the natural source of British information concerning the Indian Army, was distrusted by his regional masters and that he was purposefully being excluded from the Indian military decision-making process.

On 12 and 13 December, the Indian Air Force bombed Pakistan Army positions near the village of Palak. Gracey and Bucher immediately spoke to each other by telephone. The Pakistan Army regarded the attack by India as India reneging on a promise not to launch operations in the area. The Indian Government however insisted that the previous deal only concerned the activities of the Indian Army and not the Indian Air Force.[98] Two days later the Pakistan Army retaliated. They bombarded Indian supplies and communication routes for over 36 hours.[99] It was a simple reciprocal measure. It was not the prelude to a longer Pakistan offensive. Gracey therefore told Grafftey-Smith that, unless India planned to initiate any further counterattacks, no further Pakistan military action would be orchestrated. Grafftey-Smith welcomed Gracey's decision to downplay the Palak incident, which in other circumstances could have resulted in further grave repercussions.[100] This time, however, the Pakistan response had been forceful, limited and proportionate. Furthermore, this limited response paved the way for both sides to consider the need for a ceasefire.

On 30 December, Bucher told Gracey that India formally wanted to negotiate a ceasefire.[101] A period of intense consultation was followed on 1 January 1949 with the ceasefire being signed by Gracey on behalf of Pakistan and Bucher for India. The two British generals at the very heart of the informal discussions, on either side of the conflict, for the past year were the appropriate signatories. India and Pakistan agreed that the ceasefire line was to be monitored by United Nations observers. On 5 January, the United Nations Committee on India and Pakistan announced that the future of Kashmir would be settled by a referendum. British peace enforcement had been achieved.

Bucher and Gracey had both prevented a wider war. Gracey had definitely avoided greater political violence by refusing to implement Jinnah's October 1947 order to send the regular Pakistan Army into Kashmir. In addition, Bucher had prevented the war from spreading in 1948 by pushing for a ceasefire when India was gaining the upper hand.[102] Both generals had kept in close contact with each other and both were powerful voices for moderation in a highly charged and tempestuous conflict.[103] The ceasefire had arrived just in time. On 15 January, Lt-General K.M. Cariappa replaced Bucher as the Commander in Chief of the Indian Army. Cariappa had already revealed that he was an independent thinker, distrusted by Bucher, and that he was quite prepared to operate outside of the control of his line manager. In fairness, Cariappa had merely demonstrated the degree to which the Indian Army had successfully been nationalised. It had managed to achieve operational independence from its British advisers. The Indian armed forces were not British puppets. Mountbatten had already left India and Bucher was the last senior British person close to the Indian leadership. Furthermore, Bucher need not have feared his successor. Cariappa's first act concerning Kashmir was to reconfirm the terms of the ceasefire at an India–Pakistan conference held in New Delhi. Cariappa did not reopen the conflict. A degree of stability had been achieved. On 27 July, a further conference in Karachi worked out the diplomatic niceties needed to maintain the ceasefire, and on 3 November official demarcation lines and border points were established between India and Pakistan in Kashmir.[104]

The crisis in Kashmir may have ended in a stalemate. But in East Pakistan problems of political violence and decolonisation continued. In 1950, a mere four battalions defended East Bengal. Gracey considered it impossible to defend East Pakistan from 1,100 miles away in West Pakistan. Any urgent supplies or troop reinforcements would have to be transported around Indian territory, and India was the natural adversary in any dispute concerning East Pakistan. Gracey was fully aware that the violence in Kashmir had been abated by referral of the Kashmir war to the United Nations and deft footwork by Gracey and Bucher in pushing India and Pakistan towards a ceasefire. It appeared logical to Gracey that the Bengal crisis should also be put for resolution before the United Nations Security Council.

Following the Kashmir ceasefire, Nehru had much more time to focus upon Bengal. Gracey believed that Nehru would now seek to reinforce his bargaining position and thereby negotiate from a position of strength. A sudden show of Indian force could promote a more acceptable settlement for India. Circumstances in Kashmir had already demonstrated the power of using paramilitary forces in clandestine operations to further the political demands of a sovereign nation state. Pakistan had benefited from the swift actions of the Pathan tribesmen and the Azad Kashmir forces. Gracey now feared a similar situation in Bengal. A Hindu militia, supported across the border by the Indian Army, could easily engage in political violence on behalf of the Hindu population in East Bengal.[105]

Bengal stood on the precipice. But this was a very different crisis from the Kashmir war. During the Kashmir dispute, British attempts at peace enforcement had benefited from both sides maintaining an open dialogue through the senior British officers in the Indian and the Pakistan armed forces. But although, in the short term, Pakistan was still dependent upon Gracey and a number of British military personnel, Nehru had sought to nationalise the Indian armed forces by removing all Indian dependency upon these foreign specialists.[106] When Bucher had retired, Britain and Gracey were highly concerned about who would replace Bucher as Commander in Chief of the Indian Army. Gracey had wanted Nehru to appoint Lt.-General Kumar Shri Rajendrasinjhi, who had led the police action to incorporate the princely state of Hyderabad into India. Gracey did not consider Rajendrasinjhi to be necessarily the brightest candidate available for the position, but he did have considerable experience in balancing peace-enforcement duties with outbreaks of political violence.[107] Rajendrasinjhi later succeeded Cariappa as the second Indian Commander in Chief of the Indian Army. The crisis in East Bengal continued.

However, in January 1951 Gracey retired. General Ayub Khan was appointed as the first indigenous Commander in Chief of the Pakistan Army. Khan was a Pathan from the city of Peshawar. He had successfully served as an officer in a Punjab regiment under the British during the Second World War. He had subsequently been appointed as the Commander in Chief of the Pakistan Army in East Bengal after the partition of Pakistan from India. He therefore possessed considerable experience not least in dealing with the political violence in East Bengal. Gracey clearly had a hand in Khan's appointment. Both Gracey and the United States believed that Ayub Khan possessed pro-American sympathies.

Nevertheless, the appointment was not universally welcomed. In March 1951, Major-General Akbar Khan was arrested for plotting a coup d'état against the Pakistan Government. This was commonly known as the Rawalpindi Conspiracy. Akbar Khan had fought in the Kashmir war. He favoured a military dictatorship for Pakistan and closer ties to Moscow rather than London. He also wanted to reopen the Kashmir war with India.

Akbar Khan's arrest justified Gracey's earlier decision to depoliticise the army and to prevent the nationalisation of the Pakistan Army for as long as possible. Stability rather than militancy was required. But Akbar Khan saw himself as the natural successor to Jinnah. In the months directly after Gracey's retirement, Pakistan therefore witnessed an intense struggle between Akbar Khan and Ayub Khan. It was political tussle for the heart of the Pakistan Army and ultimately for the direction of the fledgling nation state. It was struggle between a political militant-nationalist and a political moderate. Furthermore, the crisis became epitomised as contest between pro-Kashmir elements in the Pakistan Army and those that possessed a more pro-British outlook. At the time, Gracey was greatly disturbed by Akbar Khan's political activities. He was appalled by his alcoholism and his use of women as political weapons to extract information from his opponents.[108] Akbar Khan was not the gentleman soldier that Gracey respected.[109]

However, now that the Kashmir war had been stabilised, the Pakistan Army was able to play a vital role for Britain and the United States in the early phases of the Cold War. For example in February 1949, Gracey ordered Major-General Frederick Loftus-Tottenham and a division of the Pakistan Army into Iran. This action was designed to assist British and American policy in the region. Pakistan forces also played an important role in reinforcing Baluchistan in case Britain needed military support following the nationalisation of the Anglo-Iranian oil company. Ayub Khan supported such pro-western Cold War endeavours. Furthermore, before he left office Gracey had even created 'Exercise Stalin', which was a war game designed to prepare the Pakistan Army for a possible future confrontation with the Union of Soviet Socialist Republics.[110]

As the Cold War intensified, so did the importance of the Pakistan Army to Britain and the United States. Kashmir and East Bengal would continue to remain international points of tension and conflict between India and Pakistan. But Gracey's involvement in such crises was over. Gracey had retired and he no longer had to balance the maintenance of law and order and peace-enforcement duties against popular protest, anarchy and outbursts of extreme political violence.

Conclusion

The origins of the Vietnam War are firmly rooted in a complex indigenous tussle against western imperialism in Southeast Asia at the close of the Second World War. Yet historians, for one reason or another, have often been too content to see British military operations in Vietnam and Cambodia (and subsequently in South Asia during the Kashmir crisis) within clear-cut paradigms. With Gracey's actions in Vietnam often at the forefront of such analysis, it has become fashionable for academics to view his attempts at peace enforcement from a polarised perspective, either as part of the team for the prosecution of Gracey's old-school imperialist mindset or as part of the counsel for the defence.

The arguments for the prosecution have unfortunately created the myth that Gracey's actions were predetermined, precise and pro-French, and they have certainly detracted from the reality of the British deployment in Vietnam. To this end, it would be a grave mistake for the post-war chaos facing the Allies in Southeast Asia to be underestimated. There was no intergovernmental imperial grand-strategy for the rebirth of the European colonial empires. For Britain, the prospect and subsequent consequence of Indian independence had a sharply critical effect upon the British Empire in Asia. This created a unique situation whereby the traditional binary division between imperialists and nationalists was replaced by a radical third way. This involved some senior British officers in the region (such as Gracey) actually working alongside nationalist groups in an attempt to secure some kind of continued influence. At the same time, for France, an overzealous desire for the restoration of the formal French Empire in the Far East, in order to eradicate the stain of collaboration with Nazi Germany and Imperial Japan, led to a striking contrast with British actions in the region.

Nevertheless, the purpose of this book has not been to reiterate the case for Gracey's defence. It would be erroneous merely to excuse

Gracey's actions, the weaknesses of the British response to the crises in Vietnam and Cambodia (and later Kashmir) or the more general mistakes that Britain made during the unravelling of empire. Rather, by placing Gracey's actions within a wider geopolitical context, this study has suggested that a more meaningful British response would also have failed. In doing so, it has been possible to highlight how misrepresented Gracey has often been by the historical profession. Gracey was no rabid racial colonialist. His background may have been deeply rooted in the history of the British involvement in India, and in this context Gracey could surely have been accused of being a highly paternalistic imperialist. He was, after all, fluent in the native tongue of his Gurkha troops, and he was deeply interested in their welfare. But on the whole, the 20th Indian Division was a happy one, and in this regard it naturally reflected the character and the panache of its commanding officer.

Gracey's operational experiences gleaned during the Burma Campaign unquestionably influenced his approach to other complex Asian political violence scenarios, such as the crises in Vietnam, Cambodia and Kashmir. It was in Burma that he first had the opportunity to intensively educate and shape an operational division in his own image. This enabled Gracey to build up a tightly knit and, eventually, extremely effective divisional unit, which justly received copious amounts of praise from Slim and others. Gracey's leadership skills were readily demonstrated by the 20th Indian Division's ability to work in the densest and toughest of jungle conditions. Whether in the Kabaw Valley, at the Shenam Saddle or during the crossing of the Irrawaddy River, Gracey resolutely conducted the most difficult of military operations against a determined Japanese foe. These endeavours were often carried out with limited and uninspiring supplies. Yet, despite a dearth of adequate resources, Gracey successfully used mechanical and animal transport with speed and diligence to patrol and ultimately to liberate significant portions of central Burma from Japanese control. In doing so, Gracey developed an astute ability to work alongside indigenous militia forces such as Aung San's nationalists and also the ethnic Karen minority. In addition, once the formal Japanese resistance to the British advance in Burma had been broken, Gracey was successfully able to combat Japanese counterinsurgency warfare in the Pegu Yomas mountain range.

Therefore, following a highly successful Burma Campaign, Gracey and elements of the 20th Indian Division were deployed to Allied liberation and humanitarian duties in southern French Indo-China. Gracey did not create the power vacuum in Vietnam at the end of the Second World War. Nor was Gracey to blame for the chaotic state of affairs that he inherited in the south. Even so, Gracey's previous Burmese experience of jungle operations, counterinsurgency warfare and his ability to work alongside indigenous nationalists fully demonstrated that he was not ignorant in such dealings should similar situations arise.

However, decisions made in London dictated that Gracey had to manage the emancipation of southern Vietnam with an exceedingly limited number of British–Indian troops and a universal lack of military resources. In administering his liberation duties, Gracey did not actively seek a confrontation with Asian nationalism (whether practised by the Vietminh or other nationalist groups). Yet this was what greeted him in Saigon and dogged all of his Vietnamese activities. In spite of such inauspicious circumstances, Gracey certainly sought to avoid any unnecessary violence. His reminder to the former Japanese administration of their obligation to maintain Truman's instruction to ensure law and order verified this stance. Similarly Gracey's subsequent and highly controversial use of Japanese prisoners of war as Allied peace enforcers demonstrated his desire to prevent the general administrative state of affairs from slipping out of his control. Franco-Vietnamese anarchy had to be avoided at all costs. Gracey desperately wanted to avoid the possibility of a humanitarian disaster engulfing both the colonial and the indigenous populations. To this end, Gracey fully upheld his international legal obligations, as outlined under the terms of the Hague Convention, to maintain law and order under the most difficult of liberation scenarios. In addition, when possible, Gracey keenly engaged in the organisation of humanitarian operations in order to ensure adequate food security and improve the overall living conditions for both of the resident populations in southern Vietnam. British–Indian forces for this reason found themselves actively overseeing food convoys, ensuring electricity supply and operating the Saigon dockyard facilities in a British co-ordinated logistical response.

In spite of the subsequent French support for Gracey's handling of the political violence in Saigon, the spirit of French activities in southern Indo-China and the reckless method by which the French resurrected their colonial rule profoundly disturbed Gracey. Solemn promises given by the French representatives in Saigon to Gracey, prior to the coup d'état, to use the smallest amount of force needed, turned out to be fallacious. As a matter of fact, Gracey was exceedingly troubled by the universal disposition of the French modus operandi in southern French Indo-China. In Gracey's judgement, French manoeuvres, in opposition to the Vietminh, were being executed with unwarranted cruelty. In this regard, Gracey's personal opinions differ from earlier historians' allegations that he was a narrow-minded imperialist who was keenly seeking to reinstate French colonial hegemony at any cost. Indeed, Gracey correctly prophesied that the enduring results of these French actions would be devastating for French rule in Vietnam and would make further conflict unavoidable.

At the same time, in Cambodia, Gracey was prepared to work with emergent Asian nationalism. This was not a new phenomenon for Gracey. It reflected his previous experience of working in Burma alongside Aung San's nationalist movement and also the ethnic Karen minority against the Japanese. Yet by integrating the narrative of Gracey's operations in Cambodia into his deployment in Vietnam, a very important French Indo-Chinese contrast can be made that casts new illumination upon earlier assertions regarding Gracey's fervent belief in empire building and bigotry. If Gracey had truly been an old-fashioned dyed in the wool imperialist, he would have engaged in parallel strategies in Cambodia and Vietnam in a hard-nosed and homogeneous effort to re-establish the French Empire. This would have been carried out with little regard for either the indigenous Cambodian or Vietnamese inhabitants. Time and again, this has been contended by Gracey's accusers, based solely upon his deeds in Vietnam. Yet curiously, at the same time as his complex Vietnamese venture, Gracey had radically argued that for Cambodia, Britain should work with the Cambodian nationalist movement. This attitude of operating alongside nationalists in Cambodia is revealing. It not only successfully counters the subsequent view of Gracey as some kind of nineteenth-century colonialist, but it also demonstrates that he was in fact very far-sighted. For in Burma and Cambodia, Gracey had successfully anticipated what would eventually become the main thrust of British post-war imperial policy – i.e. cultivating co-operative nationalist politicians and 'sitting on' the extremists.

However, for the moment, in French Indo-China, Gracey was faced with the new dynamic of one of Britain's first contemporary Asian peace enforcement deployments (a union of British diplomatic, military and humanitarian policies). The United Nations had emerged during a humanitarian emergency at the end of the Second World War. It was directly encountering numerous instances of power vacuums, economic disruptions, social displacements and food shortages. The United Nations clearly did not possess the knowledge, the skills or the resources to practise effective peacekeeping. Instead, peace enforcement was the only realistic resolution as the old world colonial order started to fall apart and the new world's cry for decolonisation gained momentum.

Conclusion 135

In such circumstances, Attlee and the British Labour Government were simply unprepared for the challenges at hand. They lacked a lucid policy towards many post-war issues and they clearly had no understanding of the local situations on the ground in Vietnam and Cambodia. In this context Britain, and Attlee in particular, made a number of critical errors that directly influenced the effectiveness of Gracey's actions in southern French Indo-China.

Hence, the chaos of liberation duties, political expediency, financial costs and general misconceptions prevented Attlee and Alanbrooke from fully supporting Gracey. This undoubtedly led to Attlee temporarily breaking the Prime Minister's duty of care towards the British–Indian forces in Saigon. But could he have done anything different? The problem of India loomed large. This was a much bigger and a far more important conundrum for the Labour Government to tackle compared with dubious liberation duties elsewhere in Asia, especially if such emancipation obligations were not in former British colonies. British actions towards Cambodia and Vietnam were therefore not without fault, and they certainly create a wider contextual commentary on the nature of peacekeeping versus peace enforcement, which is something that should serve as a warning for future liberation and humanitarian missions.

Similarly, the dynamic of the Gracey–Mountbatten association has clearly clouded the interpretation of Gracey's crisis management activities in southern Vietnam. This was a complicated relationship and occasionally far from harmonious. Yet some historians have been too quick to fall for Mountbatten's charm, his condemnation of Gracey in his report to the Combined Chiefs of Staff and his pro-indigenous nationalist utterances. But in such a controversial setting, should historians merely trust Mountbatten's word over Gracey's? Were the sentiments expressed in Mountbatten's dialogues really because he believed in what he was saying or was he merely rewriting history to preserve his legacy? The evidence does not wholly favour Mountbatten's perspective. Gracey vehemently denied the charges made against him that were contained within Mountbatten's report to the Combined Chiefs. Meanwhile Dening, the senior Foreign Office official attached to Mountbatten's headquarters staff, brutally laid bare Mountbatten's inconsistencies and self-promotion to Bevin, the British Foreign Secretary. In addition, there was the curious episode in which Mountbatten was awarded the French Legion of Honour.

It would also be erroneous for any analysis of Gracey's actions in Vietnam to state that, despite all other observations, the British–Indian deployment in Vietnam and Gracey's handling of the political violence in Saigon was not without controversy. At times, the battle-hardened British–Indian troops from the Burma Campaign acted more like subjugators than liberators.[1] Indeed, British–Indian, French, Japanese and Vietnamese casualties continued to accrue after the formal Japanese surrender. The only difference from previous Second World War losses was that some Japanese prisoners of war were now serving and giving their lives as Allied peace enforcers.

Nonetheless, the unravelling of empire that Gracey confronted in Vietnam and Cambodia was purely in connection with the future of the French Empire in Southeast Asia. However, when in August 1947, India and Pakistan broke away from the British Empire, this was met with brutality and bloodshed in South Asia. Gracey was as a result presented with political violence in the former British colony of British India. Once again, Attlee's conduct did not assist Gracey. The high-policy ignorance that had plagued government policy towards southern French Indo-China also hampered the response towards the crises in India and Pakistan. The Labour Government was for a second time caught out by the speed of localised events on the ground, and it again lacked a coherent approach to decolonisation in South Asia.

For the moment, Gracey was not directly caught up in the crisis in East Bengal. However, his professional character, veracity and his modus operandi in southern French Indo-China were brought into review during an informative high-level dialogue between Mountbatten and Jinnah as to the appointment of a temporary governor-general for the province. In view of how delicate the situation in Bengal had turned out to be during the division of British India, it was enlightening that Mountbatten considered Gracey worthy of such a major role; without a doubt, the state of affairs in East Bengal necessitated that an extraordinary individual was needed to handle a highly explosive situation. In this context, Mountbatten tellingly did not consider Gracey's previous exploits in Vietnam and Cambodia as unmitigated disasters.

Despite eventually not being appointed to the governor-general's position in East Bengal, Gracey did play a significant role in the subsequent Kashmir conflict. This was, perhaps, the most important of the unresolved issues following the independence of India and Pakistan. In particular, Gracey's involvement in the Kashmir crisis once again illustrates how misrepresented Gracey has been as an old-school British imperialist. In tense and exceedingly delicate conditions, Gracey was prepared to work alongside Jinnah and other indigenous nationalists. Additionally, this episode also demonstrates how Gracey's prior familiarity with events in Vietnam and Cambodia fashioned both his

Conclusion 137

comprehension of the local situation on the ground in Kashmir and his wider geopolitical crisis management skills for the duration of another demanding episode of Asian political violence. Hence, Gracey displayed singular initiative and intuition by liaising with British officers behind the scenes in both India and Pakistan to prevent a wider Kashmir war.

Likewise, it was unthinkable that Gracey's knowledge of the situations in Vietnam, Cambodia and Kashmir did not have some bearing upon his securely held conviction in 1950 that the continuing and exceedingly unpredictable circumstances in East Bengal should be referred to the United Nations. This once more demonstrated how Gracey had willingly learned fundamental lessons in one location and then used them to influence his operational philosophy in a later setting of political violence. In addition, Gracey was also able to secure a wider British sphere of influence in the region by deploying Loftus-Tottenham and a divisional taskforce from the Pakistan Army to Iran to safeguard vital British interests. This reflected Gracey's commitment to a radical third way (of being neither an imperialist nor nationalist) in order to preserve continued British advantage in South Asia.

Thus, Gracey's actions in Vietnam, Cambodia and Kashmir represent a complex fusion of imperial, diplomatic and humanitarian efforts at a crucial moment in the history of the British Empire. At the same time, Gracey's deployments staggeringly reveal that Attlee's government had no real understanding of local situations in South and Southeast Asia. Government policy was fashioned in London, and it was driven by Whitehall political and diplomatic pragmatism, which due to conflicting priorities prevented Attlee from developing a coherent policy towards the crises in Vietnam, Cambodia and Kashmir. Hence Attlee must be to blame for Britain's sordid first attempts at postwar peace enforcement. For political expediency and financial reasons, Attlee decided that he could not speed up the arrival of French forces in Vietnam by one month. Attlee thereby left British–Indian troops in Saigon under-equipped and under resourced. He did what future American presidents have done – he committed Britain fully enough to become entwined in Vietnamese issues but not adequately enough to create an effective resolution.[2] This was something that the Americans should have later learned from Britain's curious involvement in Vietnam and Cambodia in 1945.

Select Chronology

1940

March	Gracey appointed Assistant Commandant of the Staff College at Quetta
June	Vichy France Government established
September	Japanese troops occupy French Indo-China
October–May	Franco-Thai War

1941

May	Gracey given the command of the 17th Indian Brigade
	17th Indian Brigade sent to Iraq
June	17th Indian Brigade involved in the invasion of Vichy-Syria
December	Japanese attack Pearl Harbor

1942

April	Formation of the 20th Indian Division in Hyderabad and Ceylon
	Gracey appointed General Officer Commanding 20th Indian Division
October	Inter-divisional war games on Ceylon

1943

April	20th Indian Division moved to Ranchi
July	20th Indian Division transferred to Imphal
October	20th Indian Division moved to the front line at Imphal

1944

February	20th Indian Division advance down the Kabaw Valley
March–July	Battle of Imphal
March	Moreh abandoned
April	Sustained attack by the Japanese upon the Shenam Saddle
June–November	Liberation of France
July	20th Indian Division rested
December	20th Indian Division crosses the Chindwin and advances down the Kabaw Valley

1945

January	Monywa captured by the 20th Indian Division
February	20th Indian Division crosses the Irrawaddy River
March	Japanese coup d'état in French Indo-China
	20th Indian Division captures the fort at Mandalay
April	Allanmyo falls to the 20th Indian Division
May	20th Indian Division captures Prome
July–August	Potsdam Conference
August	Two atomic bombs dropped on Japan
	20th Indian Division sent to Rangoon to prepare for Malaya
August–September	Cambodia and Vietnam declare independence from France
September	20th Indian Division arrives in southern Vietnam and Cambodia
	Emergency proclamation issued by Gracey
	French counter-revolution in southern Indo-China
October	Franco-British treaty signed in London

1946

January	Mountbatten hands over all security issues in Indo-China to France
	Gracey departs Indo-China
March	20th Indian Division disbanded
	Gracey appointed to Northern Command (India)

1947

February	British Cabinet decides that Britain should withdraw from India
June	Mountbatten criticises Gracey in a report to the Combined Chiefs of Staff
July	Stand down order given to British forces in India and Pakistan
August	Crisis in Bengal
	Mountbatten urges Jinnah to appoint Gracey as Governor of East Bengal
	Pakistan and India gain their independence
	Standstill agreement signed between Kashmir and Pakistan
	Gracey appointed Deputy Commander in Chief of Pakistan Armed Forces
October	Standstill agreement breaks down
	Pathan tribesmen invade Kashmir
	Outbreak of the First Kashmir War
	Hari Singh signs Act of Accession with India
	Indian troops airlifted into Kashmir
	Gracey prevents Jinnah from sending Pakistan military into Kashmir

1948

February	Gracey appointed Commander in Chief of Pakistan Armed Forces
May	Gracey advises that Pakistan forces should be moved into Kashmir
June	Mountbatten departs South Asia
July	Police strike in Dacca, East Bengal
August	United Nations delegation visits Kashmir
September	Death of Jinnah
November	Pakistan and India agree to hold plebiscites over the future of Kashmir
	Bucher and Gracey confer in Karachi

1949

January	Cessation of the First Kashmir War
	India–Pakistan Conference in New Delhi confirms the ceasefire
July	Karachi Conference works out the diplomatic implications of the ceasefire
November	Demarcation lines established between India and Pakistan in Kashmir

1950

	Gracey believes that the Bengal crisis should be sent to the United Nations
February	Gracey orders a division of the Pakistan Army into Iran

1951

January	Gracey retires
March	Rawalpindi Conspiracy

Select Personalia

Britain

Alanbrooke. Field Marshal Sir Alanbrooke. Chief of the Imperial General Staff 1941–1946.

Alexander. Lord Alexander (Albert Alexander). First Lord of the Admiralty 1929–1931, 1940–1945, 1945–1946; Member of the Cabinet Delegation to India 1946; Minister of Defence 1947–1950.

Attlee. Clement Attlee. Lord President of the Council and Deputy Prime Minister 1943–1945; Prime Minister 1945–1951.

Auchinleck. Field Marshal Sir Claude Auchinleck. Member of the Viceroy's Executive Council 1943–1946; Supreme Commander in India and Pakistan 1947.

Bennett. John Sterndale Bennett. Head of Far Eastern Department Foreign Office 1944–1946; Minister in Sophia 1947–1949; Deputy Commissioner General Southeast Asia 1950–1953.

Bevin. Ernest Bevin. Foreign Secretary 1945–1951.

Bickersteth. Major Anthony Bickersteth. Commander of Princess Mary's 4/10th Gurkha Rifles in Gracey's 20th Indian Division.

Bucher. Major-General Sir Roy Bucher. Major-General in charge of Administration Southern Army India 1942–1945; General Officer Commanding Bengal and Assam Area 1946–1947; Chief of Staff Area Headquarters Indian Army 1947; Commander in Chief Indian Army 1948–1949.

Cadogan. Sir Alexander Cadogan. Permanent Under-Secretary of State Foreign Office 1938–1945; Permanent British Representative United Nations Security Council 1945–1950.

Christison. Lt.-General Sir Philip Christison. General Officer Commanding XV Corps in Burma 1943–1945.

Churchill. Winston Churchill. Prime Minister and Minister of Defence 1940–1945.

Cunningham. Sir George Cunningham. Governor of the North-West Frontier Province in Pakistan 1947.

142 *Select Personalia*

Dening. Maberly Esler Dening. Chief Political Adviser to the Supreme Allied Commander SEAC 1943–1946; Assistant Under-Secretary of State Foreign Office 1946–1950.

Driberg. Tom Driberg. Labour Member of Parliament.

Eden. Anthony Eden. Foreign Secretary 1940–1945.

Elmhirst. Air Vice Marshal Thomas Walker Elmhirst. Commander in Chief of the Indian Air Force 1947–1950.

Evans. Brigadier Geoffrey Evans. Commander of 123rd Indian Brigade 1944; Promoted Major-General and General Officer Commanding 5th Indian Division 1944; General Officer Commanding 7th Indian Division 1944; General Officer Commanding Allied Land Forces Siam (Thailand) 1945–1946.

Gracey. Major-General Sir Douglas Gracey. Commander of the 20th Indian Division 1942–1945; Allied Liberation Force Commander southern Indo-China 1945–1946; General Officer Commanding Northern Command India 1946; Commander of I Indian Corps 1946–1947; Chief of Staff of the Pakistan Army 1947–1948; Commander in Chief of the Pakistan Army 1948–1951.

Grafftey-Smith. Sir Lawrence Grafftey-Smith. High Commissioner in Pakistan 1947–1951.

Halifax. Lord Halifax (Edward Wood). Ambassador to US 1941–1946.

Harvey. Sir Oliver Harvey. Assistant Under-Secretary Foreign Office 1943–1946: Deputy Under-Secretary 1946–1948; Ambassador to France 1948–1954.

Hollis. Major-General Leslie Hollis. War Cabinet Secretariat 1939–1946; Deputy Military Secretary to the Cabinet 1946–1949.

Ismay. General Hastings Ismay. Chief of Staff to Churchill in his role as Minister of Defence 1940–1945 and Deputy Secretary to the War Cabinet 1940–1945; Chief of Staff to Mountbatten 1947; Secretary of State for Commonwealth Relations 1951–1952.

Killearn. Lord Killearn (Sir Miles Lampson). Ambassador to Egypt 1936–1946; Special Commissioner to Southeast Asia 1946–1948.

Lawson. John Lawson. Secretary of State for War 1945–1946.

Lockhart. General Sir Rob Lockhart. Military Secretary at the India Office 1941–1944; General Officer Commanding Southern Command India 1945–1947; Acting Governor of Northwest Frontier Province 1947; Commander in Chief Indian Army 1947.

Loftus-Tottenham. Major-General Frederick Loftus-Tottenham. Commander of 33rd Indian Brigade 1943–1944; General Officer Commanding 81st West African

Division in Burma and India 1944-1945; General Officer Commanding Force 401 1946-1947; Commander of 'Operation Venus' and General Officer Commanding 7th Division 1948.

Meiklereid. E.W. Meiklereid. Consul-General Saigon 1946-1948.

Mountbatten. Admiral Lord Louis Mountbatten. Supreme Allied Commander SEAC 1943-1946; Viceroy of India 1947; Governor-General of India 1947-1948.

Mudie. Sir Robert Francis Mudie. Governor of West Punjab in Pakistan 1947-1949.

Murray. Lt.-Colonel E.D. Murray (Brigadier 1945). Allied Liberation Force Commander Phnom Penh 1945-1946.

Noel-Baker. Philip Noel-Baker. Minister of State Foreign Office 1945-1946; Secretary of State for Air 1946-1947; Secretary of State for Commonwealth Relations 1947-1950.

Perry-Keene. Air Vice-Marshal Allan Perry Keene. Air Officer in Charge Administration Air Headquarters India 1946; Air Commander Royal Pakistan Air Force 1947-1949.

Scoones. General Sir Geoffrey Scoones. General Officer Commanding IV Corps Burma 1942-1944; General Officer Commanding in Chief Central Command India 1945-1946; Principal Staff Officer Commonwealth Relations Office 1947-1953.

Shone. Sir Terrence Shone. High Commissioner in India 1946-1948.

Slim. Field Marshal Sir William Slim. Commander XV Corps 1942; General Officer Commanding 14th Army 1943-1945; Commander in Chief Land Forces Burma 1945; Commander in Chief Allied Liberation Force Southeast Asia Command 1945-1946; Commander of the Imperial Defence College 1946-1948; retired 1948; reinstated to become Chief of the Imperial General Staff 1949-1952.

Stopford. Lt.-General Montagu Stopford. General Officer Commanding XXXIII Corps Burma 1943-1945.

Thompson. Geoffrey Thompson. Minister and then Ambassador to Siam (Thailand).

Wavell. Field Marshal Lord Wavell (Archibald Wavell). Commander in Chief India 1941-1943; Viceroy and Governor-General 1943-1947.

Woodford. Brigadier E.C.J. Woodford. Commander of the 32nd Indian Infantry Brigade within the 20th Indian Division.

France

Alessandri. General Marcel Alessandri. Commander of the French retreat in Indo-China March 1945.

Bidault. Georges Bidault. Foreign Minister 1944–1946.

Cedile. Jean Cedile. Colonial Administrator Indo-China.

Clarac. Pierre Clarac. French negotiator with Thailand.

D'Argenlieu. Admiral Thierry D'Argenlieu. High Commissioner to Indo-China 1945–1947.

Houard. Lt.-Colonel. Commander of two companies of French commandos sent to Phnom Penh 1945.

Leclerc. General Philippe Leclerc. Liberated Paris 1944; Commander French Expeditionary Corps to the Far East; Commander in Chief French Forces in Indo-China 1945–1946.

Massigli. René Massigli. Ambassador to Britain.

Petain. Marshal Henri Philippe Petain. Head of Vichy France 1940–1944.

United States

MacArthur. General Douglas MacArthur. Supreme Allied Commander Southwest Pacific; Commander Occupational Forces Japan 1945–1951; Commander in Chief United Nations Forces in Korea 1950–1951.

Marshall. General George Marshall. Army Commander in Chief 1939–1945; diplomatic mission to China December 1945; Secretary of State 1947–1949; Secretary of Defence 1950–1951.

Patti. Major Archimedes Patti. Head of the Office for Strategic Services Mission to Indo-China 1945.

Roosevelt. Franklin Delano Roosevelt. President 1933–1945.

Truman. Harry S. Truman. President 1945–1952.

Vietnam and Cambodia

Bao Dai. Vietnamese Emperor 1926–1945; abdicated; Adviser to the Democratic Republic of Vietnam 1946; exiled; returned as nationalist leader and Head of State.

Ho Chi Minh. Leader of the Vietminh; Leader of the Indo-Chinese Communist Party 1945–1969; President of the Democratic Republic of Vietnam 1945–1969; Prime Minister 1945–1955.

Khim Tit. Cambodian Defence Minister.

Norodom Sihanouk. King of Cambodia 1941–1955.

Pham Van Bach. Head of the Vietminh in southern Indo-China.

Son Ngoc Thanh. Pro-Japanese Cambodian Nationalist; Foreign Minister 1945; Prime Minister 1945.

Tran Trong Kim. Vietnamese academic and Bao Dai's Prime Minister 1945.

Vo Nguyen Giap. Member of the Indo-Chinese Communist Party; Leader of the Vietnamese Liberation Army; Minister of the Interior.

India and Pakistan

Cariappa. General K.M. Cariappa. Major-General and Deputy Chief of General Staff August–November 1947; Promoted Lt.-General, General Officer Commander in Chief Eastern Command November 1947–January 1948; General Officer and Commander in Chief Delhi and East Punjab January 1948–January 1949; Promoted General, Commander in Chief Indian Army 1949–1953.

Jinnah. Muhammad Ali Jinnah. Leader of the All-India Muslim League 1913–1947; Governor-General of Pakistan 1947–1948.

Khan. Major-General Akbar Khan. Initiator of the Rawalpindi Conspiracy to enact a coup d'état in Pakistan in March 1951.

Khan. General Ayub Khan. Commander in Chief of the Pakistani Army 1951–1958.

Liaquat. Ali Khan Liaquat. General Secretary All-India Muslim League 1936–1947; Finance Minister in the Interim Government 1946; Prime Minister of Pakistan 1947–1951.

Nehru. Jawaharlal Nehru. President of the Congress Party 1926–1964; Indian Prime Minister and Foreign Minister 1947–1964.

Rajendrasinjhi. Lt.-General Kumar Shri Rajendrasinjhi. Promoted General, Commander in Chief Indian Army 1953.

Singh. Hari Singh. Maharaja of Kashmir.

Others

Aung San. Chief of Staff Burma Independence Army 1941; Created the Anti-Fascist Party 1944; Deputy Chairman the Executive Council 1946; assassinated 1947.

Chiang Kai-Shek. President of China 1928–1949; President of Taiwan 1949–1975.

Korbel. Josef Korbel. Chair of the United Nations Committee on India and Pakistan.

Notes

Introduction

1. W.J. Slim, *Defeat into Victory: Field Marshal Viscount Slim*, London, 1986, p. 146.
2. N. Smart, *Biographical Dictionary of British Generals of the Second World War*, Barnsley, 2005, p. 127.
3. A.C. Bickersteth, *ODTAA: Being Extracts from the Diary of an Officer who Served with the 4/10th Gurkha Rifles in Manipur and Burma*, Aberdeen, 1953, p. v.
4. Slim, *Defeat into Victory*, pp. 146, 472.
5. F. McLynn, *The Burma Campaign: Disaster to Triumph 1942–45*, New Haven, 2011, pp. 9–15.
6. R. Mead, *Churchill's Lions: A Biographical Guide to the Key British Generals of World War II*, Stroud, 2007. p. 184.
7. P. Neville, *Britain in Vietnam: Prelude to Disaster 1945–46*, London, 2008, p. xiii.
8. E. Hammer, *The Struggle for Indochina 1940–55*, Stanford, 1966, p. 115.
9. J. Buttinger, *Vietnam: A Dragon Embattled Volume 1*, London, 1967; T. Draper, *The Abuse of Power*, London, 1967; G.M. Kahin and J.W. Lewis, *The United States and Vietnam*, New York, 1967; G. Rosie, *The British in Vietnam*, London, 1970; A. Patti, *Why Vietnam?* Berkley, 1980; B. Tuchmann, *The March of Folly: From Troy to Vietnam*, London, 1984; J. Saville, *The Politics of Continuity: British Foreign Policy and the Labour Government 1945–1946*, London, 1993.
10. For a synopsis of Patti's hypothesis that Gracey openly contributed to the outbreak of the First Vietnam War, see Neville, *Britain in Vietnam*, p. x.
11. Patti, *Why Vietnam?* pp. 322, 326, 332.
12. Rosie, *The British in Vietnam*, pp. 12, 136–137.
13. M.A. Lawrence, *Assuming The Burden: Europe and the American Commitment to War in Vietnam*, London, 2005, pp. 102–103, 110–112, 119.
14. D. Duncanson, 'General Gracey and the Vietminh', *Journal of the Royal Central Asian Society*, vol. 55, pt. 3, October 1986, p. 289.
15. F.S.V. Donnison, *British Military Administration in the Far East 1943–1946*, London, 1956, pp. 407–410.
16. P.M. Dunn, *The First Vietnam War*, London, 1985; Duncanson, 'General Gracey and the Vietminh', pp. 288–297.
17. D. Duncanson, *Government and Revolution in Vietnam*, London, 1968, p. 160; Duncanson, 'General Gracey and the Vietminh', p. 294, citing Article 43, under Section III ('Military Authority over the Territory of the Hostile State') – *Final Act of the Second Peace Conference Held at The Hague in 1907*, London, 1914, p. 51.
18. Dunn, *The First Vietnam War*; Neville, *Britain in Vietnam*, p. xi.
19. P. Dennis, *Troubled Days of Peace: Mountbatten and South East Asia Command 1945–46*, New York, 1987.

20. J. Springhall, 'Kicking out the Vietminh: How Britain Allowed France to Reoccupy South Indochina', *Journal of Contemporary History*, vol. 40, no. 1, 2005, pp. 115–130.
21. Neville, *Britain in Vietnam*, pp. xiii, 175, 177–188.
22. T.O. Smith, 'Britain and Cambodia, September 1945–November 1946: A Reappraisal', *Diplomacy and Statecraft*, vol. 17, no. 1, 2006, pp. 73–91.
23. Neville, *Britain in Vietnam*, p. xii.
24. Dennis, *Troubled Days of Peace*.
25. T.O. Smith, *Britain and the Origins of the Vietnam War: UK policy in Indo-China 1943–50*, Basingstoke, 2007.
26. T.O. Smith, 'Major-General Sir Douglas Gracey: Peacekeeper or Peace-Enforcer, Saigon 1945?' *Diplomacy and Statecraft*, vol. 21, no. 2, 2010, pp. 226–239.
27. The papers of Major-General Sir Douglas Gracey, The Liddell Hart Centre Archives, King's College London [hereafter: Gracey].
28. Hammer, *The Struggle for Indochina 1940–55*, p. 135.
29. The National Archives, Public Record Office, London [hereafter: TNA], War Office [hereafter: WO] 203/5644, Supreme Allied Commander 31st Miscellaneous Meeting Minutes, 28 September 1945.
30. Mountbatten to Jinnah, 6 August 1947, in Z.H. Zaidi, (Ed.), *Quaid-I-Azam Mohammad Ali Jinnah Papers, First Series, Volume IV, Pakistan at Last, 26 July–14 August 1947*, Islamabad, 1999, p. 271.
31. Extract from the Report to the Combined Chiefs of Staff by the Supreme Allied Commander, Southeast Asia, 30 June 1947, in *Documents Relating to British Involvement in the Indo-China Conflict 1945–1965*, London, 1965, pp. 47–52.
32. For a shattering examination of neoliberal security structures see D. Roberts, *Global Governance and Biopolitics: Regulating Human Security*, London, 2010.

1 The Prelude: Burma 1942–1945

1. Smart, *Biographical Dictionary of British Generals of the Second World War*, p. 126; Mead, *Churchill's Lions*, p. 181; Dunn, *The First Vietnam War*, pp. 161–162. For a discussion of the British campaigns against the Vichy French during the Second World War, see C. Smith, *England's Last War against France: Fighting Vichy 1940–1942*, London, 2009.
2. C. Bayly and T. Harper, *Forgotten Armies: Britain's Asian Empire and The War With Japan*, London, 2005, p. 146.
3. M. Gilbert, *Churchill and America*, London, 2006, pp. 256–257; Lord Moran, *Winston Churchill: The Struggle For Survival 1940–1965*, London, 1966, pp. 27–28, 31; M. Gilbert, *Churchill: A Life*, London, 1991, p. 719.
4. Bayly and Harper, *Forgotten Armies*, pp. 146, 269; A.J. Stockwell, 'Southeast Asia in War and Peace: The End of the European Colonial Empire', in N. Tarling (Ed.), *The Cambridge History of Southeast Asia: Volume Two, Part Two, From World War Two to the Present*, Cambridge, 1999, pp. 1–5.
5. Mead, *Churchill's Lions*, p. 181.
6. D.P. Marston, *Phoenix from the Ashes: The Indian Army in the Burma Campaign*, London, 2003, p. 100; R. Lyman, *Slim, Master of War: Burma and the Birth of Modern Warfare*, London, 2005, p. 169.

7. Slim, *Defeat into Victory*, p. 474.
8. J.P. Cross, *Jungle Warfare: Encounters and Experiences*, London, 1989, p. 13.
9. Marston, *Phoenix from the Ashes*, p. 100.
10. S. Woodburn Kirby, *The War against Japan Volume 2: India's Most Dangerous Hour*, Uckfield, 2004, p. 242; Lyman, *Slim, Master of War*, p. 170.
11. Dunn, *The First Vietnam War*, p. 162.
12. Lyman, *Slim, Master of War*, p. 169.
13. Dunn, *The First Vietnam War*, pp. 162–163.
14. Bickersteth, *ODTAA*, p. v.
15. Dunn, *The First Vietnam War*, p. 162.
16. Bickersteth, *ODTAA*, p. 2.
17. Dunn, *The First Vietnam War*, pp. 161–162.
18. M. Hastings, *Retribution: The Battle for Japan 1944–45*, New York, 2008, pp. 12, 79.
19. Marston, *Phoenix from the Ashes*, p. 100.
20. Hastings, *Retribution*, p. 80.
21. Slim, *Defeat into Victory*, p. 292.
22. B.R. Mullaly, *Bugle and Kukri: The Story of the 10th Princess Mary's Own Gurkha Rifles*, London, 1957, p. 326.
23. Marston, *Phoenix from the Ashes*, p. 101; Slim, *Defeat into Victory*, pp. 145–146.
24. McLynn, *The Burma Campaign*, 251.
25. Hastings, *Retribution*, p. 330; Slim, *Defeat into Victory*, p. 146.
26. Marston, *Phoenix from the Ashes*, p. 101.
27. G. Dunlop, *Military Economics, Culture and Logistics in the Burma Campaign 1942–1945*, London, 2009, p. 93.
28. Marston, *Phoenix from the Ashes*, pp. 102, 138.
29. Lyman, *Slim, Master of War*, p. 168; McLynn, *The Burma Campaign*, p. 294; Dunlop, *Military Economics, Culture and Logistics in the Burma Campaign 1942–1945*, p. 140.
30. Bickersteth, *ODTAA*, p. 55.
31. Marston, *Phoenix from the Ashes*, p. 138.
32. S. Woodburn Kirby, *The War against Japan Volume 3: The Decisive Battles*, Uckfield, 2004, pp. 129, 364; S.N. Prasad, K.D. Bhargava, and P.N. Khera, *Official History of the Indian Armed Forces in the Second World War 1939–45: Reconquest of Burma*, Prasad B. (Ed.), Volume 1, June 1942–June 1944, Calcutta, 1958, p. 169.
33. L. Allen, *Burma: The Longest War 1941–1945*, London, 2000, p. 189.
34. Prasad, Bhargava and Khera, *Official History of the Indian Armed Forces in the Second World War 1939–45: Reconquest of Burma*, Volume 1, June 1942–June 1944, pp. 160, 161.
35. Lyman, *Slim, Master of War*, p. 176; Allen, *Burma*, pp. 193, 206; Woodburn Kirby, *The War against Japan Volume 3*, p. 187; Bickersteth, *ODTAA*, p. 62.
36. Lyman, *Slim, Master of War*, p. 190; Marston, *Phoenix from the Ashes*, p. 148; Slim, *Defeat into Victory*, pp. 293–295.
37. Allen, *Burma*, p. 207; Dunlop, *Military Economics, Culture and Logistics in the Burma Campaign 1942–1945*, p. 122; Mullaly, *Bugle and Kukri*, p. 347; Prasad, Bhargava and Khera, *Official History of the Indian Armed Forces in the Second World War 1939–45: Reconquest of Burma*, Volume 1, June 1942–June 1944, p. 162.

38. Woodburn Kirby, *The War against Japan Volume 3*, pp. 193, 194, 197.
39. Marston, *Phoenix from the Ashes*, p. 142; Woodburn Kirby, *The War against Japan Volume 3*, p. 246; Lyman, *Slim, Master of War*, p. 193.
40. Dunlop, *Military Economics, Culture and Logistics in the Burma Campaign 1942–1945*, p. 140; McLynn, *The Burma Campaign*, p. 297; Woodburn Kirby, *The War against Japan Volume 3*, p. 241.
41. Slim, *Defeat into Victory*, p. 303; Prasad, Bhargava and Khera, *Official History of the Indian Armed Forces in the Second World War 1939–45: Reconquest of Burma, Volume 1, June 1942–June 1944*, pp. 182, 183.
42. Marston, *Phoenix from the Ashes*, pp. 143, 146, 147; McLynn, *The Burma Campaign*, p. 298; Slim, *Defeat into Victory*, p. 305.
43. Lyman, *Slim, Master of War*, p. 196; Woodburn Kirby, *The War against Japan Volume 3*, pp. 189, 191.
44. Slim, *Defeat into Victory*, p. 330; Lyman, *Slim, Master of War*, pp. 197, 217.
45. McLynn, *The Burma Campaign*, pp. 307, 308; Woodburn Kirby, *The War against Japan Volume 3*, pp. 310, 329.
46. Slim, *Defeat into Victory*, p. 337; McLynn, *The Burma Campaign*, p. 308.
47. Woodburn Kirby, *The War against Japan Volume 3*, p. 343.
48. Slim, *Defeat into Victory*, p. 348; Marston, *Phoenix from the Ashes*, pp. 149–150.
49. Woodburn Kirby, *The War against Japan Volume 3*, pp. 351, 357.
50. S.N. Prasad and P.N. Khera, *Official History of the Indian Armed Forces in the Second World War 1939–45: Reconquest of Burma*, Prasad B. (Ed.), *Volume 2, June 1944–August 1945*, Calcutta, 1959, p. 32.
51. Woodburn Kirby, *The War against Japan Volume 3*, pp. 358, 363.
52. H. Tinker (Ed.), *Burma: The Struggle For Independence 1944–1948: Documents From Official And Private Sources: Volume 1: From Military Occupation to Civil Government 1 January 1944–31 August 1946*, London, 1983, p. xlvi,
53. Slim, *Defeat into Victory*, p. 353.
54. Marston, *Phoenix from the Ashes*, pp. 174, 207.
55. Woodburn Kirby, *The War against Japan Volume 3*, p. 372.
56. Bayly and Harper, *Forgotten Armies*, p. 381.
57. S. Woodburn Kirby, *The War against Japan Volume 4: The Reconquest of Burma*, Uckfield, 2004, pp. 156–157.
58. Slim, *Defeat into Victory*, p. 389; Marston, *Phoenix from the Ashes*, p. 182.
59. Prasad and Khera, *Official History of the Indian Armed Forces in the Second World War 1939–45: Reconquest of Burma, Volume 2, June 1944–August 1945*, pp. 158–159.
60. Dunlop, *Military Economics, Culture and Logistics in the Burma Campaign 1942–1945*, p. 181.
61. Allen, *Burma*, p. 409; Slim, *Defeat into Victory*, p. 402.
62. Prasad and Khera, *Official History of the Indian Armed Forces in the Second World War 1939–45: Reconquest of Burma, Volume 2, June 1944–August 1945*, pp. 204, 205.
63. Mullaly, *Bugle and Kukri*, p. 364.
64. Prasad and Khera, *Official History of the Indian Armed Forces in the Second World War 1939–45: Reconquest of Burma, Volume 2, June 1944–August 1945*, p. 216.

65. Woodburn Kirby, *The War against Japan Volume 4*, pp. 176, 182–184; Bickersteth, *ODTAA*, pp. 122–123, Dunlop, *Military Economics, Culture and Logistics in the Burma Campaign 1942–1945*, p. 184.
66. Slim, *Defeat into Victory*, pp. 403, 417; Lyman, *Slim, Master of War*, p. 248; Bickersteth, *ODTAA*, p. 148; McLynn, *The Burma Campaign*, p. 419; Prasad and Khera, *Official History of the Indian Armed Forces in the Second World War 1939–45: Reconquest of Burma, Volume 2, June 1944–August 1945*, pp. 227–228.
67. McLynn, *The Burma Campaign*, p. 419; Woodburn Kirby, *The War against Japan Volume 4*, p. 185.
68. Prasad and Khera, *Official History of the Indian Armed Forces in the Second World War 1939–45: Reconquest of Burma, Volume 2, June 1944–August 1945*, pp. 228–229.
69. Slim, *Defeat into Victory*, p. 418; Marston, *Phoenix from the Ashes*, p. 186.
70. Woodburn Kirby, *The War against Japan Volume 4*, p. 242.
71. Marston, *Phoenix from the Ashes*, pp. 187, 203.
72. Slim, *Defeat into Victory*, p. 418; Prasad and Khera, *Official History of the Indian Armed Forces in the Second World War 1939–45: Reconquest of Burma, Volume 2, June 1944–August 1945*, pp. 259–261.
73. Hastings, *Retribution*, p. 324; McLynn, *The Burma Campaign*, p. 422.
74. Woodburn Kirby, *The War against Japan Volume 4*, p. 260.
75. Prasad and Khera, *Official History of the Indian Armed Forces in the Second World War 1939–45: Reconquest of Burma, Volume 2, June 1944–August 1945*, p. 262.
76. McLynn, *The Burma Campaign*, p. 422.
77. Marston, *Phoenix from the Ashes*, p. 187.
78. Slim, *Defeat into Victory*, p. 421.
79. Prasad and Khera, *Official History of the Indian Armed Forces in the Second World War 1939–45: Reconquest of Burma, Volume 2, June 1944–August 1945*, p. 274.
80. Mullaly, *Bugle and Kukri*, p. 373; Woodburn Kirby, *The War against Japan Volume 4*, pp. 261, 262; Bickersteth, *ODTAA*, p. v.
81. Woodburn Kirby, *The War against Japan Volume 4*, p. 282.
82. Lyman, *Slim, Master of War*, p. 248.
83. Woodburn Kirby, *The War against Japan Volume 4*, p. 292; Slim, *Defeat into Victory*, p. 496.
84. Allen, *Burma*, p. 410.
85. Woodburn Kirby, *The War against Japan Volume 4*, p. 293.
86. Slim, *Defeat into Victory*, p. 432; Prasad and Khera, *Official History of the Indian Armed Forces in the Second World War 1939–45: Reconquest of Burma, Volume 2, June 1944–August 1945*, p. 242.
87. Allen, *Burma*, p. 409.
88. Marston, *Phoenix from the Ashes*, pp. 188, 201.
89. Woodburn Kirby, *The War against Japan Volume 4*, p. 293; Slim, *Defeat into Victory*, pp. 471–472; Prasad and Khera, *Official History of the Indian Armed Forces in the Second World War 1939–45: Reconquest of Burma, Volume 2, June 1944–August 1945*, pp. 273, 289.
90. Slim, *Defeat into Victory*, p. 472.

Notes   151

91. Woodburn Kirby, *The War against Japan Volume 4*, pp. 294, 303.
92. Prasad and Khera, *Official History of the Indian Armed Forces in the Second World War 1939–45: Reconquest of Burma, Volume 2, June 1944–August 1945*, p. 363.
93. Mullaly, *Bugle and Kukri*, p. 379.
94. Slim, *Defeat into Victory*, pp. 473–474.
95. Prasad and Khera, *Official History of the Indian Armed Forces in the Second World War 1939–45: Reconquest of Burma, Volume 2, June 1944–August 1945*, p. 363; Woodburn Kirby, *The War against Japan Volume 4*, p. 303.
96. McLynn, *The Burma Campaign*, p. 422; Prasad and Khera, *Official History of the Indian Armed Forces in the Second World War 1939–45: Reconquest of Burma, Volume 2, June 1944–August 1945*, p. 363.
97. Slim, *Defeat into Victory*, p. 490.
98. Marston, *Phoenix from the Ashes*, p. 202.
99. Prasad and Khera, *Official History of the Indian Armed Forces in the Second World War 1939–45: Reconquest of Burma, Volume 2, June 1944–August 1945*, p. 382.
100. M. Charney, *A History of Modern Burma*, Cambridge, 2009, pp. 58–59.
101. TNA, WO 203/4193, Colonel F.S.V. Donnison to Deputy CCAO 14 Army, no. 240/2/998, 11 April 1945, in Tinker (Ed.), *Burma: The Struggle For Independence 1944–1948: Documents From Official And Private Sources: Volume 1*, pp. 221–222.
102. Slim, *Defeat into Victory*, pp. 490–491.
103. Prasad and Khera, *Official History of the Indian Armed Forces in the Second World War 1939–45: Reconquest of Burma, Volume 2, June 1944–August 1945*, p. 383.
104. Woodburn Kirby, *The War against Japan Volume 4*, pp. 371, 372.
105. Slim, *Defeat into Victory*, p. 492; Prasad and Khera, *Official History of the Indian Armed Forces in the Second World War 1939–1945: Reconquest of Burma, Volume 2, June 1944–August 1945*, p. 386.
106. McLynn, *The Burma Campaign*, pp. 438, 440; Charney, *A History of Modern Burma*, pp. 55, 57; Bayly and Harper, *Forgotten Armies*, p. 434.
107. Allen, *Burma*, p. 516; Woodburn Kirby, *The War against Japan Volume 4*, p. 375.
108. Bickersteth, *ODTAA*, p. v.
109. Prasad and Khera, *Official History of the Indian Armed Forces in the Second World War 1939–45: Reconquest of Burma, Volume 2, June 1944–August 1945*, pp. 431, 452.
110. S. Woodburn Kirby, *The War against Japan Volume 5: The Surrender of Japan*, Uckfield, 2004, pp. 15, 19.
111. Bickersteth, *ODTAA*, pp. 236–237.
112. Woodburn Kirby, *The War against Japan Volume 5*, pp. 36, 38.
113. Slim, *Defeat into Victory*, p. 523.
114. Woodburn Kirby, *The War against Japan Volume 5*, p. 91.
115. S. Tonnesson, *The Vietnamese Revolution of 1945: Roosevelt, Ho Chi Minh and De Gaulle in a World at War*, London, 1991, pp. 362–365.
116. Bickersteth, *ODTAA*, p. 241.

2 The Power Vacuum: Vietnam 1945

1. Meeting of the CCS, 24 July 1945, in *Foreign Relations of the United States: Diplomatic Papers: Department of State Publication* [hereafter *FRUS*], *The Conference at Berlin 1945 (The Potsdam Conference) Volume 2*, Washington D.C., 1960, p. 377.
2. Tonnesson, *The Vietnamese Revolution of 1945*, pp. 362–365.
3. TNA, WO 203/5655, Dening to Mountbatten, 7 August 1945.
4. Meeting of the CCS, 24 July 1945, in *FRUS, The Conference at Berlin 1945 (The Potsdam Conference) Volume 2*, p. 377; TNA, Foreign Office [hereafter FO], 371/F4715/47/23, Memorandum by Foulds, 1 August 1945, in R. Butler and M. Pelly (Eds.), *Documents on British Policy Overseas Series 1:Volume 1: The Conference at Potsdam, 1945*, London, 1984, p. 1145.
5. Lin Hua, 'The Chinese Occupation of Northern Vietnam 1945–1946: A Reappraisal', in H. Antlov and S. Tonnesson (Eds.), *Imperial Policy and Southeast Asian Nationalism 1930–1957*, Surrey, 1995, pp. 144–169.
6. TNA, WO 203/1934, Interservice Topographical Department, 26 August 1945, Appendix H to FPI 1st D(SEAC)/D/SP/59, Special Report on French Indo-China South of Latitude 16 Degrees North, 'Summary of Forces to be moved to Saigon'.
7. A. Short, *The Origins of the Vietnam War*, London, 1989, pp. 1–18.
8. B. Kiernan, *How Pol Pot Came to Power: A History of Communism in Kampuchea, 1930–75*, London, 2004, pp. 41, 46, 49; J.M. Burns, *Roosevelt: The Soldier of Freedom 1940–1945*, San Diego, 1970, pp. 108–109.
9. D. Lancaster, *The Emancipation of French Indochina*, London, 1961, pp. 104–107; Kiernan, *How Pol Pot Came to Power*, p. 49.
10. T.O. Smith, *Churchill, America and Vietnam, 1941–45*, Basingstoke, 2011, p. 88.
11. TNA, Prime Minister's Office [hereafter PREM], 3/178/2, Churchill to Ismay, D 72/5, 12 March 1945.
12. R.H. Spector, *Advice and Support: The Early Years of the United States Army in Vietnam 1941–1960*, Washington D.C., 1983, pp. 31, 34; TNA, WO 208/670, Sitrep 3, 15 March 1945; TNA, WO 208/670, Sitrep 4, 15 March 1945; TNA, WO 208/670, JBS/172, 14 March 1945; TNA, WO 208/670, JBS/180, 19 March 1945; TNA, WO 208/670, Noiret to Montgomery, 19 March 1945; TNA, WO 208/670, Sitrep 5, 16 March 1945; TNA, WO 208/670, Sitrep 13, 27 March 1945; TNA, WO 208/670, Sitrep 17, 27 March 1945; TNA, WO 208/670, Sitrep 19, 30 March 1945; TNA, WO 208/670, Sitrep 20, 31 March 1945; TNA, WO 208/670, Sitrep 21, 2 April 1945; M. Thomas, 'Silent Partners: SOE's French Indo-China Section 1943–1945', *Modern Asian Studies*, vol. 34, no. 4, 2000, p. 947.
13. TNA, Cabinet Office [hereafter CAB], 121/741, JSM Washington to AMSSO, no. 595, 12 March 1945.
14. TNA, PREM 3/178/3, Eden to Cooper, draft, 12 March 1945.
15. The papers of Anthony Eden, the Cadbury Research Library, University of Birmingham, 20/13/73, Eden to Churchill, 17 March 1945.
16. For a full discussion of Vietnam as an important conundrum in Allied high policy during the Second World War, see Smith, *Churchill, America and Vietnam 1941–45*.

17. TNA, CAB 121/ 741, JIC (45)91(0), 18 March 1945.
18. TNA, CAB 121/741, COS to Mountbatten, COSSEA 216, draft, undated, Annex 3.
19. TNA, PREM 3/178/3, Churchill to Eden and Ismay for COS, M 237/5, 19 March 1945.
20. TNA, CAB 121/741, COS to JSM, COS (W)686, 19 March 1945.
21. Lancaster, *The Emancipation of French Indochina*, p. 106.
22. TNA, CAB 121/741, Mountbatten to COS, SEACOS 339, 22 March 1945.
23. TNA, CAB 121/741, 'Support for French Resistance Forces in Indo-China', CCS 644/21, 29 March 1945, Enclosure B, Fenand to CCS, no. 17 MN/SE 12 TS, 27 March 1945; TNA, CAB 121/741, 'Support for French Resistance Forces in Indo-China', CCS 644/21, 29 March 1945, Enclosure C, Fenand to CCS, no. 18 MN/SE 124 TS, 27 March 1945.
24. TNA, CAB 121/741, Sterndale Bennett to Air Commodore Beaumont, 30 March 1945.
25. Neville, *Britain in Vietnam*, p. 44.
26. S. Bills, *Empire and the Cold War: The Roots of United States-Third World Antagonism*, London, 1990, pp. 83–84.
27. Lancaster, *The Emancipation of French Indochina*, p. 108.
28. R.E.M. Irving, *The First Indochina War, French and American Policy 1945–1954*, London, 1975, p. 16; citing B. Fall, *Street Without Joy*, p. 26.
29. Decisions of the People's Congress, 16 August 1945, in A.W. Cameron (Ed.), *Viet-Nam Crisis: A Documentary History. Volume 1, 1940–1956*, New York, 1971, pp. 46–48; Dunn, *The First Vietnam War*, p. 16; R.B. Smith, *Viet-Nam and the West*, London, 1968, p. 111.
30. Dunn, *The First Vietnam War*, p. 17–18; Saville, *The Politics of Continuity*, p. 178.
31. S. Tonnesson, 'Filling The Vacuum: 1945 in French Indochina, the Netherlands East Indies and British Malaya', in Antlov and Tonnesson (Eds.), *Imperial Policy and Southeast Asian Nationalism 1930–1957*, pp. 123–125.
32. TNA, CAB 121/741, Minute by Mountbatten, 9 August 1945.
33. TNA, WO 203/5642, Sweet-Escott, no. 7/16/45, 13 August 1945, in A.J. Stockwell (Ed.), *British Documents on the End of Empire, Series B, Volume 3: Malaya: Part 1: The Malayan Union Experiment 1942–1948*, London, 1995, p. 110.
34. Tonnesson, 'Filling The Vacuum: 1945 in French Indochina, the Netherlands East Indies and British Malaya', pp. 123–125.
35. Tonnesson, *The Vietnamese Revolution of 1945*, p. 364.
36. Patti, *Why Vietnam?*, p. 453; Dunn, *The First Vietnam War*, p. 22; Bills, *Empire and the Cold War*, p. 89.
37. Spector, *Advice and Support*, p. 56; J. Sainteny, *Ho Chi Minh and His Vietnam: A Personal Memoir*, Translated by H. Briffault, Chicago, 1972, p. 47.
38. Declaration of the Independence of the Republic of Vietnam, 2 September 1945, in A.B. Cole (Ed.), *Conflict In Indochina and International Repercussions: A Documentary History, 1945–1955*, New York, 1956, pp. 19–21.
39. Dunn, *The First Vietnam War*, p. 123.
40. K. Nitz, 'Independence without Nationalists? The Japanese and Vietnamese Nationalism during the Japanese period 1940–5', *Journal of Southeast Asian Studies*, vol. 15, no. 1, March 1984, p. 131.

41. Dunn, *The First Vietnam War*, pp. 23, 135–136.
42. Neville, *Britain in Vietnam*, pp. xv, 76.
43. Dunn, *The First Vietnam War*, pp. 23, 123, 136.
44. Neville, *Britain in Vietnam*, pp. 76–78.
45. L.C. Gardner, *Approaching Vietnam: From World War Two Through Dienbienphu*, London, 1988, p. 73.
46. Papers of Admiral Lord Louis Mountbatten Earl of Burma, Mountbatten Archive, University of Southampton [hereafter MB], 1/C10/3, Mountbatten to D'Argenlieu, 1 September 1945.
47. TNA, CAB 122/512, Dening to Foreign Office, 10 September 1945.
48. TNA, FO 371/46308/F6353/11/61, Government of India External Affairs Department to Secretary of State for India, no. 7670, 1 September 1945.
49. Tonnesson, 'Filling The Vacuum: 1945 in French Indochina, the Netherlands East Indies and British Malaya', pp. 122, 143; G.R. Hess, *The United States' Emergence as a Southeast Asian Power, 1940–1950*, New York, 1987, p. 164.
50. Buttinger, *Vietnam*, p. 311.
51. D.G. Marr, 'Vietnam 1945: Some Questions', *Vietnam Forum*, vol. 6, summer 1985, p. 171.
52. Balfour to Bevin, AN2597/4/45, 25 August 1945, in R.D. Crockatt (Ed.), *British Documents on Foreign Affairs: Reports and Papers from the Foreign Office Confidential Print: Series C, North America, Part 3: Volume 5: January 1945–December 1945*, University Publications of America, 1999, pp. 276–279; TNA, FO 371/46308/F6353/11/61, Secretary of State for India to the Government of India External Affairs Department, no. 19530, 3 September 1945.
53. N. Tarling, *Britain, Southeast Asia and the Onset of the Cold War 1945–1950*, Cambridge, 1998, pp. 56, 79; Dunn, *The First Vietnam War*, pp. 159–160.
54. Duncanson, 'General Gracey and the Vietminh', p. 294, citing Article 43, under Section III ('Military Authority over the Territory of the Hostile State') – *Final Act of the Second Peace Conference Held at The Hague in 1907*, London, 1914, p. 51.
55. Dunn, *The First Vietnam War*, pp. 159–160.
56. Donnison, *British Military Administration in the Far East 1943–1946*, pp. 408–409.
57. TNA, CAB 120/708, Mountbatten to Cabinet Office, SEAC(RL)91, 24 September 1945.
58. TNA, WO 203/5644, Saigon Control Commission to Mountbatten, 21 September 1945.
59. Duncanson, 'General Gracey and the Vietminh', p. 294, citing Article 43, under Section III ('Military Authority over the Territory of the Hostile State') – *Final Act of the Second Peace Conference Held at The Hague in 1907*, London, 1914, p. 51.
60. See the introduction.
61. TNA, CAB 120/708, Mountbatten to Cabinet Office, SEAC(RL)91, 24 September 1945.
62. TNA, WO 203/2173, Mountbatten to Gracey, NGS106, 24 September 1945.
63. TNA, WO 203/2173, Headquarters Southeast Asia 31st Miscellaneous Meeting, 28 September 1945; see Chapter 3.

64. TNA, WO 203/5644, Supreme Allied Commander 286th Meeting, 28 September 1945.
65. Dunn, *The First Vietnam War*, p. 233.
66. TNA, WO 203/2173, Brain to Mountbatten, SGN.COS 40, 1 October 1945.
67. Dunn, *The First Vietnam War*, p. 241; P. Ziegler, *Mountbatten*, Glasgow, 1985, p. 332.
68. MB 1/C91, Mountbatten to Driberg, SC5/1988/D, 4 October 1945.
69. TNA, PREM 8/63, Hollis to Attlee, 28 September 1945.
70. TNA, WO 203/2173, Monitoring Flash 445, 5 October 1945.
71. TNA, PREM 8/63, DO(45) 7th Meeting 18(Revise)(Secret), 'Situation in Indo-China', Defence Committee, 5 October 1945, Annex 1, JP(45)258(Final).
72. TNA, CAB 80/97, COS(45)598 1(0) 'Reoccupation of Dutch East Indies' 3 October 1945, Foreign Office to Secretary COS.
73. TNA, CAB 80/97, COS(45)589(0), Memorandum by COS Committee, 25 September 1945.
74. Bills, *Empire and the Cold War*, p. 126.
75. TNA, PREM 8/169, Memorandum by Sterndale Bennett, 9 October 1945, in Stockwell (Ed.), *British Documents on the End of Empire, Series B, Volume 3: Malaya: Part 1*, p. 169.
76. P. Ziegler (Ed.), *The Personal Diaries of Admiral, the Lord Louis Mountbatten, Supreme Commander Southeast Asia 1943–1946*, London, 1988, p. 258.
77. Saville, *The Politics of Continuity*, p. 191.
78. MB 1/C113/2, Mountbatten to Gracey, SC5/2089/G, 13 October 1945.
79. TNA, CAB 120/708, Supreme Allied Commander Southeast Asia to Cabinet Office, SEACOS513, 12 October 1945.
80. G. Hughes, 'A "Post-war" War: The British Occupation of French-Indochina, September 1945–March 1946', *Small Wars & Insurgencies*, vol. 17, no. 3, 2006, pp. 263, 272.
81. Rosie, *The British in Vietnam*, pp. 57–86; Lawrence, *Assuming The Burden*, pp. 105, 111; Hughes, 'A "Post-war" War: The British Occupation of French-Indochina, September 1945–March 1946', pp. 263–286; C. Bayly and T. Harper, *Forgotten Wars: The End of Britain's Asian Empire*, London, 2008, pp. 145–158.
82. TNA, WO 162/277, Far East Army and Navy Casualties, 4th Edition, Table 1, French Indo-China, 10 October 1945–27 January 1946.
83. Gracey 4/8, Saigon Control Commission Political Report, 13 September–9 October 1945.
84. See introduction for a list of the charges against Gracey.
85. Gracey 4/12, Gracey to Slim, 5 November 1945.
86. TNA, WO 203/2173, Headquarters Southeast Asia 31st Miscellaneous Meeting, 28 September 1945; MB 1/C91, Mountbatten to Driberg, SC5/1988/D, 4 October 1945.
87. MB 1/C10, Mountbatten to D'Argenlieu, Mokan 128, 8 November 1945.
88. Dennis, *Troubled Days of Peace*, p. 20; Patti, *Why Vietnam?* pp. 58, 67, 102, 125–129; TNA, WO 203/5440, Meiklereid to Dening, SGN.FO16, 25 October 1945.
89. Neville, *Britain in Vietnam*, pp. 90–93.

90. W.C. Gibbons, *The U.S. Government and the Vietnam War, Part 1: 1945–1960*, Princeton, 1986, p. 25.
91. MB 1/C113/2, Mountbatten to Gracey, SC5/2539/G, 4 December 1945.
92. TNA, Colonial Office 968/107/2, G. Hall to Sir H. Moore, 19 November 1945.
93. MB 1/C113/2, Mountbatten to Gracey, SC5/2539/G, 4 December 1945.
94. MB 1/C91, Mountbatten to Driberg, 17 December 1945.
95. Dunn, *The First Vietnam War*, p. 329; Saville, *The Politics of Continuity*, p. 197.
96. MB 1/C130/6, Dening to Foreign Office, no. 98, 14 January 1946.
97. MB 1/C130/10, Gibson to Captain Brockman, Singmo.62, 18 January 1946.
98. Nehru to the All India States People's Conference, 1 January 1946, in Cole (Ed.), *Conflict In Indochina and International Repercussions*, p. 50.
99. MB 1/C130/15, Governor General New Delhi to Secretary of State for India, no. 650, 22 January 1946.
100. MB 1/C10/15, Mountbatten to D'Argenlieu, SC6H/57/A, 24 January 1946.
101. MB 1/C113, Mountbatten to Gracey, SC6/1303/G, 17 July 1946; MB 1/C130, Mountbatten to Sir Alan Lascelles, SCH6/262/L, 18 March 1946.
102. TNA, FO 800/461/FE/46/9, Dening to Bevin, no. 46, 29 January 1946.
103. TNA, CAB 129/1, CP(45)112, Memorandum by Lord Keynes, 13 August 1945, in R. Hyam (Ed.), *British Documents on the End of Empire, Series A, Volume 2: The Labour Government and the End of Empire 1945–1951: Part 2: Economics and International Relations*, London, 1991, pp. 1–5; see Chapter 4.
104. R.F. Holland, 'The Imperial Factor in British Strategies From Attlee to Macmillan 1945–63', *Journal of Imperial and Commonwealth History*, vol. 12, January 1984, pp. 166, 183.
105. TNA, WO 203/5476, Sayers to Rayner, Rear 5527, 13 October 1945.
106. *Hansard House of Commons Parliamentary Debates*, vol. 414, cols. 2149–2150, 24 October 1945.
107. TNA, FO 800/461/FE/46/10, Bevin to Dening, no. 81, 29 January 1949.
108. Dunn, *The First Vietnam War*, pp. 342–343.
109. B. Fall, *The Two Vietnams*, London, 1963, p. 3.
110. MB 1/C91, Mountbatten to Driberg, autumn 1945, (undated).
111. Extract from the Report to the Combined Chiefs of Staff by the Supreme Allied Commander, Southeast Asia, 30 June 1947, in *Documents Relating to British Involvement in the Indo-China Conflict 1945–1965*, pp. 47–52.
112. Mountbatten to Jinnah, 6 August 1947, in Zaidi (Ed.), *Quaid-I-Azam Mohammed Ali Jinnah Papers, First Series, Volume IV, Pakistan at Last, 26 July–14 August 1947*, p. 271.

3 The Sideshow: Cambodia 1945

1. Tonnesson, *The Vietnamese Revolution of 1945*, pp. 362–365.
2. D. Chandler, *A History of Cambodia*, Washington D.C., 1999, p. 137.
3. Kiernan, *How Pol Pot Came to Power*, pp. 41, 46, 49.
4. Burns, *Roosevelt*, pp. 108–109.
5. Kiernan, *How Pol Pot Came to Power*, pp. 41, 46, 49.
6. Chandler, *A History of Cambodia*, p. 81.

7. Lancaster, *The Emancipation of French Indochina*, pp. 94–95.
8. A. Suhrke 'Irredentism Contained: The Thai-Muslim Case', *Comparative Politics*, vol. 7, no. 2, January 1975, p. 195; T.O. Smith, 'Lord Killearn and British Diplomacy Regarding French Indo-Chinese Rice Supplies, 1946–1948', *History*, vol. 96, no. 324, 2011, pp. 482–484; for a detailed discussion of the resolution of the Cambodian–Thai border dispute see Smith, 'Britain and Cambodia, September 1945–November 1946: A Reappraisal', pp. 78–87; and for a detailed discussion of Anglo-Thai relations and the post-war peace process see Tarling, *Britain, Southeast Asia and the onset of the Cold War 1945–1950*, pp. 108–128.
9. Chandler, *A History of Cambodia*, p. 170.
10. M. Vickery, *Kampuchea: Politics, Economics and Society*, London, 1986, p. 8; Chandler, *A History of Cambodia*, p. 171.
11. Centre for the Archives of France Overseas, Aix en Provence [hereafter CAOM], Government General of Indo-China files, GGI/65498, 'Etudes sur les movements rebelles au Cambodge 1942–1952', Annnex, 'Le Nationalisme Khmer', p. 3.
12. Chandler, *A History of Cambodia*, p. 171.
13. Tonnesson, *The Vietnamese Revolution of 1945*, p. 362.
14. V.M. Reddi, *A History of the Cambodian Independence Movement 1863–1955*, Triupati, 1973, p. 108.
15. Kiernan, *How Pol Pot Came to Power*, p. 51.
16. CAOM, Government General of Indo-China files, GGI/65498, 'Etudes sur les movements rebelles au Cambodge 1942–1952', Annnex, 'Le Nationalisme Khmer', pp. 19–21.
17. Chandler, *A History of Cambodia*, p. 171.
18. TNA, WO 172/7009, Secret War Diary Headquarters Allied Land Forces Phnom Penh, ALF/PP/23/G, HQ 20th Division 9–31 October 1945, 4 November, Lt.-Col. Commanding Allied Force; WO 208/636, no. 14569, 12 November 1945; CAOM, Government General of Indo-China files, GGI/65498, 'Etudes sur les movements rebelles au Cambodge 1942–1952', Annnex, 'Le Nationalisme Khmer', pp. 12–13.
19. TNA, WO 203/2151, Gracey to Mountbatten, Signal 99, COS 29, 25 September 1945.
20. TNA, WO 203/5644, Supreme Allied Commander 31st Miscellaneous Meeting Minutes, 28 September 1945.
21. Neville, *Britain in Vietnam*, p. 107.
22. For a full discussion of the current historiography, see the introduction.
23. TNA, WO 203/5644, Supreme Allied Commander 31st Miscellaneous Meeting Minutes, 28 September 1945.
24. TNA, WO 203/5644, Supreme Allied Commander 286th Meeting, 28 September 1945.
25. TNA, FO 371/46323/F6043/52/61, Balfour to Foreign Office, no. 5903, 28 August 1945.
26. TNA, WO 203/5644, Supreme Allied Commander 286th Meeting, 28 September 1945.
27. Reddi, *A History of the Cambodian Independence Movement 1863–1955*, pp. 108–111; Lancaster, *The Emancipation of French Indochina*, pp. 94, 111.
28. TNA, FO 371/46323/F6043/52/61, Minute by A.C.S. Adams, 31 August 1945.

29. TNA, WO 106/4820, FE(0)(45)19, 1 September 1945, Treatment of the boundary between Siam and Indo-China in the proposed Siamese settlement.
30. TNA, CAB 21/1950, Minute by E.A. Armstrong, 6 September 1945.
31. TNA, WO 203/894, Headquarters Supreme Allied Commander SEAC Joint Logistical Planning Committee, 1 September 1945.
32. See previous chapter.
33. TNA, CAB 121/741, Dening to Foreign Office, no. 543, 27 September 1945.
34. TNA, CAB 21/1950, Cabinet Far Eastern Committee, FE(0)(45)31, Minute by E.A. Armstrong, 21 September 1945.
35. N. Sihanouk, *Souvenirs Doux et Amers*, Paris, 1981, pp. 113–114.
36. TNA, WO 172/7009, Secret War Diary Headquarters Allied Land Forces Phnom Penh, ALF/PP/23/G, HQ 20th Division 9–31 October 1945, 4 November, Lt.-Colonel Commanding Allied Force.
37. TNA, WO 172/7009, Allied Land Forces Phnom Penh, Instruction no. 1, 10 October 1945.
38. TNA, WO 203/2178, Gracey to CGS, no. 02210, 16 October 1945.
39. D.P. Marston, *Phoenix from the Ashes: The Indian Army in the Burma Campaign*, London, 2003, p. 251; TNA, WO 172/7009, Allied Land Forces Phnom Penh, Instruction no. 1, 10 October 1945.
40. Meeting of the CCS, 24 July 1945, in *FRUS, The Conference at Berlin 1945 (The Potsdam Conference) Volume 2*, p. 377; TNA, WO 203/2173, HQSEA 31st Miscellaneous Meeting, 28 September 1945; MB 1/C10/11, Mountbatten to D'Argenlieu, Mokan 128, 8 November 1945; Gracey 4/13, Mountbatten to Gracey, SC5/2205/G, 31 October 1945.
41. TNA, WO 172/7009, Secret War Diary Headquarters Allied Land Forces Phnom Penh, ALF/PP/23/G, HQ 20th Division 9–31 October 1945, 4 November, Lt.-Colonel Commanding Allied Force.
42. TNA, WO 172/7009, Secret War Diary Headquarters Allied Land Forces Phnom Penh, ALF/PP/23/G, HQ 20th Division, Appendix, no. J2, 12 October 1945.
43. Neville, *Britain in Vietnam*, p. 106.
44. TNA, WO 172/7009, Secret War Diary Headquarters Allied Land Forces Phnom Penh, ALF/PP/23/G, HQ 20th Division 9–31 October 1945, 4 November, Lt.-Colonel Commanding Allied Force.
45. TNA, WO 172/7009, Secret War Diary Headquarters Allied Land Forces Phnom Penh, ALF/PP/23/G, HQ 20th Division, Appendix, no. J3, 12 October 1945.
46. TNA, WO 172/7009, Secret War Diary Headquarters Allied Land Forces Phnom Penh, ALF/PP/23/G, HQ 20th Division, Appendix, no. J4, 13 October 1945.
47. N. Tarling, 'Some Rather Nebulous Capacity: Lord Killearn's Appointment in Southeast Asia', *Modern Asian Studies*, vol. 20, no. 3, 1986, pp. 559–560.
48. Gracey 4/8, Gracey to the Recorder SEAC, no. 1/DDG, 3 October 1946.
49. Neville, *Britain in Vietnam*, p. 106; TNA, WO 203/2178, Gracey to CGS, no. 02210, 16 October 1945.
50. TNA, WO 172/7009, Secret War Diary Headquarters Allied Land Forces Phnom Penh, ALF/PP/23/G, HQ 20th Division 9–31 October 1945, 4 November, Lt.-Colonel Commanding Allied Force.

51. TNA, Air Ministry [hereafter AIR], 40/1451, Sum 172, 22 October 1945.
52. Report by Mountbatten to CGS, 30 June 1947, in *Documents Relating to British Involvement in the Indochina Conflict 1945–65*, pp. 47–52.
53. CAOM, Government General of Indo-China Files, GGI/65498, 'Etudes sur les movements rebelles au Cambodge 1942–1952', Annnex, 'Le Nationalisme Khmer', pp. 1–35.
54. TNA, WO 172/7009, Secret War Diary Headquarters Allied Land Forces Phnom Penh, ALF/PP/23/G, HQ 20th Division, ALF/PP/1/G, 26 October 1945.
55. Mullaly, *Bugle and Kuri*, p. 401.
56. TNA, WO 172/7009, Secret War Diary Headquarters Allied Land Forces Phnom Penh, ALF/PP/23/G, HQ 20th Division, ALF/PP/1/G, 26 October 1945.
57. TNA, WO 172/7009, Secret War Diary Headquarters Allied Land Forces Phnom Penh, ALF/PP/23/G, HQ 20th Division ALF Phnom Penh to 20th Indian Division, 31 October 1945.
58. TNA, WO 172/7009, Secret War Diary Headquarters Allied Land Forces Phnom Penh, ALF/PP/23/G, 1–30 November Report, 3 December 1945.
59. TNA, WO 172/7009, Secret War Diary Headquarters Allied Land Forces Phnom Penh, ALF/PP/23/G, 1–31 December Report, 4 January 1946.
60. TNA, CAB 121/742, Southeast Asia Chiefs of Staff to COS, no. 560, 2 December 1945.
61. TNA, WO 203/4432, Gracey to Headquarters Supreme Allied Commander Southeast Asia, COS 47, 15 December 1945.
62. TNA, WO 203/ 2463, Evans to Pyman, no. 0/220, 20 December 1945.
63. TNA, WO 203/2463, Headquarters Supreme Allied Commander Southeast Asia Commission 1 Saigon to Headquarters Southeast Asia, no. COS/168, 28 December 1945.
64. TNA, WO 203/2463, Gracey to Evans, no. COS184, 7 January 1946.
65. TNA, WO 203/2463, Evans to Gracey, no. 03189, 9 January 1946.
66. TNA, CAB 121/742, COS to Supreme Allied Commander Southeast Asia, COSSEA 448, 24 December 1945; TNA, CAB 121/742, Supreme Allied Commander Southeast Asia to Colonial Office for COS, SEACOS 611, 11 January 1946; TNA, WO 203/4455, COS to Mountbatten, COSSEA 448, 30 December 1945.
67. TNA, CAB 121/742, Mountbatten to COS, SEACOS 626, 26 January 1946.
68. TNA, CAB 121/742, JIC(46)4(0), 6 January 1946, Annex 14(45).
69. TNA, CAB 21/1950, Dening to Foreign Office, no. 353, 3 March 1946.
70. TNA, CAB 21/1950, Dening to Foreign Office, no. 354, 3 March 1946.
71. TNA, CAB 21/1950, Meiklereid to Foreign Office, no. 66, 16 March 1946; TNA, CAB 21/1950, Meiklereid to Foreign Office, no. 68, 17 March 1946.
72. TNA, CAB 21/1950, Foreign Office to Bangkok, no. 208, 9 March 1946; TNA, CAB 21/1950, Thompson to Killearn, no. 296, 26 March 1946.
73. TNA, CAB 21/1950, Foreign Office to Killearn, no. 56, 28 March 1946.
74. TNA, CAB 21/1950, Meiklereid to Foreign Office, no. 66, 16 March 1946.
75. The papers of Sir Miles Lampson, the Middle East Centre Archive, St Anthony's College, University of Oxford [hereafter Lampson], 6/2, p. 97, 26 March 1946.
76. Lampson 6/2, p. 125, 1 May 1946.

77. Lampson 6/3, p. 207, 12 August 1946; Lampson 6/3, pp. 211–212, 15 August 1946.
78. TNA, CAB 21/1951, Dominions Office to Australia, Canada, New Zealand, South Africa, no. 544, 28 May 1946.
79. Lampson 6/2, pp. 146–147, 30 May 1946.
80. TNA, CAB 21/1951, Dominions Office to Australia, Canada, New Zealand, South Africa, no. 631, 5 June 1946.
81. TNA, CAB 21/1951, Dominions Office to Australia, Canada, New Zealand, South Africa, no. 632, 5 June 1946.
82. TNA, CAB 21/1951, Dominions Office to Australia, Canada, New Zealand, South Africa, no. 362, 17 August 1946.
83. TNA, CAB 21/1951, Dominions Office to Australia, Canada, New Zealand, South Africa, no. 850, 13 September 1946; CAB 21/1951, Dominions Office to Australia, Canada, New Zealand, South Africa, no. 362, 17 August 1946.
84. TNA, CAB 21/1951, Dominions Office to Australia, Canada, New Zealand, South Africa, no. 850, 13 September 1946.
85. TNA, CAB 21/1951, Meiklereid to Bangkok, no. 100, 26 August 1946.
86. TNA, CAB 21/1951, Report of H.J.K. Toms, Straits Steamship C. Ltd. visit to Thailand 15–26 August 1946, circulated at Cabinet 3 October 1946.
87. TNA, CAB 119/201, Foreign Office to COS, COS 1346/6, 3 November 1946.
88. TNA, CAB 119/201, COS to Supreme Allied Commander Southeast Asia, COSSEA 586, 9 November 1946.
89. TNA, CAB 119/201, Stopford to COS, SEACOS 784, 12 November 1946.
90. TNA CAB 119/201, COS 14 63/6, 22 December 1946, Annex 1 letter from the Foreign Office, F16703/10/40, 21 November 1946; TNA, CAB 119/201, COS 14 63/6, 22 December 1946, Annex 2, Foreign Office to COS, 22 November 1946; TNA, CAB 119/201, COS 14 63/6, 22 December 1946, Annex 3, Draft to Supreme Allied Commander Southeast Asia (undated), agreed COS(46)171, 25 November 1946; TNA, CAB 119/201, Stopford to COS, SEACOS 793, 25 November 1946.
91. TNA, CAB 121/742, Meiklereid to Foreign Office, no. 16, 8 January 1947.
92. C.E. Goscha, *Thailand and the Southeast Asian Networks of the Vietnamese Revolution, 1885–1954*, Richmond, 1999, pp. 201–203.
93. Smith, 'Lord Killearn and British Diplomacy Regarding French Indo-Chinese Rice Supplies, 1946–1948', p. 485.
94. For a detailed discussion of British foreign policy towards French Indo-China during the formative years of the Vietminh's guerrilla warfare offensive (1946–1950), see Smith, *Britain and the Origins of the Vietnam War*; and for a useful volume of collected essays concerning the wider geo-historical interplay of decolonisation, the Cold War and the history of Southeast Asia, see C.E. Goscha and C.F. Ostermann (Eds.), *Connecting Histories: Decolonization and the Cold War in Southeast Asia, 1945–1962*, Stanford, 2009.

4 The Enforcement: Indo-China 1945–1946

1. Duncanson, 'General Gracey and the Vietminh', p. 294, citing Article 43, under Section III ('Military Authority over the Territory of the Hostile State') – *Final Act of the Second Peace Conference Held at The Hague in 1907*, London, 1914, p. 51.

2. Bayly and Harper, *Forgotten Wars*, pp. 60–190.
3. TNA, WO 203/1934, Inter-service Topographical Department, 26 August 1945, Appendix H to FPI 1st D(SEAC)/D/SP/59, Special Report on French Indo-China South of Latitude 16 Degrees North, 'Summary of Forces to be moved to Saigon'.
4. Neville, *Britain in Vietnam*, p. 76.
5. *The Pentagon Papers, The Defense Department History of United States Decision Making on Vietnam*, vol. 1, Gravel Edition, Boston, 1971, pp. 17–18; G.C. Herring, 'The Truman Administration and the Restoration of French Sovereignty in Indochina', *Diplomatic History*, vol. 1, no. 2 (Spring 1977), p. 114; M.A. Lawrence, 'Transnational Coalition Building The Making of the Cold War in Indochina', *Diplomatic History*, vol. 26, no. 3 (Summer 2002), p. 472; Lawrence, *Assuming the Burden*, pp. 112–113, 309. For a detailed discussion concerning the supply of British military aid to French Indo-China 1945–7, see T.O. Smith, 'Resurrecting the French Empire: British Military Aid to Vietnam 1945–7', *University of Sussex Journal of Contemporary History*, vol. 11, 2007, pp. 1–13.
6. For a discussion concerning globalisation and the rise of the American economic empire, see T.O. Smith, 'Europe, Americanization and Globalization', Review Article, *European History Quarterly*, vol. 37, no. 2, 2007, pp. 301–309.
7. TNA, Board of Trade [hereafter BT] 64/2864, War Office to Supreme Allied Commander Southeast Asia, 74087 cipher CA17, 15 September 1945; TNA, WO 203/4117, Leclerc to Brigadier Montague-Jones Movements and Transports Department, no. 180/ECO/LI (Undated).
8. TNA, BT 64/2864, Sanders to Harden, 13 September 1945; TNA, BT 64/2864, Harden to Sanders, 28 September 1945.
9. TNA, PREM 8/63, DO(45) 7th Meeting 18(Revise)(Secret), 5 October 1945.
10. TNA, PREM 8/63, Mountbatten to Cabinet and JSM, SEACOS 489, 24 September 1945.
11. Dunn, *The First Vietnam War*, p. 241; Ziegler, *Mountbatten*, p. 332; TNA, PREM 8/63, Mountbatten to Cabinet and JSM, SEACOS 489, 24 September 1945.
12. Dunn, *The First Vietnam War*, p. 233.
13. TNA, WO 203/2178, Lt.-Colonel Dawson, no. 79006/SD4, 28 August 1945.
14. TNA, WO 203/2235, Supreme Allied Commander Southeast Asia to Commander in Chief India, SAC 21266, 8 September 1945.
15. Hess, *The United States' Emergence of a Southeast Asian Power 1940–1950*, pp. 149–150, 162–163.
16. TNA, PREM 8/63, SACSEA to Cabinet and JSM, SEACOS 490, 24 September 1945.
17. TNA, PREM 8/63, Hollis to Attlee, 28 September 1945.
18. Saville, *The Politics of Continuity*, p. 195; TNA, PREM 8/63, Supreme Allied Commander Southeast Asia to Cabinet and JSM, SEACOS 489, 24 September 1945.
19. TNA, PREM 8/63, Hollis to Attlee, 28 September 1945.
20. TNA, PREM 8/63, 'R.B.' to Hollis, 29 September 1945.
21. TNA, FO 371/46309/F8070/11/G61, Hollis to Attlee, 4 October 1945; for the counter argument that the violence in Saigon did place a maximum number on British troop deployments to French Indo-China, see D.G. Marr, *Vietnam 1945: The Quest For Power*, Berkley, 1995, p. 542.

22. TNA, PREM 8/63, DO(45) 7th Meeting 18(Revise)(Secret), 'Situation in Indo-China', Defence Committee, 5 October 1945; TNA, PREM 8/63, DO(45) 7th Meeting 18(Revise)(Secret), 'Situation in Indo-China', Defence Committee, 5 October 1945, Annex 1, JP(45)258(Final).
23. TNA, PREM 8/63, DO(45) 7th Meeting 18(Revise)(Secret), 5 October 1945, Enclosure to Annex 1.
24. TNA, PREM 8/63, DO(45) 7th Meeting 18(Revise)(Secret), 5 October 1945, Enclosure to Annex 1; TNA, CAB 80/97, COS(45)598 1(0) 'Reoccupation of Dutch East Indies' 3 October 1945, Foreign Office to Secretary COS.
25. TNA, CAB 80/97 COS(45)607(0), 'Dutch East Indies and French Indo-China', 9 October 1945, Annex, DO OCC/2B, Slim to Alanbrooke, 6 October 1945.
26. TNA, CAB 80/97, COS(45)619(0), 'French Indo-China' Memorandum by the War Office, 13 October 1945, Annex 1, Cabinet to Supreme Allied Commander Southeast Asia.
27. *Hansard*, vol. 414, cols. 2149–2150, 24 October 1945.
28. For a full discussion of British liberation duties in the Dutch East Indies, see R. McMillan, *The British Occupation of Indonesia 1945–1946: Britain, the Netherlands and the Indonesian Revolution*, London, 2005.
29. TNA, CAB 121/742, Mountbatten to COS and JSM, SEACOS 555, 27 November 1945.
30. TNA, CAB 121/742, COS(45)333, Memorandum by the First Sea Lord, 24 December 1945.
31. TNA, WO 203/2236, Allied Land Forces Southeast Asia to ARM India, Major Weaver, no. 2131SD2, December 1945.
32. TNA, WO 203/2236, Troopers to East Africa, no. 78730LM3, 10 October 1945.
33. Meeting of the CCS, 24 July 1945, in *FRUS, The Conference at Berlin 1945 (The Potsdam Conference), Volume 2*, p. 377.
34. TNA, FO 371/46304/F1269/11/61G, Sterndale Bennett to Dening, 14 April 1945; TNA, CAB 81/46, PHP(45)29(0) Final, *British Documents on the End of Empire, Series A, Volume 1*: in S.R. Ashton, and S.E. Stockwell, (Eds.), *Imperial Policy and Colonial Practice 1925–1945: Part 1: Metropolitan Reorganisation, Defence and International Relations, Political Change and Constitutional Reform*, London, 1996, pp. 231–244.
35. TNA, WO 203/4292, War Office to Commander in Chief India and Supreme Allied Commander Southeast Asia, no. 81090Q(AE), 2 October 1945.
36. TNA, WO 203/2236, Headquarters Allied Land Forces Southeast Asia to Troopers, Major Weaver, tel. 146 (undated); TNA, WO 203/2236, Troopers to Headquarters Allied Land Forces Southeast Asia, no. 89364/WSC, 14 December 1945.
37. TNA, WO 203/2236 Allied Land Forces to Supreme Allied Commander Southeast Asia, Major Weaver, no. 2120SD2, 24 December 1945.
38. TNA, WO 203/2599 Allied Land Forces to CG USF IBT, Major Weaver, tel. 161, no. 31512/SD2 (undated).
39. For a discussion of Britain's subsequent Cold War debate over whether or not to supply military aid to the French armed forces in Indo-China see T.O. Smith, 'Protecting the British Empire: the Dilemma of Sending Military Aid to French Indo-China 1948–1950', *Historical Yearbook*, the Nicolae Iorga History Institute of the Romanian Academy, vol. 9, 2012, pp. 123–37.

40. TNA, WO 203/6066, Allied Land Forces Southeast Asia to Supreme Allied Commander Southeast Asia, Report of GSO OPS1, I/SM to French Indo-China Saigon 6–9 March 1946, Summary Report, no. 10410/G(0)1, 11 March 1946.
41. TNA, WO 203/6419, Browning to Maunsell, SAC 7486, 22 February 1946.
42. TNA, WO 203/6419, War Office to Allied Land Forces Southeast Asia, 99235Q(OPS)1, 27 February 1946.
43. TNA, WO 203/4292, D of ST to PSTO Middle East, DST France, SSTO Southern France, 21 December 1945, ALFSEA to War Office, 6 December 1945.
44. TNA, CAB 21/1950, Halifax to Foreign Office for the Cabinet, no. 464, 20 January 1946.
45. TNA, CAB 119/200, JSM to Cabinet, JSM 175, 26 January 1946.
46. TNA, CAB 119/205, COS(46) 14th Meeting, 28 January 1946.
47. TNA, CAB 121/742, Annex to JP(46)30(Final), 19 February 1946, COS com Joint Planning Staff, 'Responsibility for French Indo-China', draft telegram Cabinet to JSM, sent 20 February 1946.
48. TNA, CAB 121/742, COS(46) 31st Meeting, 25 February 1946.
49. TNA, CAB 121/742, COS to Mountbatten, COSSEA 480, 1 March 1946.
50. TNA, WO 203/4933, Sir Keith Park, Supreme Allied Commander 325th Meeting, 22 March 1946.
51. TNA, CAB 121/742, COS to Supreme Allied Commander, COSSEA 506, 29 March 1946.
52. TNA, WO 203/4924, Chiang Kai-Shek to Mountbatten, 28 August 1945.
53. MB 1/C53/51, Mountbatten to Chiang Kai-Shek, SC(?)/1763/C, 1 September 1945.
54. TNA, CAB 21/1950, Cabinet 68/6th meeting, Conclusions of the working party of the Far Eastern Committee, 4 September 1945.
55. TNA, BT 64/2864, Kenrick to Fisher, 3 August 1945.
56. TNA, BT 64/2864, Kenrick to Fisher, 8 September 1945; TNA, BT 64/2864, Harden to Sanders, 28 September 1945.
57. TNA, BT 64/2864, Kenrick to Fisher, 8 September 1945.
58. TNA, BT 64/2864, War Office to Mountbatten, 74087 cypher CA17, 15 September 1945.
59. TNA, WO 203/4117, Leclerc to Brigadier Montague-Jones, no. 180/ECO/LI (Undated).
60. Duncanson, 'General Gracey and the Vietminh', p. 294, citing Article 43, under Section III ('Military Authority over the Territory of the Hostile State') – *Final Act of the Second Peace Conference Held at The Hague in 1907*, London, 1914, p. 51.
61. TNA, WO 203/5476, Mountbatten to Saigon Control Commission, NGS 213, 9 October 1945.
62. TNA, AIR 23/2376, Headquarters Supreme Allied Commander Southeast Asia to Air Attaché Chungking, 15 October 1945.
63. TNA, CAB 121/74, Brain to Foreign Office, no. 688, 1 November 1945.
64. TNA, WO 172/1789, Gracey to Mountbatten, SGN. 241, COS 67, 26 October 1945.
65. TNA, WO 172/7009, Secret War Diary Headquarters Allied Land Forces Phnom Penh, ALF/PP/23/G, HQ 20th Division, ALF/PP/1/G, 26 October

1945; Gracey 4/8, Gracey to the Recorder, SEAC, London, no. 1/DDG, 3 October 1946.
66. TNA, FO 371/46309/F9668/11/61, SLAO (Far East)(45)109, 1 November 1945, Cabinet Committee On Supply Questions in Liberated and Conquered Areas Sub-Committee on the Far East, Minute by Kenrick; TNA, CAB 122/512, Saigon to Foreign Office, tel. 28, 22 December 1945.
67. TNA, WO 203/4432, Mountbatten to Supreme Allied Commander Southeast Asia Commission no. 1, ngs. 510, 15 December 1945.
68. TNA, CAB 122/512, Précis of Colonel Walker-Chapman's report on Indo-China, Autumn 1945.
69. TNA, CAB 121/742, JIC(46)4(0), 6 January 1946, Annex, JIC14(45).
70. TNA, WO 203/4432, 'Points discussed with General Gracey', Saigon, 5 January 1946.
71. TNA, WO 203/5440, Dening to Mountbatten, no. 7a, 7 January 1945.
72. TNA, FO 371/53957/F1393/8/61, Meiklereid to Foreign Office, no. 4, 7 January 1946.
73. TNA, CAB 121/742, Brain to Foreign Office, no, 688, 1 November 1945.
74. TNA, CAB 121/742, Meiklereid to Foreign Office, no. 25, 24 January 1946.
75. TNA, CAB 21/1950, Halifax to Foreign Office for the Cabinet, no. 464, 20 January 1946; TNA, CAB 119/205, COS(46) 14th Meeting, 28 January 1946.
76. TNA, CAB 121/742, Annex to JP(46)30(Final), 19 February 1946, COS com Joint Planning Staff, 'Responsibility for French Indo-China', draft telegram Cabinet to JSM, sent 20 February 1946.
77. TNA, CAB 121/742, Mountbatten to COS, SEACOS 627, 28 January 1946.
78. TNA, CAB 121/742, Meiklereid to Foreign Office, no. 25, 24 January 1946.
79. TNA, WO 203/6263, Brief for Mountbatten, Flag L, 28 February 1946.
80. TNA, WO 203/6263, Brief for Mountbatten, 28 February 1946.
81. TNA, CAB 121/ 742, Mountbatten to COS, SEACOS 662, 17 March 1946.
82. TNA, CAB 121/742, COS(46) 45th Meeting, 22 March 1946; TNA, CAB 121/742, COS(46)88, 23 March 1946, Foreign Office to Secretary COS Committee, 22 March 1946.
83. TNA, WO 203/4933, Sir Keith Park, Supreme Allied Commander 325th Meeting, 22 March 1946; TNA, CAB 121/742, COS to Supreme Allied Commander Southeast Asia, COSSEA 506, 29 March 1946.
84. TNA, PREM 8/211, part 2, WFS(46)19, 10 February 1946, Memorandum by the Minister for Food; TNA, PREM 8/211, part 1, CP(46)28, 29 January 1946, Memorandum by the Minister for Food, Appendix.
85. S.M. Rosen, *The Combined Food Boards of the Second World War*, New York, 1951, p. 253.
86. TNA, PREM 8/211, Part 2, WFS(46), 2nd Cabinet Meeting, 12 February 1946; *Hansard*, vol. 419, cols. 1360–1361, 21 February 1946. For a full discussion of Killearn's humanitarian mission and the continuing problems associated with Indo-Chinese rice supplies issues, see Smith, 'Lord Killearn and British Diplomacy Regarding French Indo-Chinese Rice Supplies, 1946–1948', pp. 477–489.
87. N. Tarling, 'Some Rather Nebulous Capacity: Lord Killearn's Appointment in Southeast Asia', pp. 559–600.

5 The Aftermath: Bengal and Kashmir 1946–1951

1. L.J. Butler, *Britain and Empire: Adjusting to a Post-Imperial World*, London, 2002, pp. 40–42, 71–72.
2. TNA, FO 800/461/FE/46/9, Dening to Bevin, no. 46, 29 January 1946; TNA, FO 800/461/FE/46/10, Bevin to Dening, no. 81, 29 January 1949.
3. S. Wolpert, *Shameful Flight: The Last Days of the British Empire In India*, Oxford, 2009, p. 188.
4. Mead, *Churchill's Lions*, p. 184.
5. TNA, CAB 129/1, CP(45)112, Memorandum by Lord Keynes, 13 August 1945, in Hyam (Ed.), *British Documents on the End of Empire, Series A, Volume 2: The Labour Government and the End of Empire 1945–1951: Part 2*, pp. 1–5.
6. Butler, *Britain and Empire*, pp. 64–67, 72–73.
7. A. Lamb, *Birth of a Tragedy: Kashmir 1947*, Hertingfordbury, 1994, p. 61.
8. Butler, *Britain and Empire*, p. 73.
9. Wolpert, *Shameful Flight*, p. 176. For a full discussion of the historiography concerning the number of Indians and Pakistanis killed in the political violence between the nations in 1947, see I. Talbot, 'The 1947 Partition of India', in D. Stone, (Ed.), *The Historiography of Genocide*, London, 2010, pp. 420–437.
10. Butler, *Britain and Empire*, p. 73.
11. Wolpert, *Shameful Flight*, pp. 173–175.
12. For a detailed discussion of many of the unique problems associated with Kashmir studies, see C. Zutshi, 'Whither Kashmir Studies?: A Review', *Modern Asian Studies*, vol. 46, no. 4, July 2012, pp. 1033–1047; and for a useful overview of British high-policy towards Kashmir 1947–1949, see R. Ankit, 'Great Britain and Kashmir 1947–49', *India Review*, vol. 12, no. 1, January 2013, pp. 20–40.
13. S. Raghavan, *War and Peace in Modern India: A Strategic History of the Nehru Years*, London, 2010, p. 170.
14. Wolpert, *Shameful Flight*, p. 179.
15. Mountbatten to Jinnah, 6 August 1947, in Zaidi (Ed.), *Quaid-I-Azam Mohammed Ali Jinnah Papers, First Series, Volume IV, Pakistan at Last, 26 July–14 August 1947*, p. 271.
16. Extract from the Report to the Combined Chiefs of Staff by the Supreme Allied Commander, Southeast Asia, 30 June 1947, in *Documents Relating to British Involvement in the Indo-China Conflict 1945–1965*, pp. 47–52.
17. Dunn, *The First Vietnam War*, pp. 164–166.
18. Mountbatten to Jinnah, 6 August 1947, in Zaidi (Ed.), *Quaid-I-Azam Mohammed Ali Jinnah Papers, First Series, Volume IV, Pakistan at Last, 26 July–14 August 1947*, p. 271.
19. Lamb, *Birth of a Tragedy*, p. 66.
20. Wolpert, *Shameful Flight*, pp. 183–184.
21. B. Cloughley, *A History of the Pakistan Army: Wars and Insurrections*, Oxford 2000, p. 13.
22. C. Dasgupta, *War and Diplomacy in Kashmir 1947–48*, London, 2002, pp. 18–19.
23. Wolpert, *Shameful Flight*, pp. 183–184; Lamb, *Birth of a Tragedy*, pp. 66–67, 69, 73, 79, 86, 104.

24. D. Lapierre and L. Collins, *Freedom at Midnight*, Noida, 1997, pp. 542–543.
25. Dasgupta, *War and Diplomacy in Kashmir 1947–48*, p. 52.
26. Cloughley, *A History of the Pakistan Army*, p. 13.
27. Lapierre and Collins, *Freedom at Midnight*, pp. 542–543.
28. Dasgupta, *War and Diplomacy in Kashmir 1947–48*, p. 44.
29. R.J. Moore, *Making the New Commonwealth*, Oxford, 1987, p. 52.
30. S.N. Prasad and D. Pal, *History of Operations in Jammu and Kashmir, 1947–48*, Dehra Dun, 2005, p. 27.
31. A. Campbell-Johnson, *Mission with Mountbatten*, London 1985, p. 241; P.S. Jha, *The Origins of a Dispute: Kashmir 1947*, London, 2003, p. 133.
32. Prasad and Pal, *History of Operations in Jammu and Kashmir*, p. 27.
33. Jha, *The Origins of a Dispute*, pp. 119, 124–125.
34. Moore, *Making the New Commonwealth*, p. 52.
35. Jha, *The Origins of a Dispute*, pp. 124–125.
36. J. Korbel, *Danger in Kashmir*, Princeton, 1954, p. 87.
37. Lord Ismay, *The Memoirs of General the Lord Ismay*, London, 1960, p. 444.
38. Jha, *The Origins of a Dispute*, p. 133.
39. P.P. Barua, *Gentlemen of the Raj: The Indian Army Officer Corps 1817–1949*, London, 2003, p. 133.
40. A. Jalal, *The State of Martial Rule: The origin's of Pakistan's political economy of defence*, Cambridge, 1990, p. 44.
41. Lamb, *Birth of a Tragedy*, p. 133.
42. A. Lamb, *Incomplete Partition: The Genesis of the Kashmir Dispute 1947–1948*, Hertingfordbury, 1997, p. 234.
43. Raghavan, *War and Peace in Modern India*, p. 109.
44. Prasad and Pal, *History of Operations in Jammu and Kashmir*, p. 27.
45. Lamb, *Birth of a Tragedy*, p. 134.
46. Barua, *Gentlemen of the Raj*, pp. 132–133.
47. Wolpert, *Shameful Flight*, p. 186.
48. Jalal, *The State of Martial Rule*, pp. 118–119.
49. Moore, *Making the New Commonwealth*, p. 83.
50. A. Lamb, *Crisis in Kashmir*, London, 1966, p. 49.
51. Dasgupta, *War and Diplomacy in Kashmir 1947–48*, pp. 57, 202.
52. Lamb, *Crisis in Kashmir*, pp. 49–50.
53. G. Rizvi, 'Nehru and the Indo-Pakistan Rivalry Over Kashmir 1947–1963', *Contemporary South Asia*, vol. 4, no. 1, March 1995, pp. 17–38.
54. Lamb, *Birth of a Tragedy*, pp. 113–115, 118, 147, 151.
55. Raghavan, *War and Peace in Modern India*, pp. 133–134.
56. V. Schofield, *Kashmir in Conflict: India, Pakistan and the Unending War*, London, 2003, p. 65.
57. TNA, Dominions Office [hereafter DO], 142/521, Comments on the New Delhi Telegram, no. 4026, 20 November 1948.
58. Raghavan, *War and Peace in Modern India*, pp. 133–134.
59. Communication from the Pakistan Commander in Chief, General Sir Douglas Gracey, to the Government of Pakistan, 20 April 1948, in K.S. Hasan (ed.), *Documents on the Foreign Relations of Pakistan: The Kashmir Question*, Karachi, 1966, pp. 174–176.
60. Dasgupta, *War and Diplomacy in Kashmir 1947–1948*, pp. 135, 138–139, 140–142, 205–206; for a full discussion of British policy towards Kashmir

at the United Nations, see R. Ankit, 'Britain and Kashmir 1948: "The Arena of the UN"', *Diplomacy and Statecraft*, vol. 24, no. 2, June 2013, pp. 273–290.
61. Communication from the Pakistan Commander in Chief, General Sir Douglas Gracey, to the Government of Pakistan, 20 April 1948, in K.S. Hasan (ed.), *Documents on the Foreign Relations of Pakistan: The Kashmir Question*, Karachi, 1966, pp. 174–176.
62. Raghavan, *War and Peace in Modern India*, pp. 133–134.
63. H.A. Rizvi, *Military, State and Society in Modern Pakistan*, London, 2000, p. 77.
64. Moore, *Making the New Commonwealth*, p. 83.
65. Raghavan, *War and Peace in Modern India*, pp. 133–135.
66. Moore, *Making the New Commonwealth*, p. 83.
67. Dasgupta, *War and Diplomacy in Kashmir 1947–48*, pp. 143–144, 146–147.
68. Moore, *Making the New Commonwealth*, pp. 83–84.
69. Dasgupta, *War and Diplomacy in Kashmir 1947–48*, pp. 147, 206.
70. TNA, DO 142/521, Comments on the New Delhi Telegram, no. 4026, 20 November 1948.
71. Lamb, *Incomplete Partition*, p. 241.
72. Communication from the Pakistan Commander in Chief, General Sir Douglas Gracey, to the Government of Pakistan, 20 April 1948, in K.S. Hasan (ed.), *Documents on the Foreign Relations of Pakistan: The Kashmir Question*, Karachi, 1966, pp. 174–176; Schofield, *Kashmir in Conflict*, p. 65; Korbel, *Danger in Kashmir*, pp. 138–139.
73. Lamb, *Incomplete Partition*, p. 247.
74. Jha, *The Origins of a Dispute*, pp. 164–165.
75. TNA, DO 142/521, Comments on the New Delhi Telegram, no. 4026, 20 November 1948.
76. Dasgupta, *War and Diplomacy in Kashmir 1947–48*, p. 150.
77. Jalal, *The State of Martial Rule*, p. 85.
78. Dasgupta, *War and Diplomacy in Kashmir 1947–48*, pp. 151, 153–154.
79. Korbel, *Danger in Kashmir*, p. 138.
80. Lamb, *Incomplete Partition*, p. 242.
81. Wolpert, *Shameful Flight*, p. 187.
82. Dasgupta, *War and Diplomacy in Kashmir 1947–48*, p. 167.
83. Lamb, *Incomplete Partition*, pp. 245–246.
84. Dasgupta, *War and Diplomacy in Kashmir 1947–48*, pp. 174–176.
85. TNA, DO 142/521, Shone to Noel-Baker, no. 1395, 18 November 1948.
86. Dasgupta, *War and Diplomacy in Kashmir 1947–48*, p. 178.
87. TNA, DO 142/521, Foreign Office to UK Delegation United Nations General Assembly Paris, no. 534, 19 November 1948.
88. TNA, DO 142/521, Grafftey-Smith to Noel-Baker, no. 4018, 19 November 1948.
89. TNA, DO 142/521, Grafftey-Smith to Noel-Baker, no. 4050, 22 November 1948.
90. TNA, DO 142/521, Grafftey-Smith to Noel-Baker, no. 4041, 22 November 1948.
91. TNA, DO 142/521, Noel-Baker to Attlee, no. 100/48, 22 November 1948.
92. Raghavan, *War and Peace in Modern India*, p. 143.

93. N.S. Sarila, *The Shadow of the Great Game: The Untold Story of India's Partition*, London, 2005, pp. 360, 395; Dasgupta, *War and Diplomacy in Kashmir 1947–48*, pp. 174, 183–184,
94. Raghavan, *War and Peace in Modern India*, p. 143.
95. Dasgupta, *War and Diplomacy in Kashmir 1947–48*, p. 185.
96. TNA, CAB 128/13, CM(48)79, Conclusions, 9 December 1948.
97. TNA, CAB 195/6, CM(48)79, 9 December 1948.
98. Dasgupta, *War and Diplomacy in Kashmir 1947–48*, pp. 186–187.
99. Moore, *Making the New Commonwealth*, p. 95.
100. Dasgupta, *War and Diplomacy in Kashmir 1947–48*, pp. 187–188.
101. Lamb, *Incomplete Partition*, p. 247.
102. Schofield, *Kashmir in Conflict*, pp. 69, 72.
103. Lamb, *Crisis in Kashmir*, p. 54.
104. Lamb, *Incomplete Partition*, p. 247.
105. Raghavan, *War and Peace in Modern India*, pp. 170–175-6.
106. Dasgupta, *War and Diplomacy in Kashmir 1947–48*, p. 18.
107. Barua, *Gentlemen of the Raj*, p. 148.
108. H. Tinker, *India and Pakistan: A Short Political Guide*, London, 1962, p. 78; Jalal, *The State of Martial Rule*, pp. 119–122.
109. Barua, *Gentlemen of the Raj*, p. 148.
110. Tinker, *India and Pakistan*, p. 78; Jalal, *The State of Martial Rule*, pp. 119–122.

Conclusion

1. Rosie, *The British in Vietnam*, pp. 57–86; Lawrence, *Assuming The Burden*, pp. 105, 111; Hughes, 'A "Post-war" War: The British Occupation of French-Indochina, September 1945–March 1946', pp. 263–286; Bayly, and Harper, *Forgotten Wars*, pp. 145–158.
2. H. Kissinger, *Diplomacy*, London, 1994, p. 626.

Bibliography

Archival sources

Britain
The National Archives, Public Record Office, London:
Air Ministry:
AIR 23 Overseas Commands
AIR 40 Directorate of Intelligence and other Intelligence Papers

Board of Trade:
BT 64 Industries and Manufacturers Department

Cabinet Office:
CAB 21 Registered Files 1916–1965
CAB 69 War Cabinet Defence Committee (Operations)
CAB 79 War Cabinet Chiefs of Staff Committee Minutes
CAB 80 War Cabinet Chiefs of Staff Committee Memoranda
CAB 84 War Cabinet Joint Planning Committees
CAB 119 Joint Planning Staff Files
CAB 120 Minister of Defence: Secretariat Files
CAB 121 Special Secret Information Centre
CAB 122 British Joint Staff Mission: Washington Office Files
CAB 128 Cabinet Minutes 1945–1981
CAB 134 Cabinet Miscellaneous Committees: Minutes and Papers
CAB 195 Cabinet Secretary's Notebooks 1942–1963

Colonial Office:
CO 968 Defence Department and Successors: Original Correspondence

Dominions Office:
DO 142 Commonwealth Relations Office: India

Foreign Office:
FO 371 Political Departments: General Correspondence
FO 800 Private Offices: Various Ministers and Officials Papers (Ernest Bevin)
FO 959 Consulates, French Indochina: Various Papers 1945–1959

Special Operations Executive:
HS 1 Far East: Registered Files

Prime Minister:
PREM 3 Prime Minister's Papers 1940–1945
PREM 4 Prime Minister's Papers 1940–1945
PREM 8 Prime Minister's Papers 1945–1951

War Office:
WO 32 Registered Papers General Series
WO 106 Directorate of Military Operations and Intelligence
WO 162 Adjutant General

WO 172 SEAC War Diaries
WO 203 Far East Forces
WO 208 Directorate of Military Intelligence
WO 220 Directorate of Civil Affairs

The British Library, London:
India Office

The Cadbury Research Library, University of Birmingham:
Papers of Anthony Eden, Lord Avon.

Liddell Hart Centre Archives, King's College London:
Papers of Major-General Sir Douglas Gracey

Middle East Centre Archive, St Anthony's College, University of Oxford:
Papers of Sir Miles Lampson, Lord Killearn.

Mountbatten Archive, University of Southampton Library:
Papers of Admiral Lord Louis Mountbatten Earl of Burma

France
Centre des Archives d'Outre-Mer, Aix-en-Provence:
Governement General de L'Indochine
Indochine Nouveau Fonds

Published primary sources

British Documents on the End of Empire, Series A, Volume 1: Ashton, S.R., and Stockwell, S. E. (Eds.).
  Imperial Policy and Colonial Practice 1925–1945: Part 1: Metropolitan Reorganisation, Defence and International Relations, Political Change and Constitutional Reform, London, 1996.
British Documents on the End of Empire, Series A, Volume 2: Hyam, R. (Ed.),
  The Labour Government and the End of Empire 1945–1951: Part 1: High Policy, London, 1991.
  The Labour Government and the End of Empire 1945–1951: Part 2: Economics and International Relations, London, 1991.
  The Labour Government and the End of Empire 1945–1951: Part 3: Strategy, Policies and Constitutional Change, London, 1991.
  The Labour Government and the End of Empire 1945–1951: Part 4: Race Relations and the Commonwealth, London, 1991.
British Documents on the End of Empire, Series B, Volume 3: Stockwell, A.J. (Ed.),
  Malaya: Part 1: The Malayan Union Experiment 1942–1948, London, 1995.
British Documents on Foreign Affairs: Reports and Papers from the Foreign Office Confidential Print: Series C, North America, Part 3: Crockatt, R.D. (Ed.),
  Volume 5: January 1945–December 1945, University Publications of America, 1999.
British Documents on Foreign Affairs: Reports and Papers from the Foreign Office Confidential Print: Series C, North America, Part 4: Crockatt, R.D. (Ed.),
  Volume 1: January–December 1946, University Publications of America, 1999.
  Volume 2: January–December 1947, University Publications of America, 1999.

Bibliography 171

Volume 3: January 1948–December 1949, University Publications of America, 1999.
Burma: The Struggle For Independence 1944–1948: Documents from Official and Private Sources: Tinker, H. (Ed.),
  Volume 1: From Military Occupation to Civil Government 1 January 1944–31 August 1946, London, 1983.
  Volume 2: From General Strike to Independence 31 August 1946–4 January 1948, London, 1984.
Conflict in Indochina and International Repercussions: A Documentary History, 1945–1955, Cole, A.B. (Ed.), New York, 1956.
Constitutional Relations Between Britain and India: The Transfer of Power 1942–7: Mansergh, N. (Ed.),
  Volume 3: Reassertion of Authority, Gandhi's Fast and the Succession of the Viceroyalty 21 September 1942–12 June 1943, London, 1971.
  Volume 4: The Bengal Famine and the New Viceroyalty 15 June 1943–31 August 1944, London, 1973.
  Volume 5: The Simla Conference: Background and Proceedings 1 September 1944–28 July 1945, London, 1974.
  Volume 6: The Post War Phase: New Moves by the Labour Government 1 August 1945–22 March 1946, London, 1976.
  Volume 7: The Cabinet Mission 23 March–29 June 1946, London, 1977.
  Volume 8: The Interim Government 31 July–1 November 1946, London, 1979.
  Volume 9: The Fixing of a Time Limit 4 November 1946–22 March 1947, London, 1980.
  Volume 10: The Mountbatten Viceroyalty: Formulation of a Plan 22 March–30 May 1947, London, 1981.
  Volume 11: The Mountbatten Viceroyalty: Announcement and Reception of the 3 June Plan 31 May–7 July 1947, London, 1982.
  Volume 12: The Mountbatten Viceroyalty: Princes, Partition and Independence 8 July–15 August 1947, London, 1984.
Documents on British policy overseas series 1:
  Butler, R. and Pelly, M. (Eds.), Volume 1: The Conference at Potsdam, 1945, London, 1984.
Documents Relating to British Involvement in the Indochina Conflict 1945–65, London, 1965.
Documents on the Foreign relations of Pakistan:
  Hasan, K.S. (Ed.), The Kashmir Question, Karachi, 1966.
Foreign Relations of the United States: Diplomatic Papers: Department of State Publication:
  1943: Volume 3: The British Commonwealth, Eastern Europe, The Far East, Washington D.C., 1963.
  1944: Volume 3: The British Commonwealth, Europe, Washington D.C., 1965.
  1944: Volume 5: The Near East, South Asia, Africa, The Far East, Washington D.C., 1965.
  The Conference at Berlin 1945 (The Potsdam Conference) Volume 1, Washington D.C., 1960.
  The Conference at Berlin 1945 (The Potsdam Conference) Volume 2, Washington D.C., 1960.
  1945: Volume 1: General: The United Nations, Washington D.C., 1967.

1945: Volume 6: The British Commonwealth, The Far East, Washington D.C., 1969.
1946: Volume 1: General: The United Nations, Washington D.C., 1972.
1946:Volume 5: The British Commonwealth, Western and Central Europe, Washington D.C., 1969.
1947: Volume 1: General: The United Nations, Washington D.C., 1973.
1947: Volume 3: The British Commonwealth, Europe, Washington D.C., 1972.
1948: Volume 1: General: The United Nations, Part 1, Washington D.C., 1975.
1948: Volume 1: General: The United Nations, Part 2, Washington D.C., 1976.
1948: Volume 5: The Near East, South Asia, and Africa, Part 1, Washington D.C., 1975.
1948: Volume 5: The Near East, South Asia, and Africa, Part 2, Washington D.C., 1976.
1949: Volume 2: The United Nations, the Western Hemisphere, Washington D.C., 1975.
1949: Volume 6: The Near East, South Asia, and Africa, Washington D.C., 1977.
1950: Volume 2: The United Nations, the Western Hemisphere, Washington D.C., 1976.
1950: Volume 5: The Near East, South Asia, and Africa, Washington D.C., 1978.
Hansard House of Commons Parliamentary Debates, 1943–1950, Volumes 386–476, London, 1943–1945.
La Guerre D'Indochine 1945–54: Textes et Documents, Volume 1, Le Retour de la France en Indochine1945–1946, Bordinier, G. (Ed.), Vincennes, 1987.
The Pentagon Papers, The Defense Department History of United States Decision Making on Vietnam, Volume 1, Gravel Edition, Boston, 1971.
Quaid-I-Azam Mohammad Ali Jinnah Papers, First Series, Zaidi, Z.H. (Ed.):
  Volume 1, Part 1, Prelude To Pakistan, 20 February–2 June 1947, Islamabad, 1993.
  Volume 1, Part 2, Prelude To Pakistan, 20 February–2 June 1947, Islamabad, 1993.
  Volume 3, On the Threshold of Pakistan, 1 July–25 July 1947, Islamabad, 1996.
  Volume 4, Pakistan at Last, 26 July–14 August 1947, Islamabad, 1999.
  Volume 5, Pakistan: Pangs of Birth, 15 August–30 September 1947, Islamabad, 2000.
Smith, R.B., and Stockwell, A.J. (Eds.), *British Policy and the Transfer of Power in Asia: Documentary Perspectives*, London, 1988.
Vietnam, the Definitive Documentation of Human Decisions. Volume 1, Porter, G., (Ed.), Philadelphia, 1979.

Published memoirs and diaries

Bickersteth, A.C., *ODTAA: Being extracts from the diary of an Officer who served with the 4/10th Gurkha Rifles in Manipur and Burma*, Aberdeen, 1953.
Boucher De Crevecoeur, J., *La Liberation Du Laos 1945–46*, Vincennes, 1985.
Campbell-Johnson, A., *Mission with Mountbatten*, London 1985.
D' Argenlieu, G.T., *Chronique D'Indochine 1945–1947*, Paris, 1985.
Ismay, Lord, *The Memoirs of General the Lord Ismay*, London, 1960.
Korbel, J., *Danger in Kashmir*, Princeton, 1954.
Moon, P. (Ed.), *Wavell: The Viceroy's Journal*, London, 1973.

Moran, Lord, *Winston Churchill: The Struggle For Survival 1940–1965*, London, 1966.
Patti, A., *Why Vietnam?* Berkley, 1980.
Sainteny, J., *Histoire d'une Paix Manquee: Indochine 1945–1947*, Paris, 1967.
Sainteny, J., *Ho Chi Minh and His Vietnam: A Personal Memoir*, translated by H. Briffault, Chicago, 1972.
Sihanouk, N., *Souvenirs Doux et Amers*, Paris, 1981.
Singh, K., *Heir Apparent*, Oxford, 1983.
Slim, W.J., *Defeat into Victory: Field Marshal Viscount Slim*, London, 1986.
Wedemeyer, A.C., *Wedemeyer Reports*, New York, 1958.
Ziegler, P. (Ed.), *The Personal Diaries of Admiral, the Lord Louis Mountbatten, Supreme Commander Southeast Asia 1943–1946*, London, 1988.

Secondary sources

Adamthwaite, A., 'Britain and the World 1945–9: The View from The Foreign Office', *International Affairs*, vol. 61, no. 2, Spring 1985, pp. 223–235.
Aldrich, R., 'Imperial Rivalry: British and American Intelligence in Asia 1942–6', *Intelligence and National Security*, vol. 3, no. 1, January 1988, pp. 5–55.
Allen, L., *Burma: The Longest War 1941–1945*, London, 2000.
Anderson, D.M., *Policing and Decolonisation: Politics, Nationalism and the Police 1917–1965*, Manchester, 1992.
Ankit, R., 'Great Britain and Kashmir 1947–49', *India Review*, vol. 12, no. 1, January 2013, pp. 20–40.
Ankit, R., 'Britain and Kashmir 1948: "The Arena of the UN"', *Diplomacy and Statecraft*, vol. 24, no. 2, June 2013, pp. 273–290.
Antlov, H., and Tonnesson, S. (Eds.), *Imperial Policy and Southeast Asian Nationalism 1930–1957*, Surrey, 1995.
Barua, P.P., *Gentlemen of the Raj: The Indian Army Officer Corps 1817–1949*, London, 2003.
Bayly, C., and Harper, T., *Forgotten Armies: Britain's Asian Empire and the War with Japan*, London, 2005.
Bayly, C., and Harper, T., *Forgotten Wars: The End of Britain's Asian Empire*, London, 2008.
Bills, S., *Empire and the Cold War: The Roots of United States-Third World Antagonism*, London, 1990.
Birdwood, Lord, 'Kashmir', *International Affairs*, vol. 28, no. 3, July 1952, pp. 299–309.
Blaxland, G., *The Regiments Depart: A History of the British Army 1945–1970*, London, 1971.
Brown, J.M., *Modern India: The Origins of an Asian Democracy*, Oxford, 1985.
Brown, J.M., *Nehru: A Political Life*, London, 2003.
Bullock, A., *Ernest Bevin Foreign Secretary 1945–51*, London, 1983.
Burns, J.M., *Roosevelt: The Soldier of Freedom 1940–1945*, San Diego, 1970.
Butler, L.J., *Britain and Empire: Adjusting to a Post-Imperial World*, London, 2002.
Butler, L.J., 'British Decolonization', in Thomas, M., Moore, B., and Butler, L.J. (Eds.), *Crises of Empire: Decolonization and Europe's Imperial States, 1918–1975*, London, 2008, pp. 17–96.
Buttinger, J., *Vietnam: A Dragon Embattled Volume 1*, London, 1967.

Carmichael, C., and Maguire, R. (Eds.), *The Routledge History of Genocide*, London, 2015.
Chandler, D.P., 'The Kingdom of Kampuchea, March–October 1945: Japanese Sponsored Independence in Cambodia in World War Two', *Journal of Southeast Asian Studies*, vol. 17, no. 1, March 1986, pp. 80–93.
Chandler, D.P., *A History of Cambodia*, Washington D.C., 1999.
Charmley, J., *Churchill's Grand Alliance: The Anglo-American Special Relationship 1940–57*, London, 1995.
Charney, M., *A History of Modern Burma*, Cambridge, 2009.
Chen, K.C., *Vietnam and China 1938–54*, Princeton, 1969.
Clarke, P., *The Last Thousand Days of the British Empire: Churchill, Roosevelt and the Birth of the Pax Americana*, New York, 2008.
Cloughley, B., *A History of the Pakistan Army: Wars and Insurrections*, Oxford, 2000.
Cohen, S., *The Indian Army: Its Contributions to the Development of a Nation*, Berkeley, 1971.
Colbert, E., 'The Road Not Taken: Decolonisation and Independence in Indonesia and Indochina', *Foreign Affairs*, vol. 51, no. 3, April 1973, pp. 608–628.
Colbert, E., *Southeast Asia in International Politics 1941–1956*, London, 1977.
Cross, J.P., *Jungle Warfare: Encounters and Experiences*, London, 1989.
Cruickshank, C., *SOE in the Far East*, Oxford, 1983.
Darwin, J., 'British Decolonisation Since 1945: A Pattern or a Puzzle?' *Journal of Imperial and Commonwealth History*, vol. 12, no. 2, January 1984, pp. 187–209.
Dasgupta, C., *War and Diplomacy in Kashmir 1947–48*, London, 2002.
Dennis, P., *Troubled Days of Peace: Mountbatten and South East Asia Command 1945–46*, New York, 1987.
Donnison, F.S.V., *British Military Administration in the Far East 1943–1946*, London, 1956.
Drachman, E.R., *United States Policy towards Vietnam 1940–45*, New Jersey, 1970.
Draper, T., *Abuse of Power*, London, 1967.
Duiker, W.J., *China and Vietnam: The Roots of Conflict*, Berkley, 1986.
Duncanson, D., 'General Gracey and the Vietminh', *Journal of the Royal Central Asian Society*, vol. 55, pt. 3, October 1968, pp. 288–297.
Duncanson, D., *Government and Revolution in Vietnam*, London, 1968.
Duncanson, D., 'Ho Chi Minh and the August Revolution of 1945 in Indochina', *Lugano Review*, May 1975.
Dunlop, G., *Military Economics, Culture and Logistics in the Burma Campaign 1942–1945*, London, 2009.
Dunn, P.M., *The First Vietnam War*, London, 1985.
Fall, B., *The Two Vietnams*, London, 1963.
Fall, B., *Last Reflections on a War*, New York, 1967.
Gaddis, J.L., *Strategies of Containment*, New York, 1982.
Gardner, L.C., *Approaching Vietnam: From World War Two Through Dienbienphu*, London, 1988.
Gardner, L.C., 'How We Lost Vietnam 1940–54', in Ryan, D., and Pungong, V. (Eds.), *The United States and Decolonization, Power and Freedom*, Basingstoke, 2000, pp. 121–139.
Garrett, C.W., 'In Search of Grandeur: France in Vietnam 1940–1946', *The Review of Politics*, vol. 29, no. 3, July 1967, pp. 303–323.

Gibbons, W.C., *The U.S. Government and the Vietnam War, Part 1: 1945–1960*, Princeton, 1986.
Gilbert, M., *Churchill: A Life*, London, 1991.
Gilbert, M., *Churchill and America*, London, 2006.
Gilbert, M., *Winston Spencer Churchill, Volume 8: Never Despair 1945–1965*, London, 1988.
Gormly, J.L., *From Potsdam to the Cold War: Big Three Diplomacy 1945–7*, Delaware, 1990.
Goscha, C.E., *Thailand and the Southeast Asian Networks of the Vietnamese Revolution, 1885–1954*, Richmond, 1999.
Goscha, C.E., and Ostermann, C. (Eds.), *Connecting Histories: Decolonization and the Cold War in Southeast Asia, 1945–1962*, Stanford, 2009.
Guha, R., *India after Gandhi: The History of the World's Largest Democracy*, New York, 2008.
Gupta, P.S., *Imperialism and the British Labour Movement 1914–1965*, London, 1975.
Habibuddin, S.M., 'Franklin D. Roosevelt's Anti-colonial Policy Towards Asia. Its Implications for India, Indo-china and Indonesia 1941–5', *Journal of Indian History*, vol. 53, 1975, pp. 497–522.
Hammer, E., *The Struggle for Indochina 1940–55*, Stanford, 1966.
Hastings, M., *Retribution: The Battle for Japan 1944–45*, New York, 2008.
Herman, A., *Gandhi and Churchill: The Epic Rivalry that Destroyed an Empire and Forged Our Age*, New York, 2009.
Herring, G.C., 'The Truman Administration and the Restoration of French Sovereignty in Indochina', *Diplomatic History*, vol. 1, no. 2, spring 1977, pp. 97–117.
Hess, G.R., 'United States Policy and the Origins of the Vietminh War 1945–1946', *Peace and Change*, vol. 3, no. 2–3, Summer and Fall, 1975, pp. 24–33.
Hess, G.R., *The United States' Emergence as a Southeast Asian Power, 1940–1950*, New York, 1987.
Hesse-D'Alzon, C., *Presence Militaire Francaise En Indochine 1940–1945*, Vincennes, 1985.
Holland, R.F., 'The Imperial Factor in British Strategies From Attlee to Macmillan 1945–63', *Journal of Imperial and Commonwealth History*, vol. 12, no. 2, January 1984, pp. 165–185.
Hughes, G., 'A "Post-war" War: The British Occupation of French-Indochina, September 1945–March 1946', *Small Wars & Insurgencies*, vol. 17, no. 3, 2006, pp. 263–286.
Hutton, C., *A Policy of Neglect: British Diplomacy towards French Indochina 1943–45*, PhD thesis, UEA, 1995.
Hyam, R., *Britain's Declining Empire: The Road to Decolonisation 1918–1968*, Cambridge, 2006.
Irving, R.E.M., *The First Indochina War, French and American Policy 1945–1954*, London, 1975.
Jackson, W.J., *Withdrawal from Empire*, London, 1988.
Jacobson, M., 'Winston Churchill and the Third Front', *Journal of Strategic Studies*, vol. 14, no. 3, September 1991, pp. 337–362.
Jalal, A., *The State of Martial Rule: The Origin's of Pakistan's Political Economy of Defence*, Cambridge, 1990.

Jalal, A., *The Sole Spokesman: Jinnah, the Muslim League and the Demand for Pakistan*, Cambridge, 1994.
Jha, P.S., *The Origins of a Dispute: Kashmir 1947*, London, 2003.
Kahin, G.M., and Lewis, J.W., *The United States and Vietnam*, New York, 1967.
Kanh, Huynh Kim., 'The Vietnamese August Revolution Reinterpreted', *Journal of Asian Studies*, vol. 30, no. 4, August 1971, pp. 761–782.
Kennedy, G. (Ed.), *Imperial Defence: The Old World Order 1856–1956*, London, 2008.
Kent, J., 'Anglo-French Co-operation 1939–49', *Journal of Imperial and Commonwealth History*, vol. 17, no. 1, 1988, pp. 55–82.
Kiernan, B., *How Pol Pot came to Power: A History of Communism in Kampuchea, 1930–75*, London, 2004.
Kissinger, H., *Diplomacy*, London, 1994.
Lamb, A., *Birth of a Tragedy: Kashmir 1947*, Hertingfordbury, 1994.
Lamb, A., *Crisis in Kashmir*, London, 1966.
Lamb, A., *Kashmir: A Disputed Legacy*, Hertingfordbury, 1991.
Lamb, A., *Incomplete Partition: The Genesis of the Kashmir Dispute 1947–1948*, Hertingfordbury, 1997.
Lancaster, D., *The Emancipation of French Indochina*, London, 1961.
Lapierre, D., and Collins, L., *Freedom at Midnight*, Noida, 1997.
Lawrence, M.A., 'Transnational Coalition Building The Making of the Cold War in Indochina', *Diplomatic History*, vol. 26, no. 3, Summer 2002, pp. 453–480.
Lawrence, M.A., *Assuming the Burden: Europe and the American Commitment to War in Vietnam*, London, 2005.
Lawrence, M.A., and Logevall, F. (Eds.), *The First Vietnam War: Colonial Conflict and Cold War Crisis*, Massachusetts, 2007.
Lin, Hua., 'The Chinese Occupation of Northern Vietnam 1945–1946: A reappraisal', in Antlov, H., and Tonnesson, S. (Eds.), *Imperial Policy and Southeast Asian Nationalism 1930–1957*, Surrey, 1995, pp. 144–169.
Logevall, F., *Embers of War: The Fall of an Empire and the Making of America's Vietnam*, New York, 2012.
Louis, W.R., *Imperialism at Bay: The United States and the Decolonisation of the British Empire 1941–5*, New York, 1978.
Lowe, P., *Contending With Nationalism and Communism: British Policy towards Southeast Asia 1945–65*, London, 2009.
Lyman, R., *Slim, Master of War: Burma and the Birth of Modern Warfare*, London, 2005.
Marr, D.G., 'Vietnam 1945: Some Questions', *Vietnam Forum*, vol. 6, Summer 1985, pp. 155–193.
Marr, D.G., *Vietnam 1945: The Quest For Power*, Berkley, 1995.
Marsot, A., 'The Crucial Year: Indochina 1945', *Journal of Contemporary History*, vol. 19, no. 2, April 1984, pp. 337–354.
Marston, D.P., *Phoenix from the Ashes: The Indian Army in the Burma Campaign*, London, 2003.
McLane, C.B., *Soviet Strategies in South-East Asia*, Princeton, 1966.
McLynn, F., *The Burma Campaign: Disaster to Triumph 1942–45*, New Haven, 2011.
McMillan, R., *The British Occupation of Indonesia 1945–1946: Britain, the Netherlands and the Indonesian Revolution*, London, 2005.

Mead, R., *Churchill's Lions: A Biographical Guide to the Key British Generals of World War II*, Stroud, 2007.
Merrill, D., 'The Ironies of History: The United States and the Decolonization of India', in Ryan, D., and Pungong V. (Eds.), *The United States and Decolonization: Power and Freedom*, Basingstoke, 2000, pp. 102–120.
Moore, R.J., *Making the New Commonwealth*, Oxford, 1987.
Mullaly, B.R., *Bugle and Kuri: The Story of the 10th Princess Mary's Own Gurkha Rifles*, London, 1957.
Neville, P., *Britain in Vietnam: Prelude to Disaster 1945–46*, London, 2008.
Nitz, K., 'Independence without Nationalists? The Japanese and Vietnamese Nationalism during the Japanese Period 1940–5', *Journal of Southeast Asian Studies*, vol. 15, no. 1, March 1984, pp. 108–133.
Nong, Van Dan., *Churchill, Eden and Indo-China, 1951–1955*, London, 2010.
Palleson, E.S., *United States Policy toward Decolonization in Asia 1945–50*, DPhil thesis, Oxford, 1995.
Prasad, S.N., Bhargava, K.D. and Khera, P.N., (edited by Prasad, B.) *Official History of the Indian Armed Forces in the Second World War 1939–45: Reconquest of Burma, Volume 1, June 1942–June 1944*, Calcutta, 1958.
Prasad, S.N., Khera, P.N., (edited by Prasad, B.) *Official History of the Indian Armed Forces in the Second World War 1939–45: Reconquest of Burma, Volume 2, June 1944–August 1945*, Calcutta, 1959.
Prasad, S.N. and Pal, D., *History of Operations in Jammu and Kashmir, 1947–48*, Dehra Dun, 2005.
Raghavan, S., *War and Peace in Modern India: A Strategic History of the Nehru Years*, London, 2010.
Reddi, V.M., *A History of the Cambodian Independence Movement 1863–1955*, Tirupati, 1973.
Remme, T., *Britain and Regional Cooperation in South-East Asia 1945–49*, London, 1995.
Rizvi, G., 'Nehru and the Indo-Pakistan Rivalry Over Kashmir 1947–1963', *Contemporary South Asia*, vol. 4, no. 1, March 1995, pp. 17–38.
Rizvi, H.A., *Military, State and Society in Modern Pakistan*, London, 2000.
Robb, P., *A History of India*, London, 2011.
Roberts, A., *Eminent Churchillians*, New York, 1995.
Roberts, D., *Global Governance and Biopolitics: Regulating Human Security*, London, 2010.
Robinson, R., 'Imperial Theory as a Question of Imperialism after Empire', *Journal of Imperial and Commonwealth History*, vol. 12, no. 2, January 1984, pp. 42–54.
Rosen, S.M., *The Combined Food Boards of the Second World War*, New York, 1951.
Rosie, G., *The British in Vietnam*, London, 1970.
Ryan, D., and Pungong, V. (Eds.), *The United States and Decolonization: Power and Freedom*, Basingstoke, 2000.
Sainsbury, K., *Churchill and Roosevelt at War: The War They Fought and the Peace They Hoped to Make*, London, 1994.
Sarila, N.S., *The Shadow of the Great Game: The Untold Story of India's Partition*, London, 2005.
Saville, J., *The Politics of Continuity: British Foreign Policy and the Labour Government 1945–1946*, London, 1993.

178 Bibliography

Schofield, V., *Kashmir in Conflict: India, Pakistan and the Unending War*, London, 2003.
Schofield, V., *Wavell: Soldier and Statesman*, Barnsley, 2010.
Shiraishi, T., and Furuta, M. (Eds.), *Indochina in the 1940s and 1950s*, New York, 1992.
Short, A., *The Origins of the Vietnam War*, London, 1989.
Siracusa, J.M., 'The United States, Viet-Nam and the Cold War: A Re-appraisal', *Journal of Southeast Asian Studies*, vol. 5, no. 1, 1974, pp. 82–101.
Smart, N., *Biographical Dictionary of British Generals of the Second World War*, Barnsley, 2005.
Smith, C., *England's Last War against France: Fighting Vichy 1940–1942*, London, 2009.
Smith, R.B., *An International History of the Vietnam War Volume 1: Revolution Versus Containment 1955–61*, London, 1983.
Smith, R.B., *Changing Visions of East Asia, 1943–93: Transformations and Continuities*, Mitcham, C. (Ed.), London, 2007.
Smith, R.B., *Pre-Communist Indochina*, Mitcham, C. (Ed.), London, 2009.
Smith, R.B., *Viet-Nam and the West*, London, 1968.
Smith, T.O., 'Britain and Cambodia, September 1945–November 1946: A Reappraisal', *Diplomacy and Statecraft*, vol. 17, no. 1, 2006, pp. 73–91.
Smith, T.O., 'Europe, Americanization and Globalization', Review Article, *European History Quarterly*, vol. 37, no. 2, 2007, pp. 301–309.
Smith, T.O., *Britain and the Origins of the Vietnam War: UK Policy in Indo-China 1943–1950*, Basingstoke, 2007.
Smith, T.O., 'Resurrecting the French Empire: British Military Aid to Vietnam 1945–7', *University of Sussex Journal of Contemporary History*, vol. 11, 2007, pp. 1–13.
Smith, T.O., 'Major-General Sir Douglas Gracey: Peacekeeper or Peace-Enforcer?' *Diplomacy and Statecraft*, vol. 21, no. 2, 2010, pp. 226–239.
Smith, T.O., 'Lord Killearn and British Diplomacy Regarding French Indo-Chinese Rice Supplies, 1946–1948', *History*, vol. 96, no. 324, 2011, pp. 477–489.
Smith, T.O., *Churchill, America and Vietnam: 1941–45*, Basingstoke, 2011.
Smith, T.O., 'Protecting the British Empire: The Dilemma of Sending Military Aid to French Indo-China 1948–1950', *Historical Yearbook*, the Nicolae Iorga History Institute of the Romanian Academy, vol. 9, 2012, pp. 123–137.
Smith, T.O., 'Britain in Vietnam: A Myth Re-examined', *Historical Yearbook*, the Nicolae Iorga History Institute of the Romanian Academy, vol. 10, 2013, pp. 68–76.
Smith, T.O., 'Cambodia: Paranoia, Xenophobia, Genocide and Auto-Genocide', in Carmichael, C., and Maguire, R. (Eds.), *The Routledge History of Genocide*, London, 2015.
Sockeel-Richarte, P., 'Le Probleme De La Soverainte Francaise Sur L'Indochine', in Institut Charle De Gaulle (Eds.), *General De Gaulle Et L'Indochine 1940–61*, Actes Etablis par G. Pilleul, Paris, 1982.
Soustelle, J., 'Indochina and Korea: One Front', *Foreign Affairs*, vol. 29, no. 1, 1950, pp. 56–66.
Spector, R.H., *Advice and Support: The Early Years of the United States Army in Vietnam 1941–1960*, Washington D.C., 1983.

Springhall, J., 'Kicking out the Vietminh: How Britain Allowed France to Reoccupy South Indochina', *Journal of Contemporary History*, vol. 40, no. 1, 2005, pp. 115–130.
Stockwell, A.J., 'Southeast Asia in War and Peace: The End of the European Colonial Empire', in Tarling, N., (Ed.), *The Cambridge History of Southeast Asia: Volume Two, Part Two, From World War Two to the Present*, Cambridge, 1999, pp. 1–57.
Stone, D. (Ed.), *The Historiography of Genocide*, London, 2010.
Suhrke, A., 'Irredentism Contained: The Thai-Muslim Case', *Comparative Politics*, vol. 7, no. 2, January 1975, pp. 187–203.
Talbot, I., *Pakistan: A Modern History*, London, 2005.
Talbot, I., 'The 1947 Partition of India', in Stone, D. (Ed.), *The Historiography of Genocide*, London, 2010, pp. 420–437.
Tarling, N., *Britain, Southeast Asia and the Onset of the Cold War 1945–1950*, Cambridge, 1998.
Tarling, N., 'Some Rather Nebulous Capacity: Lord Killearn's Appointment in Southeast Asia', *Modern Asian Studies*, vol. 20, no. 3, 1986, pp. 559–600.
Tarling, N. (Ed.), *The Cambridge History of Southeast Asia: Volume Two, Part Two, From World War Two to the Present*, Cambridge, 1999.
Thien, Ton That., 'The Influence of Indo-China on the Evolution of the French Union', *India Quarterly*, vol. 10, part 4, 1954, pp. 295–313.
Thomas, M., *Fight or Flight: Britain, France and the Roads from Empire*, Oxford, 2014.
Thomas, M., 'French Decolonization', in Thomas, M., Moore, B. and Butler, L.J. (Eds.), *Crises of Empire: Decolonization and Europe's Imperial States, 1918–1975*, London, 2008, pp. 127–269.
Thomas, M., 'Processing Decolonization: British Strategic Analysis of Conflict in Vietnam and Indonesia, 1945–1950', in Goscha, C.E. and Ostermann, C. (Eds.), *Connecting Histories: Decolonization and the Cold War in Southeast Asia, 1945–1962*, Stanford, 2009, pp. 84–120.
Thomas, M., 'Silent Partners: SOE's French Indo-China Section 1943–1945', *Modern Asian Studies*, vol. 34, no. 4, 2000, pp. 943–976.
Thomas, M., Moore, B. and Butler, L.J., *Crises of Empire: Decolonization and Europe's Imperial States, 1918–1975*, London, 2008.
Thorne, C., *Allies of a Kind: The United States, Britain and the War against Japan, 1941–1945*, London, 1979.
Thorne, C., 'Indochina and Anglo-American Relations 1942–5', *Pacific Historical Review*, vol. 45, no. 1, 1976, pp. 73–96.
Tinker, H., *India and Pakistan: A Short Political Guide*, London, 1962.
Tinker, H., 'The Contradiction of Empire in Asia 1945–48: The Military Dimension', *Journal of Imperial and Commonwealth History*, vol. 16, no. 2, January 1988, pp. 218–233.
Tonnesson, S., 'Filling The Vacuum: 1945 in French Indochina, the Netherlands East Indies and British Malaya', in Antlov, H., and Tonnesson, S. (Eds.), *Imperial Policy and Southeast Asian Nationalism 1930–1957*, Surrey, 1995, pp. 110–143.
Tonnesson, S., 'The Longest Wars: Indochina 1945–75', *Journal of Peace Research*, vol. 22, no. 1, 1985, pp. 9–29.
Tonnesson, S., *The Vietnamese Revolution of 1945: Roosevelt, Ho Chi Minh and De Gaulle in a World at War*, London, 1991.
Tonnesson, S., *Vietnam 1946: How the War Began*, London, 2009.

Tuchmann, B., *The March of Folly: From Troy to Vietnam*, London, 1984.
Vickery, M., *Kampuchea: Politics, Economics and Society*, London, 1986.
Watt, D.C., *Succeeding John Bull, America in Britain's Place, 1900–1975*, Cambridge, 1984.
Windrow, M., *The Last Valley: Dien Bien Phu and the French Defeat in Vietnam*, London, 2004.
Wirsing, R.G., *India, Pakistan and the Kashmir Dispute: On Regional Conflict and its Resolution*, Basingstoke, 1998.
Wolpert, S., *India*, Berkley, 2009.
Wolpert, S., *Shameful Flight: The Last Days of the British Empire in India*, Oxford, 2009.
Woodburn Kirby, S., *The War against Japan Volume 2: India's Most Dangerous Hour*, Uckfield, 2004.
Woodburn Kirby, S., *The War against Japan Volume 3: The Decisive Battles*, Uckfield, 2004.
Woodburn Kirby, S., *The War against Japan Volume 4: The Reconquest of Burma*, Uckfield, 2004.
Woodburn Kirby, S., *The War against Japan Volume 5: The Surrender of Japan*, Uckfield, 2004.
Ziegler, P., *Mountbatten*, Glasgow, 1985.
Zutshi, C., 'Whither Kashmir Studies? A Review', *Modern Asian Studies*, vol. 46, no. 4, July 2012, pp. 1033–1047.

Index

Abuse of Power (1967, Draper), 3
Alanbrooke, Field Marshal, 2, 52, 56, 84, 86, 92, 135
Alessandri, General Marcel, 36–8
Alexander of Hillsborough, Earl, 116
Allied invasion, 36, 59
Allied liberation forces
 in Cambodia, 67–70, 72–3, 77
 civilians dependence, 93–4
 complexiety, 3
 in the Far East, 42
 France in 1944, 35, 59
 in French Indo-China, 85–6, 90, 97
 Gracey's administration, 50
 on-the-ground actions, 4, 33
 in Saigon, 46, 93
 during Second World War, 55
 under Slim's leadership, 46
 in Southeast Asia, 109
 in southern Indo-China, 78–9, 96
 Vietminh announcement, 39–40
 in Thailand, 75–6
 20th Indian Division, 132
Allied troops, 40, 45, 77
American Army Air Force, 37
American military aid, 37, 89
ammunition, 17, 21, 38–9, 41, 43, 82, 116, 120
Anglo-American war, 32
Anglo-centric approach, 1, 6–7
armour, 21, 39
Asian *Blitzkrieg*, 11
Asian nationalists, 43, 53, 95
Assuming the Burden: Europe and the American Commitment to War in Vietnam (2005, Lawrence), 4
atomic bombs, 31, 33, 57
Attlee, Clement, 55, 83–5, 87, 89, 105–6, 116, 125–6, 135–7
Aung San, 7, 29, 62, 132, 134
The Axis powers, 34–5
Azad Kashmir, 111, 116–18, 120, 128

Bao, Dai, 36, 39–40, 43
Bengal famine, 79
Bevin, Ernest, 42, 49, 54–5, 85–6, 102, 126, 135
Bickersteth, Major Anthony, 2, 14, 30
Bidault, Georges, 64
Bourne, Frederick, 110
Brain, Harry N., 47, 54
Britain in Vietnam: Prelude to Disaster 1945–46 (2008, Neville), 6
British advance, 24, 27, 30, 132
British Army, 12–13, 22, 30
British control, 23, 33, 44, 104, 106
British defence, 13, 16, 116
British Empire
 consequence of Indian independence, 131, 136
 decline of, 1
 disintegration of, 11
 Gracey's operational philosophy, 137
 high-Victorian ideals, 10
 political destiny of India, 104
 resolution at the United Nations, 106
 separation of India and Pakistan, 107
British forces, 11–12, 28–9, 48, 84
British Foreign Office, 33, 49, 74–5, 122
British–Indian forces, 33, 37, 42, 44–5, 48–50, 54, 61, 64, 67, 70, 81, 83–6, 89, 97, 133, 135
British–Indian operations, 48, 52, 56, 63, 92
British–Indian troops, 42, 44–6, 50, 54–5, 82–3, 86, 94, 96, 133, 136–7
British–Indian–Japanese operations, 50–1
British in Vietnam The (1970, Rosie), 3
British Labour Government, 55, 106, 135

182   Index

British liberation force, 62, 67
British Malaya, 32, 66
British Military Administration in the Far East 1943–1946 (1956, Donnison), 5
British Singapore, 32
British Special Operations Executive, 37, 40
British victories, 15, 29, 35
British War Office, 48, 57, 86, 89, 95
Brockman, Ronald, 118–19
Bucher, Major-General Roy, 117–20, 122–9
Budalin episode, 23–4
Burma Campaign
  British–Indian troops in, 42, 136
  4/10th Gurkha Rifles, 23, 31
  Gracey's role, 1–3, 7, 13–14, 21, 132
  Slim's observation, 2
Burmese National Army, 29, 31

Cabinet Defence Committee, 83–7, 89
Cambodia
  allied liberation forces in, 67–70, 72–3, 77
  British Foreign Office's role, 74–5
  British–Indian forces in, 61, 64, 67, 70
  British liberation force, 62, 67
  diplomatic mission, 57, 61
  Franco-Cambodian treaties, 60
  French colonial control, 59–60, 63, 65, 67, 77
  French population, 62, 65
  Green Shirts (Cambodian militia), 60, 67, 70–1
  Mountbatten's operations, 62, 65–6
  political situation, 57–8
  political violence, 72
  during Second World War, 58–62
Cambodian independence, 59–61, 65
Cambodian nationalism, 60, 64, 68
Cambodian nationalist movement, 7, 62–3, 134
Cambodian railways, 68, 70
Cao Dai (religious community), 43
Cariappa, Lt. General K.M., 125–9
Cedile, Jean, 40, 46, 63
Central Intelligence Agency, 39

Ceylon, 15, 91
Chiang Kai-Shek, 61, 94
Chief of the Imperial General Staff, 52, 84
  see also Alanbrooke, Field Marshal
China Theatre, 33, 37
Chinese nationalists, 33, 39, 52, 94, 96, 100
Christison, Lt General Philip, 15
Churchill, Winston, S., 11, 37–8
civilian population, 5, 29, 68, 78–9, 86, 91, 97–8, 117, 119
Clarac, Pierre, 66, 74–5
Cold War, 2, 6, 52, 90, 114, 130
Corps Leger, 37
Cunningham, Sir George, 114–15

D'Argenlieu, G.T., 43, 47, 49, 51, 53, 73, 74, 75, 76, 99, 101
Dasgupta, C., 118
Democratic Republic of Vietnam, 61, 65, 70, 98–100
Dening, Maberly Esler, 43, 54–6, 66, 74–6, 92, 99, 135
Dennis, P., 5
Dewey, Lt. Colonel Peter, 52
Didier, General de Saint, 37
Diplomacy and Statecraft (2006, Smith), 6
disaster management, 46, 95
Donnison, F.S.V., 5
Driberg, Tom, 47–8, 51, 53, 56
Duncanson, D., 4, 5
Dunn, P.M., 5
Dutch East Indies, 5–6, 11, 32, 54, 87, 91, 99
Dyer, Brigadier G.M., 30

East Bengal
  communist elements, 122
  crisis management, 109–10, 129, 136–7
  Hindu population, 128
  Pakistan's control, 108–9
  political violence, 128
Eden, Anthony, 37
Elmhirst, Thomas, 124
Evans, Brigadier Geoffrey, 19, 30, 73–4

Index 183

XV Corps, 15
see also Slim, Field Marshal Sir William
First Kashmir War, 8–9, 106
First Vietnam War The (1985, Dunn), 5
food
  crisis, 93–4, 99–100
  shortages, 28–9, 97, 134
  supplies, 8, 23, 79, 93–4, 96–9, 102
IV Corps, 15, 19
14th Army
  in Burma warfare, 12, 15, 18, 22, 25
  against Japanese, 21, 23
  food shortage, 28–9
  Gracey's complaint, 19
  in Second World War, 2
Franco-Cambodian treaties, 60
Franco-Thai treaty, 77
Frank Messrvy, Major-General, 2
Free Cambodia Party, 72
French administration, 32, 35, 46–8, 51, 53, 72, 80, 85, 93, 98–9
French authorities, 55, 58, 66, 96
French colonialism, 5, 32–3, 36, 39, 41, 43, 46, 58, 65, 70, 91
  colonial administration, 39, 41, 58, 63, 78–9, 97
  colonial control, 35, 51, 59–60, 63, 65, 67, 77, 78, 86, 97–8
French Empire, 7, 36, 40, 58, 80, 89, 94, 107, 131, 134, 136
French forces, 37–8, 45, 52, 68, 81–2, 88–90, 137
French Indo-China
  Allied deployment, 37, 40
  American involvement, 51–2, 64, 92
  British approaches, 6
  British decolonisation activities, 106
  British liberation duties, 62, 78–102, 132
  counter revolution, 45
  Gracey's intervention in, 1, 7–8, 31, 42–3, 46, 50, 52–3, 55–6, 107, 109–10, 113, 133–6
  Japanese Army, 11, 32, 34–5, 59
  Mountbatten's management, 52–4, 64, 66
  Potsdam Conference, 33
  rice-producing areas, 75

SEAC operations, 48–9
20th Indian Division in, 104–5
Vichy Government, 58
French military
  American criticism, 91–2
  Attlee's cabinet debate, 85
  defeat by Thai army, 59
  equipment transfers, 90
  expedition of, 37
  with Gracey's liberation forces, 34
  Indo-China operations, 53, 58, 80, 84–5, 87
  schemeless nature, 51
  Thai attack, 76
French population, 31, 35–6, 43, 62, 65, 86
French sovereignty, 43, 45, 47, 78

Gracey, Major-General Sir Douglas
  Bengal crises, 107–30
  Burma Campaign (1942–1945), 1–3, 7, 13–14, 21, 23, 31, 42, 132, 136
  headquarters, 16, 81
  humanitarian aid, 98–9, 102
  intervention in Cambodia, 62–77
  Kashmir crises, 107–30
  Leadership, 15, 132
  role in the First Kashmir War, 1, 8–9, 106
  troops, 2, 19, 29–30, 96
  see also Allied liberation forces; French Indo-China; Gurkha Rifles; 20th Indian Division
Grafftey-Smith, Sir Lawrence, 117–18, 120, 124–5, 127
Greater Asia, 35–7
Green Shirts (Cambodian militia), 60, 67, 70–1
Gurkha Rifles
  1st Battalion, 67–8
  1st King George's, 10
  Princess Mary's 4/10th, 2, 22–3, 26, 30–1

Hague Convention, 5, 44–5, 78, 81, 97, 100, 133
Halifax, Lord, 52
Hammer, E., 3

Index

Harold Briggs, Major-General, 2
Harvey, Oliver, 84
Hieng, Sum, 65
Hirst, Brigadier, 44
Hoa Hao (religious community), 43
Ho Chi Minh, 3, 33, 39, 41, 43–4, 61, 77
Houard, Lt. Colonel, 67–8, 70
humanitarian aid, 8, 44, 78–9, 93–102
humanitarian crisis, 79, 95–7, 100

Imphal
  14th Army, 18, 22
  20th Indian Division, 15–16, 19
  Japanese advancement, 17, 20–2
India
  Bengal crisis, 108–9
  Britain's domestic financial crisis, 105–6
  British colonial administration, 103–4
  British withdrawal, 105–6
  Bucher–Gracey talks, 117–20, 122, 125–6
  decolonisation efforts (Britain), 106, 108–9, 128
  Pakistan Army in Kashmir, 111–23, 127
  partition of British India, 107
  during Second World War, 105, 129
Indian Air Force, 118, 124, 126–7
Indian Army, 10, 104, 111, 117–22, 124–9
Indian–Burmese frontier, 15–16, 22
Indian Congress Party, 53, 104, 106–7
Indian National Army, 20
Indo-Chinese Communist Party, 39, 41, 72

Japanese advance, in Burma, 11–12, 17–20
Japanese Air Force, 68
Japanese Army, 11–12, 14–18, 20–2, 24–31
Japanese assaults, 19, 58
Japanese coup, 36–8
Japanese forces, 16–17, 20–5, 28–9, 31, 36, 41–2, 46, 49–52, 65
Japanese imperialism, 35–6, 104

Japanese military, 18, 23, 25–6, 28–32, 34–5, 37–42, 58, 69, 81, 104
Japanese offensive, 13, 16–19, 21–2
Japanese Police Force, 68
Japanese prisoners, 47, 50–1, 55, 81–2, 92, 100, 133, 136
Japanese resistance, 23–4, 26, 40, 132
Japanese surrender
  administration of, 57, 61–2, 77, 92–3, 98
  formal, 40–1, 136
  Gracey's troops, 30, 40, 55
  in Second World War, 2, 136
  security duties, 97
  Truman's order, 46
  wartime compromise, 33
Japanese troops, 23–4, 29, 34–5, 41, 51–2, 58, 72
Jinnah, Mohammed Ali
  British call for a referendum, 116–17
  conflict with India, 113–14
  creation of Pakistan, 104–5
  death of, 124
  Gracey as Chief of Staff to the Pakistan Army, 110
  Gracey's refusal, 113–15, 127
  high-level discussion with Mountbatten, 107, 136
Khan, Akbar, as successor, 129
Mountbatten's recommendation of Gracey, 7–8, 56, 109
Pakistan Army into Kashmir, 112–14, 118–23, 127
separate homeland for Muslims, 104
Joint Planning Staff, 48, 81, 85
Joint Service Mission, 37, 87, 92
Journal of Contemporary History (2005, Springhall), 5
Journal of the Royal Central Asian Society (1968, Duncanson), 5

Kashmir
  Cariappa's first action, 128
  conflict between India and Pakistan, 110–12
  crisis, 8, 116, 126, 131, 136
  geopolitical anxieties, 125
  Gracey's reports to Mountbatten, 119–21

Indian Army, 117–18
Muslim population, 112
Pakistan Army into, 112–14, 118–23, 127
political violence, 116
United Nations' intervention, 116, 121
see also Azad Kashmir; Jinnah, Mohammed Ali; Kashmir war
Kashmir war, 8–9, 106, 108, 116, 118–21, 124–5, 128–30, 137
Khan, Akbar, Major-General, 129
Khan, General Ayub, 129–30
Khim, Tit, 65, 67–9, 71
Khmer Issarak, 68, 72
Killearn, Lord, 76, 102
King George VI, 54
Korbel, J., 113, 123

Lamb, A., 114
Lao Issara militia, 55
Laos, 32–4, 38, 55, 57, 59, 64
Lascelles, Sir Alan, 54
Lawrence, M.A., 4
Lawson, John, 47, 55, 64, 67
Leclerc, General Philippe, 45, 49–51, 58, 70–1, 82, 87, 92, 100
Lewis, J.W., 3
Liaquat, Ali Khan, 114–16, 123–4
Lockhart, Lt. General Sir Rob, 111–12, 117
Loftus-Tottenham, Major-General Frederick, 130, 137
Louis XIV (1643–1715), 34

MacArthur, General Douglas, 40–1
Malins, Major, 13–14
March of Folly: From Troy to Vietnam The (1984, Tuchmann), 3
Marshall, General George, 38
Marylebone Cricket Club, 2
Massigli, Rene, 37
Maunsell, Brigadier, 44
McClure, Major-General Robert, 37
MCC or Lord's. *see* Marylebone Cricket Club
Meiklereid, E.W., 53, 99–100
Monireth, Prince, 71
Montgomery, Field Marshal, 2

Monywa assault, 23–4
Mountbatten, Admiral Lord Louis
assessment of French operations, 51–5
Cambodia campaign, 63–6, 68, 71, 73–4
French Legion of Honour award, 135
on Gracey's actions in Saigon, 46–9, 56
Indo-Chinese mission, 101–2, 105–11, 115–16, 118–20, 122
Southeast Asian responsibilities, 82, 84, 86–7, 90, 92, 94
Mudie, Sir Robert, 112–15
Mullaly, B.R., 23
Murray, Lt. Colonel E.D., 67–72, 98
Muslim League, 104, 106–7

Nagaravatta (Cambodian newspaper), 60
Nazi Germany, 34, 58, 103, 131
Nehru, Jawaharlal, 9, 53, 110–11, 115–17, 124–6, 128–9
Neville, P., 6
9th Colonial Division (France), 82–4
Noel-Baker, Philip, 116, 119–21, 123, 125–6
Norodom, Sihanouk, 59–61, 65, 69, 71–2

The Office of Strategic Services, 39, 51–2

Pakistan
Army into Kashmir, 111–23, 127
army to Iran, 130
Auchinleck's commandership, 110, 113, 115–16
Bucher–Gracey discussions, 117–29
control of East Bengal, 108–9
creation of, 104–5
Gracey's role, 7–10, 109–30
as homeland for Muslims, 104
independence of, 108
Indian Air Force attack, 124
India-Pakistan conference in New Delhi, 128

Pakistan – *continued*
  Kashmir conflict, 136–7
  Khan, Ayub's commandership, 129
  Liaquat's prime-ministry, 114
  military action against India, 127
  partition of British India, 106
  secret operations in Kashmir, 111–12, 117, 121
  territorial units, 107
  see also Pathan tribesmen
Pakistan Army, 105, 109–10, 112–15, 118–23, 125–7, 129–30, 137
Pathan tribesmen, 111–12, 116–17, 122, 128–9
Patti, A., 3, 41
peace enforcement
  in Cambodia, 72
  early practice, 8–9
  French infrastructure, 81
  Gracey's methods, 78, 96, 134–5
  Gurkha personnel and, 84
  in India, 127–31
  Indo-China, 6, 42
  in Vietnam, 44, 63
peacekeeping, *see* peace enforcement
Perry-Keene, Air Vice-Marshal Allan, 124
Petain, Field Marshal Henri, 34, 58
Pham Van Bach, 42
political evolution, 33, 103
political violence
  in Cambodia, 72
  in India, 104–5, 107–10, 112–13, 116–17, 121–2, 127–30, 132, 137
  in Indo-China, 33, 42, 49–50, 52–3, 82–5, 90, 92, 96, 133
  in Thailand, 77
  in Vietnam, 39, 44–6, 56–7, 62–3, 80–1, 86, 98, 135–6
Politics of Continuity The: British Foreign Policy and the Labour Government 1945–1946 (1993, Saville), 3
Portal, Air Chief Marshal, 2
Potsdam Conference, 32–3, 57, 88, 94
public safety, 81–2, 85, 97
Pyman, Harold, 73

Quit India movement, 104

Rajendrasinjhi, Lt. General Kumar Shri, 129
Ranchi, 15
Rangoon, 25, 27–8, 30–1, 49
Roosevelt, Franklin D., 37
Rosie, G., 3, 4
Royal Air Force, 18, 24–5, 27, 87, 93, 102
Royal Hospital for the Incurables, 2

Sainteny, J., 41
Saville, J., 3
Scoones, Lt. General Geoffrey, 15, 18–19
Second World War
  Asian imperialism and, 11
  birth of United Nation, 8, 134
  Britain's financial bankruptcy, 80
  British campaigns, 2
  British coalition government, 55
  British foreign policy on Vietnam, 6
  Cambodia during, 58–62
  Foreign Office's advice, 49
  French administration in Indo-China, 32–3
  French Indo-China at, 8
  Gracey's 17th Infantry Brigade in Iraq and Syria, 10–11
  humanitarian aid, 93
  India during, 103–5, 129
  Japanese surrender, 2, 136
  official history of the Indian armed forces, 26
  peace enforcement strategy of Britain, 9
  Thailand during, 65–6, 75
  United States during, 80, 88
  Vietnam during, 34–42
Shenam defence system, 19–20
Shone, Sir Terrence, 118–19, 125
Sihanouk, N., 59, 60, 61, 65, 69, 71, 72
Singh, Hari (Hindu Maharaja), 110
Slim, Field Marshal Sir William
  on Aung San, 29
  defensive position in Imphal, 17
  Gracey's complaint on, 19
  Gracey's letter to, 51
  hold on Burma, 28

Index 187

meeting with Lawson, 47
meeting with SEAC commanders, 46
ominous warning, 49, 55
praising Gracey, 2, 15, 132
relationship with Bevin, 86
on 20th Indian Division, 12, 15, 17–18, 22, 25–8
see also 14th Army
Son Ngoc, Thanh, 7, 60–5, 67–72, 83
Southeast Asia
  British decolonisation, 6
  British–Indian forces in, 89
  food crisis, 94–5, 97, 99, 102
  French colonialism in, 5, 65, 136
  Gracey's division in, 15, 29, 137
  indigenous forces, 31
  Japanese control, 12, 31–2, 34, 58–9
  Lawson's mission, 47
  Mountbatten's operations, 32, 53–6, 62, 65–6, 109
  post-war chaos, 131
  Potsdam Conference, 33
  power vacuum in, 2, 5
  SEAC's functioning, 81–2, 92
  during Second World War, 11
  Slim's warning, 86
Southeast Asia Command (SEAC)
  in Cambodia, 75–7
  under Dening, 43, 74
  in French Indo-China, 37–8, 48–9, 53, 80–4, 87–8, 90, 92–4, 99, 102
  Japanese surrender duties, 57
  under Mountbatten, 54–6, 66
  under Pyman, 73
  under Slim, 46
  in southern Indo-China, 32–4, 96, 100–1
  talks with Vietminh representatives, 47
  in Thailand, 75–7
  United States withdrawal of participation, 51
Springhall, J., 5
Stopford, Lt. General Montagu, 21, 30
Struggle for Indo-china The 1940–55 (1955, Hammer), 3

Thai Government, 59, 66, 74–5
Thailand
  bilateral issues with France, 66, 72, 74–5
  Cambodian independence, 61, 64–5
  Foreign Office activities, 57–8
  Franco-Thai treaty, 77
  Japanese supervision, 59
  peace enforcement, 87
  rice production, 94–5
32nd Indian Infantry Brigade, 13
XXXIII Corps, 15, 21
The Times (London, newspaper), 111
Tioulong, Nhek, 65
Tran Trong Kim, 36
Troubled Days of Peace: Mountbatten and South East Asia Command 1945–46 (1987, Dennis), 5
Truman, Harry S., 41, 46, 50, 133
Tuchmann, B., 3
20th Indian Division
  Burma Campaign of 1942–1945, 7, 132
  deployment in French Indo-China, 89, 105
  elements, 104
  Gurkha Rifles, 2
  history of triumph, 12–31
  'implicitly ruthless' actions, 4
  Slim's praise, 2
  transportation, 12
221st Group, Royal Air Force, 27
268th Indian Infantry Brigade, 30

United Nations Food Commission, 94
United Nations General Assembly, 102
United Nations organisation, 2
  peacekeeping duties, 9
United Nations Security Council, 117, 121–2, 124–5, 128
United States of America
  during Cold War, 130
  French Indo-China support, 33, 87–8, 92
  hegemony, 80
  humanitarian aid, 96
  Military aid to Saigon, 79
  Office of Strategic Services team to Hanoi, 40–1, 51

United States of America – *continued*
withdrawal of participation in SEAC, 51–2
United States and Vietnam The (1967, Kahin and Lewis), 3

Vichy France, 34–6, 58–60, 70, 93, 96
Vietminh movement, 39
Vietnam
　Allied troops in, 40, 45
　American Army Air Force in, 37
　American support for self-government, 41
　British–Indian forces in, 33, 37, 42, 44–5, 48–50, 54
　French administration, 32, 35, 46–8, 51, 53
　French colonialism, 32–3, 36, 39, 41, 43, 46
　French forces in, 37–8, 45, 52
　French population, 31, 35–6, 43
　French sovereignty, 43, 45, 47
　Gracey's actions in Saigon, 46–9, 56
　Japanese forces, 36, 41–2, 46, 49–52
　Mountbatten's assessment of French operations, 51–5
　Mountbatten's operations, 32, 53–6
　peace enforcement, 44, 63
　political violence, 39, 44–6, 56–7, 62–3, 80–1, 86, 98, 135–6

Potsdam Conference, 33
Second World War, 34–42
Southeast Asia Command (SEAC) in, 37–8, 48–9, 53
United States withdrawal of participation, 51
see also Vietnam War
Vietnam: A Dragon Embattled (1966, Buttinger), 3
Vietnamese nationalism, 4, 33–4
Vietnamese populations, 7, 42, 44, 50, 70, 86
Vietnam War
　American entanglement, 3
　First, 3, 9, 56
　origins of, 131
Viwat (Prince), 66
Vo Nguyen, Giap, 41

Wainggyo Gorge endeavour, 23
Walker-Chapman, Colonel, 99
War Office, 33, 48, 57, 81, 83, 85–6, 89, 95, 101–2
Wavell, Lord, 91, 105–6
weapons, 39, 41, 44, 50, 67, 71, 116, 129
Weaver, Major F.H., 90
Woodford, E.C.J., 13–14